Eng^d by H.B. Hall, Jr. N.Y.

MARGARET FULLER.

MEMOIRS

OF

MARGARET FULLER OSSOLI.

BY

R. W. EMERSON, W. H. CHANNING, AND J. F. CLARKE.

With a Portrait and an Appendix.

Only a learned and a manly soul
  I purposed her, that should with even powers
The rock, the spindle, and the shears control
  Of Destiny, and spin her own free hours.
BEN JONSON.

Però che ogni diletto nostro e doglia
Sta in sì e nò saper, voler, potere;
Adunque quel sol può, che col dovere
Ne trae la ragion fuor di sua soglia.

Adunque tu, lettor di queste note,
S' a te vuoi esser buono, e agli altri caro,
Vogli sempre poter quel che tu debbi.
LEONARDO DA VINCI.

VOL. I.

NEW YORK:
THE TRIBUNE ASSOCIATION,
154 NASSAU STREET.
1869.

PREFACE.

THE present edition of my sister's Memoirs appears without change, as it came from the hands of the accomplished editors whose names appear on the title-page. Theirs was a work of love, to diffuse wide a knowledge of my sister's eventful life and noble character; and most lovingly and well has their work been done.

I have, however, while refraining from changes, made some additions to this volume, on my own responsibility, which I trust will enhance its value to the reader. As a frontispiece appears the beautiful engraving of Hicks's portrait of Margaret Fuller, which was painted by him from life during her residence in Rome, only a year or two before her death. It is the only painting in existence which serves to perpetuate her likeness. No daguerreotype, engraving, or portrait, seems, to many of her friends, to present her to the eye just as she remains in their memories; but this is doubtless the most authentic likeness which the public can ever now possess, and will "grow upon" the love and favor of those who attentively study it.

The Appendix contains two articles, published, the one in the New England Historical and Genealogical Register for October, 1859, where a "Genealogy of the Fuller Family" also appears, and the other in the Quarterly Journal of the American Unitarian Association for October, 1859; and also some poetical tributes. The historical article first named is inserted as giving some information in reference to the various members of my sister's family, to whom many of the letters in these volumes are addressed. Several of these loved ones — a brother, a sister, a mother — have entered the "spirit land" since these Memoirs first appeared; and in how few years will all have gone there to rejoin that "great and noble soul," who, reaching first those eternal shores, has by none of us been, or ever can be, forgotten! I would fain twine their memories, as were their lives, in one wreath together.

This sketch, however, finds its place here chiefly as serving to remove, in some degree, a most unintentional injustice to my father's memory, which has been done by the autobiographical sketch in the first pages of these Memoirs. This conveys an impression that he was stern and exacting, and utterly overlooked the physical health of his daughter by tasking to the utmost her extraordinary powers. My sister never would have published this sketch — which she herself entitled an autobiographical romance — without such modifications as would have shown our father to have been a most judicious and tender one, erring, perhaps, in stimulating too much the rare intellect of his first child, but erring through no lack of love or general good judgment, but as all the educators of his time erred, and as would have harmed none but one possessing a mind so precocious and unusual. This error, too, he saw, and avoided in the education of his other children. He was a man whose memory deserves to be entirely honored, and to perpetuate which Margaret desired to write a memoir of one whom she, each year of life, saw more and more was a person to be deeply loved and respected. I feel that the insertion of this brief record in part accomplishes an object she herself once had in view, and would be entirely in harmony with her own wishes.

The memorial of my sainted mother deserves also a place here. Bearing the same name, this mother and daughter shared also the same pure, noble spirit, and in their separate spheres were alike remarkable and excellent. This brief sketch of the mother's history finds fitting place in her daughter's Memoirs, since both "were lovely and pleasant in their lives," and now are "not divided."

One word only remains to be said. The reader of these Memoirs who desires a thorough knowledge of Margaret Fuller's intellectual life and spiritual character must read, not them alone, but also the volumes of her works which are now, for the first time, published in complete form, and whose ideas deserve, not only to be studied, but embodied in the lives of those who would themselves be true and noble.

ARTHUR B. FULLER.

WATERTOWN, MASS.

TABLE OF CONTENTS

FOR

VOLUME FIRST.

APPENDIX.

YOUTH.

AUTOBIOGRAPHY.

"Aus Morgenduft gewebt und Sonnenklarheit
Der Dichtung Schleir aus der Hand der Wahrheit.'

GŒTHE

"The million stars which tremble
O'er the deep mind of dauntless infancy."

TENNYSON.

"Wie leicht ward er dahin getragen,
Was war dem Glücklichen zu schwer!
Wie tanzte vor des Lebens Wagen
Die luftige Begleitung her!
Die Liebe mit dem süssen Lohne,
Das Glück mit seinem gold'nen Kranz,
Der Ruhm mit seiner Sternenkrone,
Die Wahrheit in der Sonne Glanz."

SCHILLER

( )

"What wert thou then? A child most infantine,
Yet wandering far beyond that innocent age,
In all but its sweet looks and mien divine;
Even then, methought, with the world's tyrant rage
A patient warfare thy young heart did wage,
When those soft eyes of scarcely conscious thought
Some tale, or thine own fancies, would engage
To overflow with tears, or converse fraught
With passion o'er their depths its fleeting light had wrought."

SHELLEY.

"And I smiled, as one never smiles but once;
Then first discovering my own aim's extent,
Which sought to comprehend the works of God,
And God himself, and all God's intercourse
With the human mind."

BROWNING.

I.

YOUTH.

'TIECK, who has embodied so many Runic secrets, 'explained to me what I have often felt toward myself, 'when he tells of the poor changeling, who, turned from 'the door of her adopted home, sat down on a stone and 'so pitied herself that she wept. Yet me also, the wonder-'ful bird, singing in the wild forest, has tempted on, and 'not in vain.'

Thus wrote Margaret in the noon of life, when looking back through youth to the "dewy dawn of memory." She was the eldest child of Timothy Fuller* and Margaret Crane,† and was born in Cambridge-Port, Massachusetts, on the 23d of May, 1810.

Among her papers fortunately remains this unfinished sketch of youth, prepared by her own hand, in 1840, as the introductory chapter to an autobiographical romance.

PARENTS.

'My father was a lawyer and a politician. He was 'a man largely endowed with that sagacious energy, 'which the state of New England society, for the last half

* See Appendix A. † See Appendix B.

'century, has been so well fitted to develop. His father
'was a clergyman, settled as pastor in Princeton, Mas-
'sachusetts, within the bounds of whose parish-farm was
'Wachuset. His means were small, and the great object
'of his ambition was to send his sons to college. As a
'boy, my father was taught to think only of preparing
'himself for Harvard University, and when there of
'preparing himself for the profession of Law. As a
'Lawyer, again, the ends constantly presented were to
'work for distinction in the community, and for the
'means of supporting a family. To be an honored cit-
'izen, and to have a home on earth, were made the great
'aims of existence. To open the deeper fountains of the
'soul, to regard life here as the prophetic entrance to
'immortality, to develop his spirit to perfection, — mo-
'tives like these had never been suggested to him, either
'by fellow-beings or by outward circumstances. The
'result was a character, in its social aspect, of quite the
'common sort. A good son and brother, a kind neigh-
'bor, an active man of business — in all these outward
'relations he was but one of a class, which surrounding
'conditions have made the majority among us. In the
'more delicate and individual relations, he never ap-
'proached but two mortals, my mother and myself.

'His love for my mother was the green spot on
'which he stood apart from the common-places of a
'mere bread-winning, bread-bestowing existence. She
'was one of those fair and flower-like natures, which
'sometimes spring up even beside the most dusty high-
'ways of life — a creature not to be shaped into a merely
'useful instrument, but bound by one law with the blue
'sky, the dew, and the frolic birds. Of all persons
'whom I have known, she had in her most of the angelic,

'—of that spontaneous love for every living thing, 'for man, and beast, and tree, which restores the golden 'age.'

DEATH IN THE HOUSE.

'My earliest recollection is of a death, — the death of 'a sister, two years younger than myself. Probably there 'is a sense of childish endearments, such as belong to this 'tie, mingled with that of loss, of wonder, and mystery; 'but these last are prominent in memory. I remember 'coming home and meeting our nursery-maid, her face 'streaming with tears. That strange sight of tears made 'an indelible impression. I realize how little I was of 'stature, in that I looked up to this weeping face; — and 'it has often seemed since, that — full-grown for the life 'of this earth, I have looked up just so, at times of threat-'ening, of doubt, and distress, and that just so has some 'being of the next higher order of existences looked 'down, aware of a law unknown to me, and tenderly 'commiserating the pain I must endure in emerging from 'my ignorance.

'She took me by the hand and led me into a still and 'dark chamber, —then drew aside the curtain and showed 'me my sister. I see yet that beauty of death! The 'highest achievements of sculpture are only the reminder 'of its severe sweetness. Then I remember the house all 'still and dark, — the people in their black clothes and 'dreary faces, — the scent of the newly-made coffin, — 'my being set up in a chair and detained by a gentle hand 'to hear the clergyman, — the carriages slowly going, 'the procession slowly doling out their steps to the grave. 'But I have no remembrance of what I have since been 'told I did, — insisting, with loud cries, that they should 'not put the body in the ground. I suppose that my emo-'tion was spent at the time, and so there was nothing to 'fix that moment in my memory.

'I did not then, nor do I now, find any beauty in these 'ceremonies. What had they to do with the sweet play-'ful child? Her life and death were alike beautiful, but 'all this sad parade was not. Thus my first experience 'of life was one of death. She who would have been the 'companion of my life was severed from me, and I was 'left alone. This has made a vast difference in my lot. 'Her character, if that fair face promised right, would 'have been soft, graceful and lively; it would have tem-'pered mine to a gentler and more gradual course.

OVERWORK.

'My father, — all whose feelings were now concentred 'on me, — instructed me himself. The effect of this 'was so far good that, not passing through the hands of 'many ignorant and weak persons as so many do at pre-'paratory schools, I was put at once under discipline of 'considerable severity, and, at the same time, had a more 'than ordinarily high standard presented to me. My 'father was a man of business, even in literature; he had 'been a high scholar at college, and was warmly attached 'to all he had learned there, both from the pleasure he 'had derived in the exercise of his faculties and the asso-'ciated memories of success and good repute. He was, 'beside, well read in French literature, and in English, a 'Queen Anne's man. He hoped to make me the heir of 'all he knew, and of as much more as the income of his 'profession enabled him to give me means of acquir-'ing. At the very beginning, he made one great mistake, 'more common, it is to be hoped, in the last generation, 'than the warnings of physiologists will permit it to be 'with the next. He thought to gain time, by bringing 'forward the intellect as early as possible. Thus I had 'tasks given me, as many and various as the hours would 'allow, and on subjects beyond my age; with the additional disadvantage of reciting to him in the evening, 'after he returned from his office. As he was subject to 'many interruptions, I was often kept up till very late; 'and as he was a severe teacher, both from his habits of 'mind and his ambition for me, my feelings were kept on 'the stretch till the recitations were over. Thus frequently, I was sent to bed several hours too late, with 'nerves unnaturally stimulated. The consequence was a 'premature development of the brain, that made me a '"youthful prodigy" by day, and by night a victim of 'spectral illusions, nightmare, and somnambulism, which 'at the time prevented the harmonious development of 'my bodily powers and checked my growth, while, later, 'they induced continual headache, weakness and nervous 'affections, of all kinds. As these again re-acted on the 'brain, giving undue force to every thought and every 'feeling, there was finally produced a state of being both 'too active and too intense, which wasted my constitution, 'and will bring me, — even although I have learned to 'understand and regulate my now morbid temperament, '— to a premature grave.

'No one understood this subject of health then. No 'one knew why this child, already kept up so late, was still unwilling to retire. My aunts cried out upon the '"spoiled child, the most unreasonable child that ever 'was, — if brother could but open his eyes to see it, — who 'was never willing to go to bed." They did not know 'that, so soon as the light was taken away, she seemed to 'see colossal faces advancing slowly towards her, the eyes 'dilating, and each feature swelling loathsomely as they 'came, till at last, when they were about to close upon 'her, she started up with a shriek which drove them 'away, but only to return when she lay down again. 'They did not know that, when at last she went to 'sleep, it was to dream of horses trampling over her, and 'to awake once more in fright; or, as she had just read 'in her Virgil, of being among trees that dripped with 'blood, where she walked and walked and could not get 'out, while the blood became a pool and plashed over 'her feet, and rose higher and higher, till soon she 'dreamed it would reach her lips. No wonder the child 'arose and walked in her sleep, moaning all over the 'house, till once, when they heard her, and came and 'waked her, and she told what she had dreamed, her 'father sharply bid her "leave off thinking of such non-' "sense, or she would be crazy,"—never knowing that 'he was himself the cause of all these horrors of the 'night. Often she dreamed of following to the grave 'the body of her mother, as she had done that of her 'sister, and woke to find the pillow drenched in tears. 'These dreams softened her heart too much, and cast a 'deep shadow over her young days; for then, and later, 'the life of dreams,—probably because there was in it 'less to distract the mind from its own earnestness,—has 'often seemed to her more real, and been remembered 'with more interest, than that of waking hours.

'Poor child! Far remote in time, in thought, from 'that period, I look back on these glooms and terrors, 'wherein I was enveloped, and perceive that I had no 'natural childhood.'

BOOKS.

'Thus passed my first years. My mother was in deli-'cate health, and much absorbed in the care of her 'younger children. In the house was neither dog nor 'bird, nor any graceful animated form of existence. I 'saw no persons who took my fancy, and real life offered 'no attraction. Thus my already over-excited mind 'found no relief from without, and was driven for refuge 'from itself to the world of books. I was taught Latin 'and English grammar at the same time, and began to 'read Latin at six years old, after which, for some years, 'I read it daily. In this branch of study, first by my 'father, and afterwards by a tutor, I was trained to quite 'a high degree of precision. I was expected to under-'stand the mechanism of the language thoroughly, and in 'translating to give the thoughts in as few well-arranged 'words as possible, and without breaks or hesitation,—'for with these my father had absolutely no patience.

'Indeed, he demanded accuracy and clearness in every-'thing: you must not speak, unless you can make your 'meaning perfectly intelligible to the person addressed; 'must not express a thought, unless you can give a reason 'for it, if required; must not make a statement, unless 'sure of all particulars — such were his rules. "But," '"if," "unless," "I am mistaken," and "it may be '"so," were words and phrases excluded from the prov-'ince where he held sway. Trained to great dexterity in 'artificial methods, accurate, ready, with entire com-mand of his resources, he had no belief in minds that 'listen, wait, and receive. He had no conception of the 'subtle and indirect motions of imagination and feeling. 'His influence on me was great, and opposed to the nat-

'ural unfolding of my character, which was fervent, of 'strong grasp, and disposed to infatuation, and self-forget-'fulness. He made the common prose world so present 'to me, that my natural bias was controlled. I did not 'go mad, as many would do, at being continually roused 'from my dreams. I had too much strength to be 'crushed,—and since I must put on the fetters, could not 'submit to let them impede my motions. My own world 'sank deep within, away from the surface of my life; 'in what I did and said I learned to have reference to 'other minds. But my true life was only the dearer 'that it was secluded and veiled over by a thick curtain 'of available intellect, and that coarse, but wearable 'stuff woven by the ages,—Common Sense.

'In accordance with this discipline in heroic common 'sense, was the influence of those great Romans, whose 'thoughts and lives were my daily food during those plas-'tic years. The genius of Rome displayed itself in Char-'acter, and scarcely needed an occasional wave of the 'torch of thought to show its lineaments, so marble strong 'they gleamed in every light. Who, that has lived with 'those men, but admires the plain force of fact, of 'thought passed into action? They take up things 'with their naked hands. There is just the man, 'and the block he casts before you,—no divinity, no 'demon, no unfulfilled aim, but just the man and Rome, 'and what he did for Rome. Everything turns your 'attention to what a man can become, not by yielding 'himself freely to impressions, not by letting nature play 'freely through him, but by a single thought, an earnest 'purpose, an indomitable will, by hardihood, self-com-'mand, and force of expression. Architecture was the art 'in which Rome excelled, and this corresponds with the 'feeling these men of Rome excite. They did not grow, '—they built themselves up, or were built up by the 'fate of Rome, as a temple for Jupiter Stator. The 'ruined Roman sits among the ruins; he flies to no green 'garden; he does not look to heaven; if his intent is 'defeated, if he is less than he meant to be, he lives no 'more. The names which end in "*us*," seem to speak 'with lyric cadence. That measured cadence,—that 'tramp and march,—which are not stilted, because they 'indicate real force, yet which seem so when compared 'with any other language,—make Latin a study in itself 'of mighty influence. The language alone, without the 'literature, would give one the *thought* of Rome. Man 'present in nature, commanding nature too sternly to be 'inspired by it, standing like the rock amid the sea, or 'moving like the fire over the land, either impassive, or 'irresistible; knowing not the soft mediums or fine flights 'of life, but by the force which he expresses, piercing to 'the centre.

'We are never better understood than when we speak 'of a "Roman virtue," a "Roman outline." There is 'somewhat indefinite, somewhat yet unfulfilled in the 'thought of Greece, of Spain, of modern Italy; but 'ROME! it stands by itself, a clear Word. The power of 'will, the dignity of a fixed purpose is what it utters. 'Every Roman was an emperor. It is well that the 'infallible church should have been founded on this rock, 'that the presumptuous Peter should hold the keys, as 'the conquering Jove did before his thunderbolts, to be 'seen of all the world. The Apollo tends flocks with 'Admetus; Christ teaches by the lonely lake, or plucks 'wheat as he wanders through the fields some Sabbath 'morning. They never come to this stronghold; they 'could not have breathed freely where all became stone 'as soon as spoken, where divine youth found no horizon 'for its all-promising glance, but every thought put on, 'before it dared issue to the day in action, its *toga* '*virilis.*

'Suckled by this wolf, man gains a different complexion from that which is fed by the Greek honey. He 'takes a noble bronze in camps and battle-fields; the 'wrinkles of council well beseem his brow, and the eye 'cuts its way like the sword. The Eagle should never 'have been used as a symbol by any other nation: it 'belonged to Rome.

'The history of Rome abides in mind, of course, more 'than the literature. It was degeneracy for a Roman to 'use the pen; his life was in the day. The "vaunting" 'of Rome, like that of the North American Indians, is her 'proper literature. A man rises; he tells who he is, and 'what he has done; he speaks of his country and her 'brave men; he knows that a conquering god is there, 'whose agent is his own right hand; and he should end 'like the Indian, "I have no more to say."

'It never shocks us that the Roman is self-conscious. 'One wants no universal truths from him, no philosophy, 'no creation, but only his life, his Roman life felt in every 'pulse, realized in every gesture. The universal heaven 'takes in the Roman only to make us feel his individuality the more. The Will, the Resolve of Man! — it has 'been expressed,— fully expressed!

'I steadily loved this ideal in my childhood, and this 'is the cause, probably, why I have always felt that 'man must know how to stand firm on the ground, 'before he can fly. In vain for me are men more, if 'they are less, than Romans. Dante was far greater 'than any Roman, yet I feel he was right to take the 'Mantuan as his guide through hell, and to heaven.

'Horace was a great deal to me then, and is so still. 'Though his words do not abide in memory, his pres- 'ence does: serene, courtly, of darting hazel eye, a self- 'sufficient grace, and an appreciation of the world of 'stern realities, sometimes pathetic, never tragic. He is 'the natural man of the world; he is what he ought to 'be, and his darts never fail of their aim. There is a 'perfume and raciness, too, which makes life a banquet, 'where the wit sparkles no less that the viands were 'bought with blood.

'Ovid gave me not Rome, nor himself, but a view into 'the enchanted gardens of the Greek mythology. This 'path I followed, have been following ever since; and 'now, life half over, it seems to me, as in my child- 'hood, that every thought of which man is suscep- 'tible, is intimated there. In those young years, indeed, 'I did not see what I now see, but loved to creep from 'amid the Roman pikes to lie beneath this great vine, 'and see the smiling and serene shapes go by, woven 'from the finest fibres of all the elements. I knew not 'why, at that time,—but I loved to get away from the 'hum of the forum, and the mailed clang of Roman 'speech, to these shifting shows of nature, these Gods 'and Nymphs born of the sunbeam, the wave, the 'shadows on the hill.

'As with Rome I antedated the world of deeds, so I 'lived in those Greek forms the true faith of a refined 'and intense childhood. So great was the force of real- 'ity with which these forms impressed me, that I prayed 'earnestly for a sign,—that it would lighten in some particular region of the heavens, or that I might find a 'bunch of grapes in the path, when I went forth in the 'morning. But no sign was given, and I was left a 'waif stranded upon the shores of modern life!

'Of the Greek language, I knew only enough to feel 'that the sounds told the same story as the mythology; — 'that the law of life in that land was beauty, as in 'Rome it was a stern composure. I wish I had learned 'as much of Greece as of Rome,— so freely does the 'mind play in her sunny waters, where there is no chill, 'and the restraint is from within out; for these Greeks, 'in an atmosphere of ample grace, could not be impetu-'ous, or stern, but loved moderation as equable life 'always must, for it is the law of beauty.

'With these books I passed my days. The great 'amount of study exacted of me soon ceased to be a 'burden, and reading became a habit and a passion. 'The force of feeling, which, under other circumstances, 'might have ripened thought, was turned to learn the 'thoughts of others. This was not a tame state, for the 'energies brought out by rapid acquisition gave glow 'enough. I thought with rapture of the all-accom-'plished man, him of the many talents, wide resources, 'clear sight, and omnipotent will. A Cæsar seemed 'great enough. I did not then know that such men 'impoverish the treasury to build the palace. I kept 'their statues as belonging to the hall of my ancestors, 'and loved to conquer obstacles, and fed my youth and 'strength for their sake.

'Still, though this bias was so great that in earliest 'years I learned, in these ways, how the world takes hold 'of a powerful nature, I had yet other experiences. None 'of these were deeper than what I found in the happiest haunt of my childish years,—our little garden. Our 'house, though comfortable, was very ugly, and in a 'neighborhood which I detested,—every dwelling and its 'appurtenances having a *mesquin* and huddled look. I 'liked nothing about us except the tall graceful elms 'before the house, and the dear little garden behind. 'Our back door opened on a high flight of steps, by 'which I went down to a green plot, much injured in 'my ambitious eyes by the presence of the pump and 'tool-house. This opened into a little garden, full of 'choice flowers and fruit-trees, which was my mother's 'delight, and was carefully kept. Here I felt at home. 'A gate opened thence into the fields,—a wooden gate 'made of boards, in a high, unpainted board wall, and 'embowered in the clematis creeper. This gate I used 'to open to see the sunset heaven; beyond this black 'frame I did not step, for I liked to look at the deep gold 'behind it. How exquisitely happy I was in its beauty, 'and how I loved the silvery wreaths of my protecting 'vine! I never would pluck one of its flowers at that 'time, I was so jealous of its beauty, but often since I 'carry off wreaths of it from the wild-wood, and it 'stands in nature to my mind as the emblem of domestic 'love.

'Of late I have thankfully felt what I owe to that 'garden, where the best hours of my lonely childhood 'were spent. Within the house everything was socially 'utilitarian; my books told of a proud world, but in 'another temper were the teachings of the little garden. 'There my thoughts could lie callow in the nest, and 'only be fed and kept warm, not called to fly or sing 'before the time. I loved to gaze on the roses, the vio- 'lets, the lilies, the pinks; my mother's hand had planted 'them, and they bloomed for me. I culled the most 'beautiful. I looked at them on every side. I kissed 'them, I pressed them to my bosom with passionate 'emotions, such as I have never dared express to any 'human being. An ambition swelled my heart to be as 'beautiful, as perfect as they. I have not kept my 'vow. Yet, forgive, ye wild asters, which gleam so 'sadly amid the fading grass; forgive me, ye golden 'autumn flowers, which so strive to reflect the glories 'of the departing distant sun; and ye silvery flowers, 'whose moonlight eyes I knew so well, forgive! Living 'and blooming in your unchecked law, ye know noth-'ing of the blights, the distortions, which beset the 'human being; and which at such hours it would seem 'that no glories of free agency could ever repay!

'There was, in the house, no apartment appropriated 'to the purpose of a library, but there was in my father's 'room a large closet filled with books, and to these I had 'free access when the task-work of the day was done. 'Its window overlooked wide fields, gentle slopes, a rich 'and smiling country, whose aspect pleased without 'much occupying the eye, while a range of blue hills, 'rising at about twelve miles distance, allured to reverie. '"Distant mountains," says Tieck, "excite the fancy, for '"beyond them we place the scene of our Paradise." 'Thus, in the poems of fairy adventure, we climb the 'rocky barrier, pass fearless its dragon caves, and dark 'pine forests, and find the scene of enchantment in the 'vale behind. My hopes were never so definite, but my 'eye was constantly allured to that distant blue range, 'and I would sit, lost in fancies, till tears fell on my cheek. I loved this sadness; but only in later years, 'when the realities of life had taught me moderation, 'did the passionate emotions excited by seeing them 'again teach how glorious were the hopes that swelled 'my heart while gazing on them in those early days.

'Melancholy attends on the best joys of a merely ideal 'life, else I should call most happy the hours in the gar- 'den, the hours in the book closet. Here were the best 'French writers of the last century; for my father had 'been more than half a Jacobin, in the time when the 'French Republic cast its glare of promise over the 'world. Here, too, were the Queen Anne authors, his 'models, and the English novelists; but among them 'I found none that charmed me. Smollett, Fielding, 'and the like, deal too broadly with the coarse actuali- 'ties of life. The best of their men and women — so 'merely natural, with the nature found every day — do 'not meet our hopes. Sometimes the simple picture, 'warm with life and the light of the common sun, can- 'not fail to charm, — as in the wedded love of Fielding's 'Amelia, — but it is at a later day, when the mind is 'trained to comparison, that we learn to prize excellence 'like this as it deserves. Early youth is prince-like: 'it will bend only to "the king, my father." Various 'kinds of excellence please, and leave their impression, 'but the most commanding, alone, is duly acknowledged 'at that all-exacting age.

'Three great authors it was my fortune to meet at 'this important period, — all, though of unequal, yet 'congenial powers, — all of rich and wide, rather than 'aspiring genius, — all free to the extent of the horizon 'their eye took in, — all fresh with impulse, racy with 'experience; never to be lost sight of, or superseded, but 'always to be apprehended more and more.

'Ever memorable is the day on which I first took a 'volume of SHAKSPEARE in my hand to read. It was on 'a Sunday.

'— This day was punctiliously set apart in our house. 'We had family prayers, for which there was no time on 'other days. Our dinners were different, and our clothes. 'We went to church. My father put some limitations 'on my reading, but — bless him for the gentleness which 'has left me a pleasant feeling for the day! — he did not 'prescribe what was, but only what was *not*, to be done. 'And the liberty this left was a large one. "You must '"not read a novel, or a play;" but all other books, 'the worst, or the best, were open to me. The distinc- 'tion was merely technical. The day was pleasing to 'me, as relieving me from the routine of tasks and reci- 'tations; it gave me freer play than usual, and there 'were fewer things occurred in its course, which 'reminded me of the divisions of time; still the church- 'going, where I heard nothing that had any connection 'with my inward life, and these rules, gave me asso- 'ciations with the day of empty formalities, and arbi- 'trary restrictions; but though the forbidden book or 'walk always seemed more charming then, I was sel- 'dom tempted to disobey. —

'This Sunday — I was only eight years old — I took 'from the book-shelf a volume lettered SHAKSPEARE. It 'was not the first time I had looked at it, but before I 'had been deterred from attempting to read, by the 'broken appearance along the page, and preferred 'smooth narrative. But this time I held in my hand '"Romeo and Juliet" long enough to get my eye fast- 'ened to the page. It was a cold winter afternoon. I 'took the book to the parlor fire, and had there been 'seated an hour or two, when my father looked up and 'asked what I was reading so intently. "Shakspeare," 'replied the child, merely raising her eye from the page. '"Shakspeare, — that won't do; that's no book for Sun-'"day; go put it away and take another." I went as 'I was bid, but took no other. Returning to my seat, 'the unfinished story, the personages to whom I was but 'just introduced, thronged and burnt my brain. I could 'not bear it long; such a lure it was impossible to resist. 'I went and brought the book again. There were sev-'eral guests present, and I had got half through the 'play before I again attracted attention. "What is that '"child about that she don't hear a word that's said '"to her?" quoth my aunt. "What are you read-'"ing?" said my father. "Shakspeare" was again 'the reply, in a clear, though somewhat impatient, tone. '"How?" said my father angrily, — then restraining 'himself before his guests, — "Give me the book and '"go directly to bed."

'Into my little room no care of his anger followed me. 'Alone, in the dark, I thought only of the scene placed 'by the poet before my eye, where the free flow of life, 'sudden and graceful dialogue, and forms, whether gro-'tesque or fair, seen in the broad lustre of his imagina-'tion, gave just what I wanted, and brought home the '*life* I seemed born to live. My fancies swarmed like 'bees, as I contrived the rest of the story; — what all 'would do, what say, where go. My confinement tor-'tured me. I could not go forth from this prison to ask 'after these friends; I could not make my pillow of the 'dreams about them which yet I could not forbear to 'frame. Thus was I absorbed when my father entered. He felt it right, before going to rest, to reason with me 'about my disobedience, shown in a way, as he consid- 'ered, so insolent. I listened, but could not feel inter- 'ested in what he said, nor turn my mind from what 'engaged it. He went away really grieved at my im- 'penitence, and quite at a loss to understand conduct 'in me so unusual.

'—Often since I have seen the same misunderstand- 'ing between parent and child,—the parent thrusting 'the morals, the discipline, of life upon the child, when 'just engrossed by some game of real importance and 'great leadings to it. That is only a wooden horse 'to the father,—the child was careering to distant 'scenes of conquest and crusade, through a country of 'elsewhere unimagined beauty. None but poets remem- 'ber their youth; but the father who does not retain 'poetical apprehension of the world, free and splendid 'as it stretches out before the child, who cannot read 'his natural history, and follow out its intimations with 'reverence, must be a tyrant in his home, and the purest 'intentions will not prevent his doing much to cramp 'him. Each new child is a new Thought, and has 'bearings and discernings, which the Thoughts older in 'date know not yet, but must learn.—

'My attention thus fixed on Shakspeare, I returned 'to him at every hour I could command. Here was a 'counterpoise to my Romans, still more forcible than 'the little garden. My author could read the Roman 'nature too,—read it in the sternness of Coriolanus, 'and in the varied wealth of Cæsar. But he viewed 'these men of will as only one kind of men; he kept 'them in their place, and I found that he, who could 'understand the Roman, yet expressed in Hamlet a deeper thought.

'In Cervantes, I found far less productive talent, — 'indeed, a far less powerful genius, — but the same wide 'wisdom, a discernment piercing the shows and sym- 'bols of existence, yet rejoicing in them all, both for 'their own life, and as signs of the unseen reality. Not 'that Cervantes philosophized, — his genius was too 'deeply philosophical for that; he took things as they 'came before him, and saw their actual relations and 'bearings. Thus the work he produced was of deep 'meaning, though he might never have expressed that 'meaning to himself. It was left implied in the whole. 'A Coleridge comes and calls Don Quixote the pure 'Reason, and Sancho the Understanding. Cervantes 'made no such distinctions in his own mind; but he 'had seen and suffered enough to bring out all his 'faculties, and to make him comprehend the higher as 'well as the lower part of our nature. Sancho is too 'amusing and sagacious to be contemptible; the Don 'too noble and clear-sighted towards absolute truth, to 'be ridiculous. And we are pleased to see manifested 'in this way, how the lower must follow and serve the 'higher, despite its jeering mistrust and the stubborn 'realities which break up the plans of this pure-minded 'champion.

'The effect produced on the mind is nowise that 'described by Byron: —

"Cervantes smiled Spain's chivalry away," &c.

'On the contrary, who is not conscious of a sincere rev- 'erence for the Don, prancing forth on his gaunt steed? 'Who would not rather be he than any of the persons 'who laugh at him? — Yet the one we would wish to 'be is thyself, Cervantes, unconquerable spirit! gaining 'flavor and color like wine from every change, while 'being carried round the world; in whose eye the serene 'sagacious laughter could not be dimmed by poverty, 'slavery, or unsuccessful authorship. Thou art to us 'still more the Man, though less the Genius, than Shak-'speare; thou dost not evade our sight, but, holding the 'lamp to thine own magic shows, dost enjoy them with 'us.

'My third friend was Molière, one very much lower, 'both in range and depth, than the others, but, as far as 'he goes, of the same character. Nothing secluded or par-'tial is there about his genius,— a man of the world, and 'a man by himself, as he is. It was, indeed, only the 'poor social world of Paris that he saw, but he viewed 'it from the firm foundations of his manhood, and every 'lightest laugh rings from a clear perception, and teaches 'life anew.

'These men were all alike in this,—they loved the '*natural history* of man. Not what he should be, but 'what he is, was the favorite subject of their thought. 'Whenever a noble leading opened to the eye new paths 'of light, they rejoiced; but it was never fancy, but 'always fact, that inspired them. They loved a thorough 'penetration of the murkiest dens, and most tangled paths 'of nature; they did not spin from the desires of their 'own special natures, but reconstructed the world from 'materials which they collected on every side. Thus 'their influence upon me was not to prompt me to follow out thought in myself so much as to detect it every-'where, for each of these men is not only a nature, but 'a happy interpreter of many natures. They taught me to distrust all invention which is not based on a wide 'experience. Perhaps, too, they taught me to overvalue 'an outward experience at the expense of inward 'growth; but all this I did not appreciate till later.

'It will be seen that my youth was not unfriended, 'since those great minds came to me in kindness. A 'moment of action in one's self, however, is worth an 'age of apprehension through others; not that our deeds 'are better, but that they produce a renewal of our being. 'I have had more productive moments and of deeper joy, 'but never hours of more tranquil pleasure than those in 'which these demi-gods visited me,— and with a smile 'so familiar, that I imagined the world to be full of such. 'They did me good, for by them a standard was early 'given of sight and thought, from which I could never 'go back, and beneath which I cannot suffer patiently 'my own life or that of any friend to fall. They did me 'harm, too, for the child fed with meat instead of milk 'becomes too soon mature. Expectations and desires 'were thus early raised, after which I must long toil 'before they can be realized. How poor the scene 'around, how tame one's own existence, how meagre and 'faint every power, with these beings in my mind! 'Often I must cast them quite aside in order to grow in 'my small way, and not sink into despair. Certainly I 'do not wish that instead of these masters I had read 'baby books, written down to children, and with such 'ignorant dulness that they blunt the senses and corrupt 'the tastes of the still plastic human being. But I do wish 'that I had read no books at all till later,— that I had lived with toys, and played in the open air. Children should not cull the fruits of reflection and observation 'early, but expand in the sun, and let thoughts come to 'them. They should not through books antedate their 'actual experiences, but should take them gradually, as 'sympathy and interpretation are needed. With me, 'much of life was devoured in the bud.]

FIRST FRIEND.

'For a few months, this bookish and solitary life was 'invaded by interest in a living, breathing figure. At 'church, I used to look around with a feeling of coldness 'and disdain, which, though I now well understand its 'causes, seems to my wiser mind as odious as it was 'unnatural. [The puny child sought everywhere for 'the Roman or Shakspeare figures, and she was met 'by the shrewd, honest eye, the homely decency, or the 'smartness of a New England village on Sunday. There 'was beauty, but I could not see it then; it was not of 'the kind I longed for.] In the next pew sat a family 'who were my especial aversion. There were five 'daughters, the eldest not above four-and-twenty,— yet 'they had the old fairy, knowing look, hard, dry, dwarfed, 'strangers to the All-Fair,— were working-day residents 'in this beautiful planet. They looked as if their 'thoughts had never strayed beyond the jobs of the day, 'and they were glad of it. Their mother was one of 'those shrunken, faded patterns of woman who have 'never done anything to keep smooth the cheek and 'dignify the brow. The father had a Scotch look of 'shrewd narrowness, and entire self-complacency. I 'could not endure this family, whose existence contra-'dicted all my visions; yet I could not forbear looking 'at them.

'As my eye one day was ranging about with its accustomed coldness, and the proudly foolish sense of being in a shroud of thoughts that were not their thoughts, it was arrested by a face most fair, and well-'known as it seemed at first glance,—for surely I had 'met her before and waited for her long. But soon I 'saw that she was a new apparition foreign to that scene, 'if not to me. Her dress,—the arrangement of her hair, 'which had the graceful pliancy of races highly cultiva-'ted for long,—the intelligent and full picture of her eye, 'whose reserve was in its self-possession, not in timidity, '—all combined to make up a whole impression, which, 'though too young to understand, I was well prepared 'to feel.

'How wearisome now appears that thorough-bred '*millefleur* beauty, the distilled result of ages of Euro-'pean culture! Give me rather the wild heath on the 'lonely hill-side, than such a rose-tree from the daintily 'clipped garden. But, then, I had but tasted the cup, 'and knew not how little it could satisfy; more, more, 'was all my cry; continued through years, till I had 'been at the very fountain. Indeed, it was a ruby-red, 'a perfumed draught, and I need not abuse the wine 'because I prefer water, but merely say I have had 'enough of it. Then, the first sight, the first knowledge 'of such a person was intoxication.

'She was an English lady, who, by a singular chance, 'was cast upon this region for a few months. Elegant 'and captivating, her every look and gesture was tuned 'to a different pitch from anything I had ever known. 'She was in various ways "accomplished," as it is 'called, though to what degree I cannot now judge. 'She painted in oils;—I had never before seen any one 'use the brush, and days would not have been too long 'for me to watch the pictures growing beneath her hand. 'She played the harp; and its tones are still to me the 'heralds of the promised land I saw before me then. She rose, she looked, she spoke; and the gentle swaying motion she made all through life has gladdened 'memory, as the stream does the woods and meadows.

'As she was often at the house of one of our neighbors, 'and afterwards at our own, my thoughts were fixed on 'her with all the force of my nature. It was my first real 'interest in my kind, and it engrossed me wholly. I had 'seen her,— I should see her,— and my mind lay steeped 'in the visions that flowed from this source. My task-'work I went through with, as I have done on similar 'occasions all my life, aided by pride that could not bear 'to fail, or be questioned. Could I cease from doing 'the work of the day, and hear the reason sneeringly 'given,—"Her head is so completely taken up with —— ' "that she can do nothing"? Impossible.

'Should the first love be blighted, they say, the mind 'loses its sense of eternity. All forms of existence seem 'fragile, the prison of time real, for a god is dead. 'Equally true is this of friendship. I thank Heaven that 'this first feeling was permitted its free flow. The years 'that lay between the woman and the girl only brought 'her beauty into perspective, and enabled me to see her 'as I did the mountains from my window, and made her 'presence to me a gate of Paradise. That which she 'was, that which she brought, that which she might 'have brought, were mine, and over a whole region of 'new life I ruled proprietor of the soil in my own right.

'Her mind was sufficiently unoccupied to delight in 'my warm devotion. She could not know what it was 'to me, but the light cast by the flame through so delicate a vase cheered and charmed her. All who saw admired her in their way; but she would lightly turn her head 'from their hard or oppressive looks, and fix a glance 'of full-eyed sweetness on the child, who, from a dis-'tance, watched all her looks and motions. She did not 'say much to me — not much to any one; she spoke in 'her whole being rather than by chosen words. Indeed, 'her proper speech was dance or song, and what was less 'expressive did not greatly interest her. But she saw 'much, having in its perfection the woman's delicate 'sense for sympathies and attractions. We walked in 'the fields, alone. Though others were present, her eyes 'were gliding over all the field and plain for the objects 'of beauty to which she was of kin. She was not cold 'to her seeming companions; a sweet courtesy satisfied 'them, but it hung about her like her mantle that she 'wore without thinking of it; her thoughts were free, for 'these civilized beings can really live two lives at the 'same moment. With them she seemed to be, but her 'hand was given to the child at her side; others did not 'observe me, but to her I was the only human presence. 'Like a guardian spirit she led me through the fields and 'groves, and every tree, every bird greeted me, and said, 'what I felt, "She is the first angel of your life."

'One time I had been passing the afternoon with her. 'She had been playing to me on the harp, and I sat lis-'tening in happiness almost unbearable. Some guests 'were announced. She went into another room to 'receive them, and I took up her book. It was Guy 'Mannering, then lately published, and the first of 'Scott's novels I had ever seen. I opened where her 'mark lay, and read merely with the feeling of continu-'ing our mutual existence by passing my eyes over the same page where hers had been. It was the description of the rocks on the sea-coast where the little Harry

'Bertram was lost. I had never seen such places, and 'my mind was vividly stirred to imagine them. The 'scene rose before me, very unlike reality, doubtless, but 'majestic and wild. I was the little Harry Bertram, and 'had lost her,— all I had to lose,— and sought her 'vainly in long dark caves that had no end, plashing 'through the water; while the crags beetled above, 'threatening to fall and crush the poor child. Absorbed 'in the painful vision, tears rolled down my cheeks. 'Just then she entered with light step, and full-beaming 'eye. When she saw me thus, a soft cloud stole over 'her face, and clothed every feature with a lovelier ten-'derness than I had seen there before. She did not ques-'tion, but fixed on me inquiring looks of beautiful love. 'I laid my head against her shoulder and wept,— dimly 'feeling that I must lose her and all,— all who spoke to 'me of the same things,— that the cold wave must rush 'over me. She waited till my tears were spent, then 'rising, took from a little box a bunch of golden ama-'ranths or everlasting flowers, and gave them to me. 'They were very fragrant. "They came," she said, '"from Madeira." These flowers stayed with me seven-'teen years. "Madeira" seemed to me the fortunate isle, 'apart in the blue ocean from all of ill or dread. When-'ever I saw a sail passing in the distance,— if it bore 'itself with fulness of beautiful certainty,— I felt that it 'was going to Madeira. Those thoughts are all gone 'now. No Madeira exists for me now,— no fortunate 'purple isle,— and all these hopes and fancies are lifted 'from the sea into the sky. Yet I thank the charms that 'fixed them here so long,— fixed them till perfumes like 'those of the golden flowers were drawn from the earth, 'teaching me to know my birth-place.

'I can tell little else of this time, — indeed, I remember 'little, except the state of feeling in which I lived. For 'I *lived*, and when this is the case, there is little to tell in 'the form of thought. We meet — at least those who 'are true to their instincts meet — a succession of per- 'sons through our lives, all of whom have some pecu- 'liar errand to us. There is an outer circle, whose exist- 'ence we perceive, but with whom we stand in no real 'relation. They tell us the news, they act on us in the 'offices of society, they show us kindness and aversion; 'but their influence does not penetrate; we are nothing 'to them, nor they to us, except as a part of the world's 'furniture. Another circle, within this, are dear and near 'to us. We know them and of what kind they are. 'They are to us not mere facts, but intelligible thoughts 'of the divine mind. We like to see how they are 'unfolded; we like to meet them and part from them; we 'like their action upon us and the pause that succeeds 'and enables us to appreciate its quality. Often we 'leave them on our path, and return no more, but we 'bear them in our memory, tales which have been told, 'and whose meaning has been felt.

'But yet a nearer group there are, beings born under 'the same star, and bound with us in a common destiny. 'These are not mere acquaintances, mere friends, but, 'when we meet, are sharers of our very existence. There 'is no separation; the same thought is given at the same 'moment to both, — indeed, it is born of the meeting, and 'would not otherwise have been called into existence at 'all. These not only know themselves more, but *are* 'more for having met, and regions of their being, which 'would else have laid sealed in cold obstruction, burst into 'leaf and bloom and song.

4

'The times of these meetings are fated, nor will either 'party be able ever to meet any other person in the same 'way. Both seem to rise at a glance into that part of 'the heavens where the word can be spoken, by which 'they are revealed to one another and to themselves. 'The step in being thus gained, can never be lost, nor can 'it be re-trod; for neither party will be again what the 'other wants. They are no longer fit to interchange 'mutual influence, for they do not really need it, and if 'they think they do, it is because they weakly pine after 'a past pleasure.

'To this inmost circle of relations but few are admit-'ted, because some prejudice or lack of courage has pre-'vented the many from listening to their instincts the 'first time they manifested themselves. If the voice is 'once disregarded it becomes fainter each time, till, at 'last, it is wholly silenced, and the man lives in this 'world, a stranger to its real life, deluded like the maniac 'who fancies he has attained his throne, while in real-'ity he is on a bed of musty straw. Yet, if the voice 'finds a listener and servant the first time of speaking, it 'is encouraged to more and more clearness. Thus it 'was with me,—from no merit of mine, but because I 'had the good fortune to be free enough to yield to my 'impressions. Common ties had not bound me; there 'were no traditionary notions in my mind; I believed in 'nothing merely because others believed in it; I had 'taken no feelings on trust. Thus my mind was open to 'their sway.

'This woman came to me, a star from the east, a 'morning star, and I worshipped her. She too was 'elevated by that worship, and her fairest self called out. 'To the mind she brought assurance that there was a 'region congenial with its tendencies and tastes, a region 'of elegant culture and intercourse, whose object, fulfilled 'or not, was to gratify the sense of beauty, not the mere 'utilities of life. In our relation she was lifted to the top 'of her being. She had known many celebrities, had 'roused to passionate desire many hearts, and became 'afterwards a wife; but I do not believe she ever more 'truly realized her best self than towards the lonely child 'whose heaven she was, whose eye she met, and whose 'possibilities she predicted.] "He raised me," said a 'woman inspired by love, "upon the pedestal of his own '"high thoughts, and wings came at once, but I did not '"fly away. I stood there with downcast eyes worthy '"of his love, for he had made me so."

['Thus we do always for those who inspire us to expect from them the best. That which they are able to 'be, they become, because we demand it of them. "We '"expect the impossible — and find it."]

'My English friend went across the sea. She passed 'into her former life, and into ties that engrossed her 'days. But she has never ceased to think of me. Her 'thoughts turn forcibly back to the child who was to her 'all she saw of the really New World. On the promised 'coasts she had found only cities, careful men and women, 'the aims and habits of ordinary life in her own land, 'without that elegant culture which she, probably, over-'estimated, because it was her home. But in the mind of 'the child she found the fresh prairie, the untrodden for-'ests for which she had longed. I saw in her the storied 'castles, the fair stately parks and the wind laden with 'tones from the past, which I desired to know. We wrote 'to one another for many years; — her shallow and delicate epistles did not disenchant me, nor did she fail tc 'see something of the old poetry in my rude characters 'and stammering speech. But we must never meet again.

'When this friend was withdrawn I fell into a pro-'found depression. I knew not how to exert myself, but 'lay bound hand and foot. Melancholy enfolded me in 'an atmosphere, as joy had done. This suffering, too, 'was out of the gradual and natural course. Those who 'are really children could not know such love, or feel 'such sorrow. "I am to blame," said my father, "in '" keeping her at home so long merely to please myself. '" She needs to be with other girls, needs play and vari-'"ety. She does not seem to me really sick, but dull '"rather. She eats nothing, you say. I see she grows '" thin. She ought to change the scene."

'I was indeed *dull.* The books, the garden, had lost 'all charm. I had the excuse of headache, constantly, 'for not attending to my lessons. The light of life was 'set, and every leaf was withered. At such an early age 'there are no back or side scenes where the mind, wea-'ry and sorrowful, may retreat. Older, we realize the 'width of the world more, and it is not easy to despair 'on any point. The effort at thought to which we are 'compelled relieves and affords a dreary retreat, like 'hiding in a brick-kiln till the shower be over. But then all 'joy seemed to have departed with my friend, and the 'emptiness of our house stood revealed. This I had not felt 'while I every day expected to see or had seen her, or 'annoyance and dulness were unnoticed or swallowed 'up in the one thought that clothed my days with beauty. 'But now she was gone, and I was roused from habits 'of reading or reverie to feel the fiery temper of the 'soul, and to learn that it must have vent, that it would 'not be pacified by shadows, neither meet without con-

'suming what lay around it. I avoided the table as much 'as possible, took long walks and lay in bed, or on the 'floor of my room. I complained of my head, and it was 'not wrong to do so, for a sense of dulness and suffoca-'tion, if not pain, was there constantly.

'But when it was proposed that I should go to school, 'that was a remedy I could not listen to with patience 'for a moment. The peculiarity of my education had 'separated me entirely from the girls around, except that 'when they were playing at active games, I would some-'times go out and join them. I liked violent bodily exer-'cise, which always relieved my nerves. But I had no 'success in associating with them beyond the mere play. 'Not only I was not their school-mate, but my book-life 'and lonely habits had given a cold aloofness to my 'whole expression, and veiled my manner with a hau-'teur which turned all hearts away. Yet, as this reserve 'was superficial, and rather ignorance than arrogance, 'it produced no deep dislike. Besides, the girls supposed 'me really superior to themselves, and did not hate me 'for feeling it, but neither did they like me, nor wish 'to have me with them. Indeed, I had gradually given 'up all such wishes myself; for they seemed to me rude, 'tiresome, and childish, as I did to them dull and strange. 'This experience had been earlier, before I was admitted 'to any real friendship; but now that I had been lifted 'into the life of mature years, and into just that atmos-'phere of European life to which I had before been tend-'ing, the thought of sending me to school filled me with 'disgust.

'Yet what could I tell my father of such feelings? 'I resisted all I could, but in vain. He had no faith in 'medical aid generally, and justly saw that this was nc 'occasion for its use. He thought I needed change of 'scene, and to be roused to activity by other children. '"I have kept you at home," he said, "because I took '"such pleasure in teaching you myself, and besides I '"knew that you would learn faster with one who is so "desirous to aid you. But you will learn fast enough '"wherever you are, and you ought to be more with '"others of your own age. I shall soon hear that you '"are better, I trust."'

SCHOOL-LIFE.

The school to which Margaret was sent was that of the Misses Prescott, in Groton, Massachusetts. And her experience there has been described with touching truthfulness by herself, in the story of "Mariana."*

'At first her school-mates were captivated with her 'ways; her love of wild dances and sudden song, her 'freaks of passion and of wit. She was always new, 'always surprising, and, for a time, charming.

'But after a while, they tired of her. She could never 'be depended on to join in their plans, yet she expected 'them to follow out hers with their whole strength. She 'was very loving, even infatuated in her own affections, 'and exacted from those who had professed any love for 'her the devotion she was willing to bestow.

'Yet there was a vein of haughty caprice in her char-'acter, and a love of solitude, which made her at times 'wish to retire apart, and at these times she would ex-'pect to be entirely understood, and let alone, yet to be 'welcomed back when she returned. She did not thwart

* Summer on the Lakes, p. 81.

'others in their humors, but she never doubted of great 'indulgence from them.

'Some singular habits she had, which, when new, 'charmed, but, after acquaintance, displeased her com- 'panions. She had by nature the same habit and power 'of excitement that is described in the spinning der- 'vishes of the East. Like them she would spin until all 'around her were giddy, while her own brain, instead of 'being disturbed, was excited to great action. Pausing, 'she would declaim verses of others, or her own, or act 'many parts, with strange catchwords and burdens, that 'seemed to act with mystical power on her own fancy, 'sometimes stimulating her to convulse the hearers with 'laughter, sometimes to melt them to tears. When her 'power began to languish, she would spin again till fired 'to re-commence her singular drama, into which she wove 'figures from the scenes of her earlier childhood, her com- 'panions, and the dignitaries she sometimes saw, with 'fantasies unknown to life, unknown to heaven or earth.

'This excitement, as may be supposed, was not good 'for her. It usually came on in the evening, and often 'spoiled her sleep. She would wake in the night, and 'cheat her restlessness by inventions that teased, while 'they sometimes diverted her companions.

'She was also a sleep-walker; and this one trait of 'her case did somewhat alarm her guardians, who, oth- 'erwise, showed the profound ignorance as to this pecu- 'liar being, usual in the overseeing of the young. They 'consulted a physician, who said she would outgrow it, 'and prescribed a milk diet.

'Meantime, the fever of this ardent and too early stim- 'ulated nature was constantly increased by the restraints 'and narrow routine of the boarding-school. She was 'always devising means to break in upon it. She had a 'taste — which would have seemed ludicrous to her mates, 'if they had not felt some awe of her, from the touch of 'genius and power that never left her — for costume and 'fancy dresses. There was always some sash twisted 'about her, some drapery, something odd in the arrange-'ment of her hair and dress; so that the methodical pre-'ceptress dared not let her go out without a careful 'scrutiny and remodelling, whose soberizing effects gen-'erally disappeared the moment she was in the free air.

'At last a vent was assured for her in private theatri-'cals. Play followed play, and in these and the rehear-'sals, she found entertainment congenial with her. The 'principal parts, as a matter of course, fell to her lot; 'most of the good suggestions and arrangements came 'from her; and, for a time, she ruled mostly, and shone 'triumphant.

'During these performances, the girls had heightened 'their bloom with artificial red; this was delightful to 'them, it was something so out of the way. But Ma-'riana, after the plays were over, kept her carmine 'saucer on the dressing-table, and put on her blushes, 'regularly as the morning. When stared and jeered at, 'she at first said she did it because she thought it made 'her look pretty; but, after a while, she became petulant 'about it, — would make no reply to any joke, but merely 'kept up the habit.

'This irritated the girls, as all eccentricity does the 'world in general, more than vice or malignity. They 'talked it over among themselves till they were wrought 'up to a desire of punishing, once for all, this sometimes 'amusing, but so often provoking non-conformist. And 'having obtained leave of the mistress, they laid, with 'great glee, a plan, one evening, which was to be carried 'into execution next day at dinner.

'Among Mariana's irregularities was a great aversion 'to the meal-time ceremonial,— so long, so tiresome, she 'found it, to be seated at a certain moment, and to wait 'while each one was served, at so large a table, where 'there was scarcely any conversation; and from day to 'day it became more heavy to sit there, or go there at 'all; often as possible she excused herself on the ever-'convenient plea of headache, and was hardly ever 'ready when the dinner-bell rang.

'To-day the summons found her on the balcony, but 'gazing on the beautiful prospect. I have heard her say 'afterwards, that she had scarcely in her life been so 'happy,— and she was one with whom happiness was a 'still rapture. It was one of the most blessed summer 'days; the shadows of great white clouds empurpled the 'distant hills for a few moments, only to leave them 'more golden; the tall grass of the wide fields waved in 'the softest breeze. Pure blue were the heavens, and 'the same hue of pure contentment was in the heart of 'Mariana.

'Suddenly on her bright mood jarred the dinner-bell. 'At first rose her usual thought, I will not, cannot go; 'and then the *must*, which daily life can always enforce, 'even upon the butterflies and birds, came, and she 'walked reluctantly to her room. She merely changed 'her dress, and never thought of adding the artificial 'rose to her cheek.

'When she took her seat in the dining-hall, and was 'asked if she would be helped, raising her eyes, she saw 'the person who asked her was deeply rouged, with a 'bright glaring spot, perfectly round, on either cheek.

'She looked at the next,—same apparition! She then 'slowly passed her eyes down the whole line, and saw 'the same, with a suppressed smile distorting every 'countenance. Catching the design at once, she deliber-'ately looked along her own side of the table, at every 'schoolmate in turn; every one had joined in the trick. 'The teachers strove to be grave, but she saw they enjoyed the joke. The servants could not suppress a 'titter.

'When Warren Hastings stood at the bar of West-'minster Hall, — when the Methodist preacher walked 'through a line of men, each of whom greeted him with 'a brickbat or rotten egg, — they had some preparation for 'the crisis, though it might be very difficult to meet it 'with an impassible brow. Our little girl was quite 'unprepared to find herself in the midst of a world 'which despised her, and triumphed in her disgrace.

'She had ruled like a queen, in the midst of her com-'panions; she had shed her animation through their 'lives, and loaded them with prodigal favors, nor once 'suspected that a popular favorite might not be loved. 'Now she felt that she had been but a dangerous play-'thing in the hands of those whose hearts she never had 'doubted.

'Yet the occasion found her equal to it, for Mariana 'had the kind of spirit which, in a better cause, had 'made the Roman matron truly say of her death-wound, '"It is not painful, Pœtus." She did not blench, — she 'did not change countenance. She swallowed her din-'ner with apparent composure. She made remarks to 'those near her, as if she had no eyes.

'The wrath of the foe, of course, rose higher, and the moment they were freed from the restraints of the din-

'ing room, they all ran off, gayly calling, and sarcastically laughing, with backward glances, at Mariana, left alone.

'Alone she went to her room, locked the door, and threw herself on the floor in strong convulsions. These had sometimes threatened her life, in earlier childhood, but of later years she had outgrown them. School-hours came, and she was not there. A little girl, sent to her door, could get no answer. The teachers became alarmed, and broke it open. Bitter was their penitence, and that of her companions, at the state in which they found her. For some hours terrible anxiety was felt, but at last nature, exhausted, relieved herself by a deep slumber.

'From this Mariana arose an altered being. She made no reply to the expressions of sorrow from her companions, none to the grave and kind, but undiscerning, comments of her teacher. She did not name the source of her anguish, and its poisoned dart sank deeply in. This was the thought which stung her so:—

'"What, not one, not a single one, in the hour of trial, "to take my part? not one who refused to take part "against me?" Past words of love, and caresses, little heeded at the time, rose to her memory, and gave fuel to her distempered heart. Beyond the sense of burning resentment at universal perfidy, she could not get. And Mariana, born for love, now hated all the world.

'The change, however, which these feelings made in her conduct and appearance, bore no such construction to the careless observer. Her gay freaks were quite gone, her wildness, her invention. Her dress was uniform, her manner much subdued. Her chief interest seemed to be now in her studies, and in music. Her 'companions she never sought; but they, partly from 'uneasy, remorseful feelings, partly that they really liked 'her much better now that she did not puzzle and 'oppress them, sought her continually. And here the 'black shadow comes upon her life, the only stain upon 'the history of Mariana.

'They talked to her, as girls having few topics natur- 'ally do, of one another. Then the demon rose within 'her, and spontaneously, without design, generally with- 'out words of positive falsehood, she became a genius of 'discord amongst them. She fanned those flames of 'envy and jealousy which a wise, true word from a third 'person will often quench forever; and by a glance, or 'seemingly light reply, she planted the seeds of dissen- 'sion, till there was scarcely a peaceful affection, or sin- 'cere intimacy, in the circle where she lived, and could 'not but rule, for she was one whose nature was to that 'of the others as fire to clay.

'It was at this time that I came to the school, and 'first saw Mariana. Me she charmed at once, for I was 'a sentimental child, who, in my early ill health, had 'been indulged in reading novels, till I had no eyes for 'the common. It was not, however, easy to approach 'her. Did I offer to run and fetch her handkerchief, she 'was obliged to go to her room, and would rather do it 'herself. She did not like to have people turn over for 'her the leaves of the music-book as she played. Did I 'approach my stool to her feet, she moved away as if to 'give me room. The bunch of wild flowers, which I 'timidly laid beside her plate, was left untouched. 'After some weeks, my desire to attract her notice really 'preyed upon me; and one day, meeting her alone in the 'entry, I fell upon my knees, and, kissing her hand, cried,

'"O, Mariana, do let me love you, and try to love me a '"little!" But my idol snatched away her hand, and 'laughing wildly, ran into her room. After that day, 'her manner to me was not only cold, but repulsive, and 'I felt myself scorned.

'Perhaps four months had passed thus, when, one 'afternoon, it became obvious that something more than 'common was brewing. Dismay and mystery were 'written in many faces of the older girls; much whisper-'ing was going on in corners.

'In the evening, after prayers, the principal bade us 'stay; and, in a grave, sad voice, summoned forth 'Mariana to answer charges to be made against her.

'Mariana stood up and leaned against the chimney-'piece. Then eight of the older girls came forward, and 'preferred against her charges,— alas! too well founded, 'of calumny and falsehood.

'At first, she defended herself with self-possession and 'eloquence. But when she found she could no more 'resist the truth, she suddenly threw herself down, 'dashing her head with all her force against the iron 'hearth, on which a fire was burning, and was taken up 'senseless.

'The affright of those present was great. Now that 'they had perhaps killed her, they reflected it would 'have been as well if they had taken warning from the 'former occasion, and approached very carefully a 'nature so capable of any extreme. After a while she 'revived, with a faint groan, amid the sobs of her com-'panions. I was on my knees by the bed, and held her 'cold hand. One of those most aggrieved took it from 'me, to beg her pardon, and say, it was impossible not to 'love her. She made no reply.

'Neither that night, nor for several days, could a word 'be obtained from her, nor would she touch food; but, 'when it was presented to her, or any one drew near 'from any cause, she merely turned away her head, and 'gave no sign. The teacher saw that some terrible ner-'vous affection had fallen upon her — that she grew 'more and more feverish. She knew not what to do.

'Meanwhile, a new revolution had taken place in the 'mind of the passionate but nobly-tempered child. All 'these months nothing but the sense of injury had 'rankled in her heart. She had gone on in one 'mood, doing what the demon prompted, without 'scruple, and without fear.

'But at the moment of detection, the tide ebbed, and 'the bottom of her soul lay revealed to her eye. How 'black, how stained, and sad! Strange, strange, 'that she had not seen before the baseness and cruelty 'of falsehood, the loveliness of truth! Now, amid the 'wreck, uprose the moral nature, which never before 'had attained the ascendant. "But," she thought, '"too late sin is revealed to me in all its deformity, and '"sin-defiled, I will not, cannot live. The main-spring '"of life is broken."

'The lady who took charge of this sad child had 'never well understood her before, but had always 'looked on her with great tenderness. And now love 'seemed, — when all around were in the greatest dis-'tress, fearing to call in medical aid, fearing to do with-'out it, — to teach her where the only balm was to be 'found that could heal the wounded spirit.

'One night she came in, bringing a calming draught. 'Mariana was sitting as usual, her hair loose, her dress 'the same robe they had put on her at first, her eyes 'fixed vacantly upon the whited wall. To the proffers 'and entreaties of her nurse, she made no reply.

'The lady burst into tears, but Mariana did not seem 'even to observe it.

'The lady then said, "O, my child, do not despair; do '"not think that one great fault can mar a whole life! '"Let me trust you; let me tell you the griefs of my sad '"life. I will tell you, Mariana, what I never expected '"to impart to any one."

'And so she told her tale. It was one of pain, of 'shame, borne not for herself, but for one near and dear 'as herself. Mariana knew the dignity and reserve of 'this lady's nature. She had often admired to see how 'the cheek, lovely, but no longer young, mantled with 'the deepest blush of youth, and the blue eyes were 'cast down at any little emotion. She had understood 'the proud sensibility of her character. She fixed her 'eyes on those now raised to hers, bright with fast-fall-'ing tears. She heard the story to the end, and then, 'without saying a word, stretched out her hand for the 'cup.

'She returned to life, but it was as one who had 'passed through the valley of death. The heart of 'stone was quite broken in her, — the fiery will fallen 'from flame to coal. When her strength was a little 'restored, she had all her companions summoned, and 'said to them, — "I deserved to die, but a generous '"trust has called me back to life. I will be worthy '"of it, nor ever betray the trust, or resent injury more. '"Can you forgive the past?"

'And they not only forgave, but, with love and ear-'nest tears, clasped in their arms the returning sister. 'They vied with one another in offices of humble love 'to the humbled one; and let it be recorded, as an 'instance of the pure honor of which young hearts are 'capable, that these facts, known to some forty persons, 'never, so far as I know, transpired beyond those walls.

'It was not long after this that Mariana was 'summoned home. She went thither a wonderfully 'instructed being, though in ways those who had sent 'her forth to learn little dreamed of.

'Never was forgotten the vow of the returning prodi-'gal. Mariana could not *resent*, could not *play false.* 'The terrible crisis, which she so early passed through, probably prevented the world from hearing much of 'her. A wild fire was tamed in that hour of penitence 'at the boarding-school, such as has oftentimes wrapped 'court and camp in a destructive glow.'

SELF-CULTURE.

Letters written to the beloved teacher, who so wisely befriended Margaret in her trial-hour, will best show how this high-spirited girl sought to enlarge and harmonize her powers.

'*Cambridge, July* 11, 1825. — Having excused myself 'from accompanying my honored father to church, which 'I always do in the afternoon, when possible, I devote 'to you the hours which Ariosto and Helvetius ask of 'my eyes, — as, lying on my writing-desk, they put me 'in mind that they must return this week to their 'owner.

'You keep me to my promise of giving you some 'sketch of my pursuits. I rise a little before five, walk 'an hour, and then practise on the piano, till seven, 'when we breakfast. Next I read French, — Sismondi's

'Literature of the South of Europe,— till eight, then two 'or three lectures in Brown's Philosophy. About half-'past nine I go to Mr. Perkins's school and study Greek 'till twelve, when, the school being dismissed, I recite, go 'home, and practise again till dinner, at two. Some-'times, if the conversation is very agreeable, I lounge 'for half an hour over the dessert, though rarely so lav-'ish of time. Then, when I can, I read two hours in 'Italian, but I am often interrupted. At six, I walk, or 'take a drive. Before going to bed, I play or sing, for 'half an hour or so, to make all sleepy, and, about 'eleven, retire to write a little while in my journal, exer-'cises on what I have read, or a series of characteristics 'which I am filling up according to advice. Thus, you 'see, I am learning Greek, and making acquaintance 'with metaphysics, and French and Italian literature.

'"How," you will say, "can I believe that my indo-'"lent, fanciful, pleasure-loving pupil, perseveres in such '"a course?" I feel the power of industry growing 'every day, and, besides the all-powerful motive of 'ambition, and a new stimulus lately given through a 'friend, I have learned to believe that nothing, no! not 'perfection, is unattainable. I am determined on dis-'tinction, which formerly I thought to win at an easy 'rate; but now I see that long years of labor must be 'given to secure even the "*succès de societé*,"—which, 'however, shall never content me. I see multitudes of 'examples of persons of genius, utterly deficient in 'grace and the power of pleasurable excitement. I 'wish to combine both. I know the obstacles in my 'way. I am wanting in that intuitive tact and polish, 'which nature has bestowed upon some, but which I 'must acquire. And, on the other hand, my powers of 'intellect, though sufficient, I suppose, are not well disci-'plined. Yet all such hindrances may be overcome by 'an ardent spirit. If I fail, my consolation shall be 'found in active employment.'

'*Cambridge, March* 5, 1826.—Duke Nicholas is to suc-'ceed the Emperor Alexander, thus relieving Europe from 'the sad apprehension of evil to be inflicted by the bru-'tal Constantine, and yet depriving the Holy Alliance of 'its very soul. We may now hope more strongly for the 'liberties of unchained Europe; we look in anxious sus-'pense for the issue of the struggle of Greece, the result 'of which seems to depend on the new autocrat. I have 'lately been reading Anastasius, the Greek Gil Blas, 'which has excited and delighted me; but I do not think 'you like works of this cast. You did not like my sombre 'and powerful Ormond, —though this is superior to Or-'mond in every respect; it translates you to another scene, 'hurls you into the midst of the burning passions of the 'East, whose vicissitudes are, however, interspersed by 'deep pauses of shadowy reflective scenes, which open 'upon you like the green watered little vales occasion-'ally to be met with in the burning desert. There is 'enough of history to fix profoundly the attention, and 'prevent you from revolting from scenes profligate and 'terrific, and such characters as are never to be met 'with in our paler climes. How delighted am I to 'read a book which can absorb me to tears and shud-'dering, —not by individual traits of beauty, but by 'the spirit of adventure,—happiness which one seldom 'enjoys after childhood in this blest age, so philosophic, 'free, and enlightened to a miracle, but far removed from 'the ardent dreams and soft credulity of the world's 'youth. Sometimes I think I would give all our gains 'for those times when young and old gathered in the 'feudal hall, listening with soul-absorbing transport to 'the romance of the minstrel, unrestrained and regard- 'less of criticism, and when they worshipped nature, 'not as high-dressed and pampered, but as just risen 'from the bath.'

'*Cambridge, May* 14, 1826. — I am studying Madame 'de Stael, Epictetus, Milton, Racine, and Castilian bal- 'lads, with great delight. There's an assemblage for you. 'Now tell me, had you rather be the brilliant De Stael or 'the useful Edgeworth? — though De Stael is useful too, 'but it is on the grand scale, on liberalizing, regenerating 'principles, and has not the immediate practical success 'that Edgeworth has. I met with a parallel the other 'day between Byron and Rousseau, and had a mind to 'send it to you, it was so excellent.'

'*Cambridge, Jan.* 10, 1827. — As to my studies, I am 'engrossed in reading the elder Italian poets, beginning 'with Berni, from whom I shall proceed to Pulci and Poli- 'tian. I read very critically. Miss Francis * and I think 'of reading Locke, as introductory to a course of English 'metaphysics, and then De Stael on Locke's system. 'Allow me to introduce this lady to you as a most inter- 'esting woman, in my opinion. She is a natural person, '— a most rare thing in this age of cant and pretension. 'Her conversation is charming,— she brings all her pow- 'ers to bear upon it; her style is varied, and she has a 'very pleasant and spirited way of thinking. I should judge, too, that she possesses peculiar purity of mind. I

* Lydia Maria Child.

'am going to spend this evening with her, and wish you 'were to be with us.'

'*Cambridge, Jan.* 3, 1828.—I am reading Sir William 'Temple's works, with great pleasure. Such enlarged 'views are rarely to be found combined with such acute- 'ness and discrimination. His style, though diffuse, is 'never verbose or overloaded, but beautifully expressive; ''t is English, too, though he was an accomplished linguist, 'and wrote much and well in French, Spanish, and Latin. 'The latter he used, as he says of the Bishop of Mun- 'ster, (with whom he corresponded in that tongue,) '"more like a man of the court and of business than a '"scholar." He affected not Augustan niceties, but his 'expressions are free and appropriate. I have also read 'a most entertaining book, which I advise you to read, '(if you have not done so already,) Russell's Tour in Ger- 'many. There you will find more intelligent and detailed 'accounts than I have seen anywhere of the state of the 'German universities, Viennese court, secret associations, 'Plica Polonica, and other very interesting matters. 'There is a minute account of the representative gov- 'ernment given to his subjects by the Duke of Wei- 'mar. I have passed a luxurious afternoon, having 'been in bed from dinner till tea, reading Rammohun 'Roy's book, and framing dialogues aloud on every 'argument beneath the sun. Really, I have not had my 'mind so exercised for months; and I have felt a gladi- 'atorial disposition lately, and don't enjoy mere light con- 'versation. The love of knowledge is prodigiously kin- 'dled within my soul of late; I study much and reflect 'more, and feel an aching wish for some person with 'whom I might talk fully and openly.

'Did you ever read the letters and reflections of Prince 'de Ligne, the most agreeable man of his day? I have 'just had it, and if it is new to you, I recommend it as 'an agreeable book to read at night just before you go to 'bed. There is much curious matter concerning Catha-'rine II.'s famous expedition into Taurida, which puts 'down some of the romantic stories prevalent on that 'score, but relates more surprising realities. Also it 'gives much interesting information about that noble 'philosopher, Joseph II., and about the Turkish tactics 'and national character.'

'*Cambridge, Jan.* 1830. — You need not fear to revive 'painful recollections. I often think of those sad experi-'ences. True, they agitate me deeply. But it was best 'so. They have had a most powerful effect on my char-'acter. I tremble at whatever looks like dissimulation. 'The remembrance of that evening subdues every proud, 'passionate impulse. My beloved supporter in those sor-'rowful hours, your image shines as fair to my mind's eye 'as it did in 1825, when I left you with my heart over-'flowing with gratitude for your singular and judicious 'tenderness. Can I ever forget that to your treatment in 'that crisis of youth I owe the true life, — the love of 'Truth and Honor?'

LIFE IN CAMBRIDGE.

BY JAMES FREEMAN CLARKE.

"Extraordinary, generous seeking."

GOETHE.

"Through, brothers, through, — this be
Our watchword in danger or sorrow,
Common clay to its mother dust,
All nobleness heavenward!"

THEODORE KOERNER.

"Thou friend whose presence on my youthful heart
Fell, like bright Spring upon some herbless plain;
How beautiful and calm and free thou wert
In thy young wisdom, when the mortal chain
Of custom thou didst burst and rend in twain,
And walk as free as light the clouds among!"

SHELLEY

"There are not a few instances of that conflict, known also to the fathers, of the spirit with the flesh, the inner with the outer man, of the freedom of the will with the necessity of nature, the pleasure of the individual with the conventions of society, of the emergency of the case with the despotism of the rule. It is this, which, while it makes the interest of life, makes the difficulty of living. It is a struggle, indeed, between unequal powers, — between the man, who is a conscious moral person, and nature, or events, or bodies of men, which either want personality or unity; and hence the man, after fearful and desolating war, sometimes rises on the ruins of all the necessities of nature and all the prescriptions of society. But what these want in personality they possess in number, in recurrency, in invulnerability. The spirit of man, an agent indeed of curious power and boundless resource, but trembling with sensibilities, tender and irritable, goes out against the inexorable conditions of destiny, the lifeless forces of nature, or the ferocious cruelty of the multitude, and long before the hands are weary or the invention exhausted, the heart may be broken in the warfare."

N. A. Review, Jan., 1817, article "*Dichtung und Wahrheit.*"

II.

CAMBRIDGE.

The difficulty which we all feel in describing our past intercourse and friendship with Margaret Fuller, is, that the intercourse was so intimate, and the friendship so personal, that it is like making a confession to the public of our most interior selves. For this noble person, by her keen insight and her generous interest, entered into the depth of every soul with which she stood in any real relation. To print one of her letters, is like giving an extract from our own private journal. To relate what she was to us, is to tell how she discerned elements of worth and beauty where others could only have seen what was common-place and poor; it is to say what high hopes, what generous assurance, what a pure ambition, she entertained on our behalf, — a hope and confidence which may well be felt as a rebuke to our low attainments and poor accomplishments.

Nevertheless, it seems due to this great soul that those of us who have been blessed and benefited by her friendship should be willing to say what she has done for us, — undeterred by the thought that to reveal her is to expose ourselves.

My acquaintance with Sarah Margaret Fuller began in 1829. We both lived in Cambridge, and from that time until she went to Groton to reside, in 1833, I saw her, or heard from her, almost every day. There was a family connection, and we called each other cousin.* During this period, her intellect was intensely active. With what eagerness did she seek for knowledge! What fire, what exuberance, what reach, grasp, overflow of thought, shone in her conversation! She needed a friend to whom to speak of her studies, to whom to express the ideas which were dawning and taking shape in her mind. She accepted me for this friend, and to me it was a gift of the gods, an influence like no other.

For the first few months of our acquaintance, our intercourse was simply that of two young persons seeking entertainment in each other's society. Perhaps a note written at this time will illustrate the easy and graceful movement of her mind in this superficial kind of intercourse.

'*March* 16*th*, 1830. *Half-past six, morning.*—I have 'encountered that most common-place of glories, sunrise, '(to say naught of being praised and wondered at by 'every member of the family in succession,) that I 'might have leisure to answer your note even as you 'requested. I thank you a thousand times for "The

* I had once before seen Margaret, when we were both children about five years of age. She made an impression on my mind which was never effaced, and I distinctly recollect the joyful child, with light flowing locks and bright face, who led me by the hand down the back-steps of her house into the garden. This was when her father lived in Cambridgeport, in a house on Cherry street, in front of which still stand some handsome trees, planted by him in the year of Margaret's birth.

'Rivals."* Alas!·! I must leave my heart in the 'book, and spend the livelong morning in reading to a 'sick lady from some amusing story-book. I tell you 'of this act of (in my professedly unamiable self) most 'unwonted charity, for three several reasons. Firstly, 'and foremostly, because I think that you, being a social-'ist by vocation, a sentimentalist by nature, and a Chan-'ningite from force of circumstances and fashion, will 'peculiarly admire this little self-sacrifice exploit. Sec-'ondly, because 't is neither conformable to the spirit of 'the nineteenth century, nor the march of mind, that 'those churlish reserves should be kept up between *the 'right and left hands,* which belonged to ages of barba-'rism and prejudice, and could only have been inculcated 'for their use. Thirdly, and lastly, the true lady-like 'reason, — because I would fain have my correspondent 'enter into and sympathize with my feelings of the 'moment.

'As to the relationship; 't is, I find, on inquiry, by no 'means to be compared with that between myself and '—; of course, the intimacy cannot be so great. But no 'matter; it will enable me to answer your notes, and you 'will interest my imagination much more than if I knew 'you better. But I am exceeding legitimate note-writing 'limits. With a hope that this epistle may be legible to 'your undiscerning eyes, I conclude,

'Your cousin only thirty-seven degrees removed,

'M.'

The next note which I shall give was written not many days after, and is in quite a different vein. It is

* "The Rivals" was a novel I had lent her, — if I remember right, by the author of "The Collegians;" a writer who in those days interested us not a little.

memorable to me as laying the foundation of a friendship which brought light to my mind, which enlarged my heart, and gave elevation and energy to my aims and purposes. For nearly twenty years, Margaret remained true to the pledges of this note. In a few years we were separated, but our friendship remained firm. Living in different parts of the country, occupied with different thoughts and duties, making other friends,— sometimes not seeing nor hearing from each other for months,— we never met without my feeling that she was ready to be interested in all my thoughts, to love those whom I loved, to watch my progress, to rebuke my faults and follies, to encourage within me every generous and pure aspiration, to demand of me, always, the best that I could be or do, and to be satisfied with no mediocrity, no conformity to any low standard.

And what she thus was to me, she was to many others. Inexhaustible in power of insight, and with a good-will "broad as ether," she could enter into the needs, and sympathize with the various excellences, of the greatest variety of characters. One thing only she demanded of all her friends,— that they should have some "extraordinary generous seeking,"* that they should not be satisfied with the common routine of life,— that they should aspire to something higher, better, holier, than they had now attained. Where this element of aspiration existed, she demanded no originality of intellect, no greatness of soul. If these were found, well; but she could love,

* These words of Goethe, which I have placed among the mottoes at the beginning of this chapter, were written by Margaret on the first page of a richly gilt and bound blank book, which she gave to me, in 1832, for a private journal. The words of Körner are also translated by herself, and were given to me about the same time

tenderly and truly, where they were not. But for a worldly character, however gifted, she felt and expressed something very like contempt. At this period, she had no patience with self-satisfied mediocrity. She afterwards learned patience and unlearned contempt; but at the time of which I write, she seemed, and was to the multitude, a haughty and supercilious person, — while to those whom she loved, she was all the more gentle, tender and true.

Margaret possessed, in a greater degree than any person I ever knew, the power of so magnetizing others, when she wished, by the power of her mind, that they would lay open to her all the secrets of their nature. She had an infinite curiosity to know individuals, — not the vulgar curiosity which seeks to find out the circumstances of their outward lives, but that which longs to understand the inward springs of thought and action in their souls. This desire and power both rested on a profound conviction of her mind in the individuality of every human being. A human being, according to her faith, was not the result of the presence and stamp of outward circumstances, but an original *monad*, with a certain special faculty, capable of a certain fixed development, and having a profound personal unity, which the ages of eternity might develop, but could not exhaust. I know not if she would have stated her faith in these terms, but some such conviction appeared in her constant endeavor to see and understand the germinal principle, the special characteristic, of every person whom she deemed worthy of knowing at all. Therefore, while some persons study human nature in its universal laws, and become great philosophers, moralists and teachers of the race, — while others study mankind in action, and, seeing the motives

6*

and feelings by which masses are swayed, become eminent politicians, sagacious leaders, and eminent in all political affairs,— a few, like Margaret, study character, and acquire the power of exerting profoundest influence on individual souls.

I had expressed to her my desire to know something of the history of her mind,— to understand her aims, her hopes, her views of life. In a note written in reply, she answered me thus:—

'I cannot bring myself to write you what you wished. 'You would be disappointed, at any rate, after all the 'solemn note of preparation; the consciousness of this 'would chill me now. Besides, I cannot be willing to 'leave with you such absolute *vagaries* in a tangible, 'examinable shape. I think of your after-smiles, of 'your colder moods. But I will tell you, when a fitting 'opportunity presents, all that can interest you, and per- 'haps more. And excuse my caution. I do not profess, 'I may not dare, to be generous in these matters.'

To this I replied to the effect that, "in my coldest mood I could not criticize words written in a confiding spirit;" and that, at all events, she must not expect of me a confidence which she dared not return. This was the substance of a note to which Margaret thus replied:—

'I thank you for your note. Ten minutes before I 'received it, I scarcely thought that anything again 'would make my stifled heart throb so warm a pulse of 'pleasure. Excuse my cold doubts, my selfish arrogance, '— you will, when I tell you that this experiment has 'before had such uniform results; those who professed 'to seek my friendship, and whom, indeed, I have often 'truly loved, have always learned to content themselves 'with that inequality in the connection which I have 'never striven to veil. Indeed, I have thought myself 'more valued and better beloved, because the sympathy, 'the interest, were all on my side. True! such regard 'could never flatter my pride, nor gratify my affections, 'since it was paid not to myself, but to the need they 'had of me; still, it was dear and pleasing, as it has 'given me an opportunity of knowing and serving many 'lovely characters; and I cannot see that there is any- 'thing else for me to do on earth. And I should rejoice 'to cultivate generosity, since (see that *since*) affections 'gentler and more sympathetic are denied me.

'I would have been a true friend to you; ever ready 'to solace your pains and partake your joy as far as 'possible. Yet I cannot but rejoice that I have met a 'person who could discriminate and reject a proffer of 'this sort. Two years ago I should have ventured to 'proffer you friendship, indeed, on seeing such an in- 'stance of pride in you; but I have gone through a sad 'process of feeling since, and those emotions, so necessa- 'rily repressed, have lost their simplicity, their ardent 'beauty. *Then*, there was nothing I might not have 'disclosed to a person capable of comprehending, had I 'ever seen such an one! Now there are many voices of 'the soul which I imperiously silence. This results not 'from any particular circumstance or event, but from a 'gradual ascertaining of realities.

'I cannot promise you any limitless confidence, but I '*can* promise that no timid caution, no haughty dread 'shall prevent my telling you the truth of my thoughts 'on any subject we may have in common. Will this 'satisfy you? Oh let it! suffer me to know you.'

In a postscript she adds, 'No other cousin or friend of 'any style is to see this note.'] So for twenty years it has lain unseen, but for twenty years did we remain true to the pledges of that period. And now that noble heart sleeps beneath the tossing Atlantic, and I feel no reluctance in showing to the world this expression of pure youthful ardor. It may, perhaps, lead some wise worldlings, who doubt the possibility of such a relation, to reconsider the grounds of their scepticism; or, if not that, it may encourage some youthful souls, as earnest and eager as ours, to trust themselves to their hearts' impulse, and enjoy some such blessing as came to us.

Let me give extracts from other notes and letters, written by Margaret, about the same period.

'*Saturday evening, May 1st,* 1830. — The holy 'moon and merry-toned wind of this night woo to a 'vigil at the open window; a half-satisfied interest 'urges me to live, love and perish! in the noble, 'wronged heart of Basil;* my Journal, which lies before 'me, tempts to follow out and interpret the as yet only 'half-understood musings of the past week. Letter-'writing, compared with any of these things, takes the 'ungracious semblance of a duty. I have, nathless, 'after a two hours' reverie, to which this resolve and its 'preliminaries have formed excellent warp, determined 'to sacrifice this hallowed time to you.

'It did not in the least surprise me that you found it impossible at the time to avail yourself of the confiden-

* The hero of a novel she was reading.

'tial privileges I had invested you with. On the contrary, I only wonder that we should ever, after such 'gage given and received, (not by a look or tone, but by 'letter,) hold any frank communication. Preparations 'are good in life, prologues ruinous. I felt this even 'before I sent my note, but could not persuade myself to 'consign an impulse so embodied, to oblivion, from any 'consideration of expediency.' * *

'*May 4th*, 1830.—* * I have greatly wished to see 'among us such a person of genius as the nineteenth 'century can afford—*i. e.*, one who has tasted in the 'morning of existence the extremes of good and ill, 'both imaginative and real. I had imagined a person 'endowed by nature with that acute sense of Beauty, '(*i. e.*, Harmony or Truth,) and that vast capacity 'of desire, which give soul to love and ambition. I 'had wished this person might grow up to manhood 'alone (but not alone in crowds); I would have placed 'him in a situation so retired, so obscure, that he 'would quietly, but without bitter sense of isolation, 'stand apart from all surrounding him. I would have 'had him go on steadily, feeding his mind with congenial love, hopefully confident that if he only nourished his existence into perfect life, Fate would, at 'fitting season, furnish an atmosphere and orbit meet for 'his breathing and exercise. I wished he might adore, 'not fever for, the bright phantoms of his mind's creation, and believe them but the shadows of external 'things to be met with hereafter. After this steady 'intellectual growth had brought his powers to manhood, 'so far as the ideal can do it, I wished this being might 'be launched into the world of realities, his heart glowing with the ardor of an immortal toward perfection, 'his eyes searching everywhere to behold it; I wished 'he might collect into one burning point those withering, 'palsying convictions, which, in the ordinary routine of 'things, so gradually pervade the soul; that he might 'suffer, in brief space, agonies of disappointment com-'mensurate with his unpreparedness and confidence. 'And I thought, thus thrown back on the representing 'pictorial resources I supposed him originally to possess, 'with such material, and the need he must feel of using 'it, such a man would suddenly dilate into a form of 'Pride, Power, and Glory, — a centre, round which ask-'ing, aimless hearts might rally, — a man fitted to act as 'interpreter to the one tale of many-languaged eyes!

'What words are these! Perhaps you will feel as if 'I sought but for the longest and strongest. Yet to my 'ear they do but faintly describe the imagined powers of 'such a being.'

Margaret's home at this time was in the mansion-house formerly belonging to Judge Dana,— a large, old-fashioned building, since taken down, standing about a quarter of a mile from the Cambridge Colleges, on the main road to Boston. The house stood back from the road, on rising ground, which overlooked an extensive landscape. It was always a pleasure to Margaret to look at the outlines of the distant hills beyond the river, and to have before her this extent of horizon and sky. In the last year of her residence in Cambridge, her father moved to the old Brattle place, — a still more ancient edifice, with large, old-fashioned garden, and stately rows of Linden trees. Here Margaret enjoyed the garden walks, which took the place of the extensive view.

During these five years her life was not diversified by events, but was marked by an inward history

Study, conversation, society, friendship, and reflection on the aim and law of life, made up her biography. Accordingly, these topics will constitute the substance of this chapter, though sometimes, in order to give completeness to a subject, we may anticipate a little, and insert passages from the letters and journals of her Groton life.

I.

FRIENDSHIP.

"Friendly love perfecteth mankind.'

BACON.

"To have found favor in thy sight
Will still remain
A river of thought, that full of light
Divides the plain."

MILNES.

"Cui potest vita esse vitalis, (ut ait Ennius,) quæ non in amici mutatâ benevolentiâ requiescat?" — CICERO.

IT was while living at Cambridge that Margaret commenced several of those friendships which lasted through her life, and which were the channels for so large a part of her spiritual activity. In giving some account of her in these relations, there is only the alternative of a prudent reserve which omits whatever is liable to be misunderstood, or a frank utterance which confides in the good sense and right feeling of the reader. By the last course, we run the risk of allowing our friend to be misunderstood; but by the first we make it certain that the most important part of her character shall not be understood at all. I have, therefore, thought it best to follow, as far as I can, her own ideas on this subject, which I find in two of her letters to myself. The first is dated, Groton, Jan. 8th, 1839. I was at that time editing a theological and literary magazine, in the West, and this letter was occasioned by my asking her to allow me to publish therein certain poems, and articles of hers, which she had given me to read.

'And I wish now, as far as I can, to give my reasons 'for what you consider absurd squeamishness in me. 'You may not acquiesce in my view, but I think you 'will respect it *as* mine, and be willing to act upon it so 'far as I am concerned.

'Genius seems to me excusable in taking the public 'for a confidant. Genius is universal, and can appeal 'to the common heart of man. But even here I would 'not have it too direct. I prefer to see the thought or 'feeling made universal. How different the confidence 'of Goethe, for instance, from that of Byron!

'But for us lesser people, who write verses merely as 'vents for the overflowings of a personal experience, 'which in every life of any value craves occasionally 'the accompaniment of the lyre, it seems to me that all 'the value of this utterance is destroyed by a hasty or 'indiscriminate publicity. The moment I lay open my 'heart, and tell the fresh feeling to any one who chooses 'to hear, I feel profaned.

'When it has passed into experience, when the flower 'has gone to seed, I don't care who knows it, or whither 'they wander. I am no longer it, — I stand on it. I do 'not know whether this is peculiar to me, or not, but I 'am sure the moment I cease to have any reserve or 'delicacy about a feeling, it is on the wane.

'About putting beautiful verses in your Magazine, I 'have no feeling except what I should have about fur-'nishing a room. I should not put a dressing-case into 'a parlor, or a book-case into a dressing-room, because, 'however good things in their place, they were not in 'place there. And this, not in consideration of the 'public, but of my own sense of fitness and harmony.'

The next extract is from a letter written to me in 1842, after a journey which we had taken to the White Mountains, in the company of my sister, and Mr. and Mrs. Farrar. During this journey Margaret had conversed with me concerning some passages of her private history and experience, and in this letter she asks me to be prudent in speaking of it, giving her reasons as follows: —

'*Cambridge, July* 31, 1842.— * * I said I was happy 'in having no secret. It is my nature, and has been 'the tendency of my life, to wish that all my thoughts 'and deeds might lie, as the "open secrets" of Nature, 'free to all who are able to understand them. I have no 'reserves, except intellectual reserves; for to speak of 'things to those who cannot receive them is stupidity, 'rather than frankness. But in this case, I alone am 'not concerned. Therefore, dear James, give heed to 'the subject. You have received a key to what was 'before unknown of your friend; you have made use 'of it, now let it be buried with the past, over whose 'passages profound and sad, yet touched with heaven-'born beauty, "let silence stand sentinel."'

I shall endeavor to keep true to the spirit of these sentences in speaking of Margaret's friendships. Yet not to speak of them in her biography would be omitting the most striking feature of her character. It would be worse than the play of Hamlet with Hamlet omitted. Henry the Fourth without Sully, Gustavus

Adolphus without Oxenstiern, Napoleon without his marshals, Socrates without his scholars, would be more complete than Margaret without her friends. So that, in touching on these private relations, we must be everywhere "bold," yet not "too bold." The extracts will be taken indiscriminately from letters written to many friends.

The insight which Margaret displayed in finding her friends, the magnetism by which she drew them toward herself, the catholic range of her intimacies, the influence which she exercised to develop the latent germ of every character, the constancy with which she clung to each when she had once given and received confidence, the delicate justice which kept every intimacy separate, and the process of transfiguration which took place when she met any one on this mountain of Friendship, giving a dazzling lustre to the details of common life, — all these should be at least touched upon and illustrated, to give any adequate view of her in these relations.

Such a prejudice against her had been created by her faults of manner, that the persons she might most wish to know often retired from her and avoided her. But she was "sagacious of her quarry," and never suffered herself to be repelled by this. She saw when any one belonged to her, and never rested till she came into possession of her property. I recollect a lady who thus fled from her for several years, yet, at last, became most nearly attached to her. This "wise sweet" friend, as Margaret characterized her in two words, a flower hidden in the solitude of deep woods, Margaret saw and appreciated from the first.

See how, in the following passage, she describes to

one of her friends her perception of character. and her power of attracting it, when only fifteen years old.

'*Jamaica Plains*, *July*, 1840.—Do you remember my 'telling you, at Cohasset, of a Mr. ——— staying with 'us, when I was fifteen, and all that passed? Well, I 'have not seen him since, till, yesterday, he came here. 'I was pleased to find, that, even at so early an age, I 'did not overrate those I valued. He was the same as 'in memory; the powerful eye dignifying an otherwise 'ugly face; the calm wisdom, and refined observation, 'the imposing *manière d'être*, which anywhere would 'give him an influence among men, without his taking 'any trouble, or making any sacrifice, and the great 'waves of feeling that seemed to rise as an attractive 'influence, and overspread his being. He said, nothing 'since his childhood had been so marked as his visit 'to our house; that it had dwelt in his thoughts 'unchanged amid all changes. I could have wished 'he had never returned to change the picture. He 'looked at me continually, and said, again and again, 'he should have known me anywhere; but O how 'changed I must be since that epoch of pride and ful'ness! He had with him his son, a wild boy of five 'years old, all brilliant with health and energy, and 'with the same powerful eye. He said,—You know 'I am not one to confound acuteness and rapidity of 'intellect with real genius; but he is for those an ex'traordinary child. He would astonish you, but I look 'deep enough into the prodigy to see the work of an 'extremely nervous temperament, and I shall make him 'as dull as I can. "*Margaret*," (pronouncing the name 'in the same deliberate searching way he used to do,)

'"I love him so well, I will try to teach him moderation. '"If I can help it, he shall not feed on bitter ashes, nor '"try these paths of avarice and ambition." It made me 'feel very strangely to hear him talk so to my old self. 'What a gulf between! There is scarce a fibre left of 'the haughty, passionate, ambitious child he remembered 'and loved. I felt affection for him still; for his charac-'ter was formed then, and had not altered, except by 'ripening and expanding! But thus, in other worlds, 'we shall remember our present selves.'

Margaret's constancy to any genuine relation, once established, was surprising. If her friends' *aim* changed, so as to take them out of her sphere, she was saddened by it, and did not let them go without a struggle. But wherever they continued "true to the original standard," (as she loved to phrase it) her affectionate interest would follow them unimpaired through all the changes of life. The principle of this constancy she thus expresses in a letter to one of her brothers: —

'Great and even *fatal* errors (so far as this life is con-'cerned) could not destroy my friendship for one in 'whom I am sure of the kernel of nobleness.'

She never formed a friendship until she had seen and known this germ of good; and afterwards judged conduct by this. To this germ of good, to this highest law of each individual, she held them true. But never did she act like those who so often judge of their friend from some report of his conduct, as if they had never known him, and allow the inference from a single act to alter the opinion formed by an induction from years of intercourse. From all such weakness Margaret stood wholly free.

I have referred to the wide range of Margaret's friendships. Even at this period this variety was very apparent. She was the centre of a group very different from each other, and whose only affinity consisted in their all being polarized by the strong attraction of her mind,— all drawn toward herself. Some of her friends were young, gay and beautiful; some old, sick or studious. Some were children of the world, others pale scholars. Some were witty, others slightly dull. But all, in order to be Margaret's friends, must be capable of seeking something,— capable of some aspiration for the better. And how did she glorify life to all! all that was tame and common vanishing away in the picturesque light thrown over the most familiar things by her rapid fancy, her brilliant wit, her sharp insight, her creative imagination, by the inexhaustible resources of her knowledge, and the copious rhetoric which found words and images always apt and always ready. Even then she displayed almost the same marvellous gift of conversation which afterwards dazzled all who knew her,— with more perhaps of freedom, since she floated on the flood of our warm sympathies. Those who know Margaret only by her published writings know her least; her notes and letters contain more of her mind; but it was only in conversation that she was perfectly free and at home.

Margaret's constancy in friendship caused her to demand it in others, and thus she was sometimes exacting. But the pure Truth of her character caused her to express all such feelings with that freedom and simplicity that they became only as slight clouds on a serene sky, giving it a tenderer beauty, and casting picturesque shades over the landscape below. From her letters to different friends I select a few examples of these feelings.

'The world turns round and round, and you too must 'needs be negligent and capricious. You have not 'answered my note; you have not given me what I 'asked. You do not come here. Do not you act so,—it 'is the drop too much. The world seems not only turning 'but tottering, when my kind friend plays such a part.'

'You need not have delayed your answer so long; 'why not at once answer the question I asked? Faith is 'not natural to me; for the love I feel to others is not in 'the idleness of poverty, nor can I persist in believing 'the best, merely to save myself pain, or keep a leaning 'place for the weary heart. But I should believe you, 'because I have seen that your feelings are strong and 'constant; they have never disappointed me, when 'closely scanned.'

'*July* 6, 1832.—I believe I behaved very badly the 'other evening. I did not think so yesterday. I had 'been too surprised and vexed to recover very easily, 'but to-day my sophistries have all taken wing, and I 'feel that nothing good could have made me act with 'such childish petulance and bluntness towards one 'who spoke from friendly emotions. Be at peace; I 'will astonish you by my repose, mildness, and self-pos-'session. No, that is silly; but I believe it cannot be 'right to be on such terms with any one, that, on the 'least vexation, I indulge my feelings at his or her 'expense. We will talk less, but we shall be very good 'friends still, I hope. Shall not we?'

In the last extract, we have an example of that genuine humility, which, being a love of truth, underlaid her whole character, notwithstanding its seeming pride. She could not have been great as she was, without it.*

'*December* 19*th*, 1829.—I shall always be glad to 'have you come to me when saddened. The melan-'cholic does not misbecome you. The lights of your 'character are *wintry*. They are generally inspiriting, 'life-giving, but, if perpetual, would glare too much on 'the tired sense; one likes sometimes a cloudy day, with 'its damp and warmer breath,—its gentle, down-look-'ing shades. Sadness in some is intolerably ungraceful 'and oppressive; it affects one like a cold rainy day in 'June or September, when all pleasure departs with the 'sun; everything seems out of place and irrelative to 'the time; the clouds are fog, the atmosphere leaden,—'but 'tis not so with you.'

Of her own truthfulness to her friends, which led her frankly to speak to them of their faults or dangers, her correspondence gives constant examples.

The first is from a letter of later date than properly belongs to this chapter, but is so wholly in her spirit of candor that I insert it here. It is from a letter written in 1843.

* According to Dryden's beautiful statement—

For as high turrets, in their airy sweep
Require foundations, in proportion deep,
And lofty cedars as far upward shoot
As to the nether heavens they drive the root;
So low did her secure foundation lie,
She was not humble, but humility.'

'I have been happy in the sight of your pure design, 'of the sweetness and serenity of your mind. In the 'inner sanctuary we met. But I shall say a few blunt 'words, such as were frequent in the days of intimacy, 'and, if they are needless, you will let them fall to the 'ground. Youth is past, with its passionate joys and 'griefs, its restlessness, its vague desires. You have 'chosen your path, you have rounded out your lot, your 'duties are before you. *Now* beware the mediocrity 'that threatens middle age, its limitation of thought and 'interest, its dulness of fancy, its too external life, and 'mental thinness. Remember the limitations that 'threaten every professional man, only to be guarded 'against by great earnestness and watchfulness. So 'take care of yourself, and let not the intellect more 'than the spirit be quenched.

'It is such a relief to me to be able to speak to you 'upon a subject which I thought would never lie open 'between us. Now there will be no place which does 'not lie open to the light. I can always say what I feel. 'And the way in which you took it, so like yourself, so 'manly and noble, gives me the assurance that I shall 'have the happiness of seeing in you that symmetry, that 'conformity in the details of life with the highest aims, 'of which I have sometimes despaired. How much 'higher, dear friend, is "the mind, the music breathing '"from the" *life*, than anything we can say! Character 'is higher than intellect; this I have long felt to be true; 'may we both live as if we knew it.

* * 'I hope and believe we may be yet very much 'to each other. Imperfect as I am, I feel myself not 'unworthy to be a true friend. Neither of us is

'unworthy. In few natures does such love for the 'good and beautiful survive the ruin of all youthful 'hopes, the wreck of all illusions.'

"'I supposed our intimacy would terminate when I 'left Cambridge. Its continuing to subsist is a matter 'of surprise to me. And I expected, ere this, you would 'have found some Hersilia, or such-like, to console you 'for losing your Natalia. See, my friend, I am three 'and twenty. I believe in love and friendship, but I 'cannot but notice that circumstances have appalling 'power, and that those links which are not riveted by 'situation, by *interest*, (I mean, not mere worldly inter-'est, but the instinct of self-preservation,) may be lightly 'broken by a chance touch. I speak not in misan-'thropy, I believe

"Die Zeit ist schlecht, doch giebts noch grosse Herzen."

'Surely I may be pardoned for aiming at the same 'results with the chivalrous "gift of the Gods." I can-'not endure to be one of those shallow beings who can 'never get beyond the primer of experience, — who are 'ever saying, —

"Ich habe geglaubt, *nun glaube ich erst recht*,
Und geht es auch wunderlich, geht es auch schlecht,
Ich bleibe in glaubigen Orden."

'Yet, when you write, write freely, and if I don't like 'what you say, let me say so. I have ever been frank, 'as if I expected to be intimate with you good three-'score years and ten. I am sure we shall always esteem 'each other. I have that much faith.'

'*Jan.* 1832. — All that relates to ——— must be interesting to me, though I never voluntarily think of him 'now. The apparent caprice of his conduct has shaken 'my faith, but not destroyed my hope. That hope, if I, 'who have so mistaken others, may dare to think I know 'myself, was never selfish. It is painful to lose a friend 'whose knowledge and converse mingled so intimately 'with the growth of my mind,—an early friend to whom 'I was all truth and frankness, seeking nothing but 'equal truth and frankness in return. But this evil may 'be borne; the hard, the lasting evil was to learn to 'distrust my own heart, and lose all faith in my power 'of knowing others. In this letter I see again that peculiar pride, that contempt of the forms and shows of 'goodness, that fixed resolve to be anything but "like '"unto the Pharisees," which were to my eye such 'happy omens. Yet how strangely distorted are all his 'views! The daily influence of his intercourse with 'me was like the breath he drew; it has become a part 'of him. Can he escape from himself? Would he be 'unlike all other mortals? His feelings are as false as 'those of Alcibiades. He influenced me, and helped 'form me to what I am. Others shall succeed him. 'Shall I be ashamed to owe anything to friendship? 'But why do I talk? — a child might confute him 'by defining the term *human being*. He will gradually 'work his way into light; if too late for our friendship, 'not, I trust, too late for his own peace and honorable 'well-being. I never insisted on being the instrument 'of good to him. I practised no little arts, no! not to 'effect the good of the friend I loved. I have prayed to 'Heaven, (surely we are sincere when doing that,) to 'guide him in the best path for him, however far from 'me that path might lead. The lesson I have learned 'may make me a more useful friend, a more efficient aid 'to others than I could be to him; yet I hope I shall 'not be denied the consolation of knowing surely, one 'day, that all which appeared evil in the companion of 'happy years was but error.'

* * * * *

'I think, since you have seen so much of my char- 'acter, that you must be sensible that any reserves with 'those whom I call my friends, do not arise from duplic- 'ity, but an instinctive feeling that I could not be under- 'stood. I can truly say that I wish no one to overrate 'me; undeserved regard could give me no pleasure; nor 'will I consent to practise charlatanism, either in friend- 'ship or anything else.'

* * * * *

'You ought not to think I show a want of generous 'confidence, if I sometimes try the ground on which I 'tread, to see if perchance it may return the echoes of 'hollowness.'

* * * * *

'Do not cease to respect me as formerly. It seems to 'me that I have reached the "parting of the ways" in 'my life, and all the knowledge which I have toiled to 'gain only serves to show me the disadvantages of each. 'None of those who think themselves my friends can 'aid me; each, careless, takes the path to which present 'convenience impels; and all would smile or stare, could 'they know the aching and measureless wishes, the sad 'apprehensiveness, which make me pause and strain 'my almost hopeless gaze to the distance. What won- 'der if my present conduct should be mottled by self- 'ishness and incertitude? Perhaps you, who *can* make 'your views certain, cannot comprehend me; though 'you showed me last night a penetration which did not 'flow from sympathy. But this I may say — though 'the glad light of hope and ambitious confidence, which 'has vitalized my mind, should be extinguished forever, 'I will not in life act a mean, ungenerous, or useless 'part. Therefore, let not a slight thing lessen your 'respect for me. If you feel as much pain as I do, when 'obliged to diminish my respect for any person, you will 'be glad of this assurance. I hope you will not think 'this note in the style of a French novel.'

POWER OF CIRCUMSTANCES.

'Do you remember a conversation we had in the gar-'den, one starlight evening, last summer, about the 'incalculable power which outward circumstances have 'over the character? You would not sympathize with 'the regrets I expressed, that mine had not been formed 'amid scenes and persons of nobleness and beauty, 'eager passions and dignified events, instead of those 'secret trials and petty conflicts which make my trans-'ition state so hateful to my memory and my tastes. 'You then professed the faith which I resigned with 'such anguish, — the faith which a Schiller could never 'attain, — a faith in the power of the human will. Yet 'now, in every letter, you talk to me of the power of 'circumstances. You tell me how changed you are. 'Every one of your letters is different from the one pre-'ceding, and all so altered from your former self. For 'are you not leaving all our old ground, and do you not 'apologize to me for all your letters? Why do you 'apologize? I think I know you very, very well; con-

'sidering that we are both human, and have the gift of 'concealing our thoughts with words. Nay, further— 'I do not believe you will be able to become anything 'which I cannot understand. I know I can sympathize 'with all who feel and think, from a Dryfesdale up to 'a Max Piccolomini. You say, you have become a 'machine. If so, I shall expect to find you a grand, 'high-pressure, wave-compelling one — requiring plenty 'of fuel. You must be a steam-engine, and move some 'majestic fabric at the rate of thirty miles an hour along 'the broad waters of the nineteenth century. None of 'your pendulum machines for me! I should, to be sure, 'turn away my head if I should hear you tick, and mark 'the quarters of hours; but the buzz and whiz of a good 'large life-endangerer would be music to mine ears. 'Oh, no! sure there is no danger of your requiring to be 'set down quite on a level, kept in a still place, and 'wound up every eight days. Oh no, no! you are not 'one of that numerous company, who

—— "live and die,
Eat, drink, wake, sleep between,
Walk, talk like clock-work too,
So pass in order due,
Over the scene,
To where the past — *is* past,
The future — nothing yet," &c. &c.

'But we must all be machines: you shall be a steam-'engine; — shall be a mill, with extensive water-privi-'leges, — and I will be a spinning jenny. No! upon 'second thoughts, I will not be a machine. I will 'be an instrument, not to be confided to vulgar hands, — 'for instance, a chisel to polish marble, or a whetstone 'to sharpen steel!'

In an unfinished tale, Margaret has given the following studies of character. She is describing two of the friends of the hero of her story. Unquestionably the traits here given were taken from life, though it might not be easy to recognize the portrait of any individual in either sketch. Yet we insert it here to show her own idea of this relation, and her fine feeling of the action and reaction of these subtle intimacies.

'Now, however, I found companions, in thought, at 'least. One, who had great effect on my mind, I may call 'Lytton. He was as premature as myself; at thirteen a 'man in the range of his thoughts, analyzing motives, 'and explaining principles, when he ought to have been 'playing cricket, or hunting in the woods. The young 'Arab, or Indian, may dispense with mere play, and 'enter betimes into the histories and practices of man'hood, for all these are, in their modes of life, closely 'connected with simple nature, and educate the body 'no less than the mind; but the same good cannot be 'said of lounging lazily under a tree, while mentally 'accompanying Gil Blas through his course of intrigue 'and adventure, and visiting with him the impure 'atmosphere of courtiers, picaroons, and actresses. This 'was Lytton's favorite reading; his mind, by nature 'subtle rather than daring, would in any case have 'found its food in the now hidden workings of char'acter and passion, the by-play of life, the unexpected 'and seemingly incongruous relations to be found there. 'He loved the natural history of man, not religiously, 'but for entertainment. What he sought, he found, but 'paid the heaviest price. All his later days were poi'soned by his subtlety, which made it impossible for him 'to look at any action with a single and satisfied eye. 'He tore the buds open to see if there were no worm 'sheathed in the blushful heart, and was so afraid of 'overlooking some mean possibility, that he lost sight 'of virtue. Grubbing like a mole beneath the surface 'of earth, rather than reading its living language above, 'he had not faith enough to believe in the flower, neither 'faith enough to mine for the gem, and remains at pen-'ance in the limbo of halfnesses, I trust not forever. 'Then all his characteristics wore brilliant hues. He 'was very witty, and I owe to him the great obligation 'of being the first and only person who has excited me 'to frequent and boundless gayety. The sparks of his 'wit were frequent, slight surprises; his was a slender 'dart, and rebounded easily to the hand. I like the 'scintillating, arrowy wit far better than broad, genial 'humor. The light metallic touch pleases me. When 'wit appears as fun and jollity, she wears a little of the 'Silenus air; — the Mercurial is what I like.

'In later days, — for my intimacy with him lasted 'many years, — he became the feeder of my intellect. He 'delighted to ransack the history of a nation, of an art 'or a science, and bring to me all the particulars. Tel-'ling them fixed them in his own memory, which was 'the most tenacious and ready I have ever known; he 'enjoyed my clear perception as to their relative value, 'and I classified them in my own way. As he was 'omnivorous, and of great mental activity, while my 'mind was intense, though rapid in its movements, and 'could only give itself to a few things of its own accord, 'I traversed on the wings of his effort large demesnes 'that would otherwise have remained quite unknown 'to me. They were not, indeed, seen to the same profit 'as my own province, whose tillage I knew, and whose 'fruits were the answer to my desire; but the fact of 'seeing them at all gave a largeness to my view, and a 'candor to my judgment. I could not be ignorant how 'much there was I did not know, nor leave out of 'sight the many sides to every question, while, by the 'law of affinity, I chose my own.

'Lytton was not loved by any one. He was not 'positively hated, or disliked; for there was nothing 'which the general mind could take firm hold of enough 'for such feelings. Cold, intangible, he was to play across 'the life of others. A momentary resentment was some-'times felt at a presence which would not mingle with 'theirs; his scrutiny, though not hostile, was recog-'nized as unfeeling and impertinent, and his mirth 'unsettled all objects from their foundations. But he 'was soon forgiven and forgotten. Hearts went not 'forth to war against or to seek one who was a mere 'experimentalist and observer in existence. For myself, 'I did not love, perhaps, but was attached to him, and 'the attachment grew steadily, for it was founded, not 'on what I wanted of him, but on his truth to himself. 'His existence was a real one; he was not without a 'pathetic feeling of his wants, but was never tempted 'to supply them by imitating the properties of any other 'character. He accepted the law of his being, and never 'violated it. This is next best to the nobleness which 'transcends it. I did not disapprove, even when I dis-'liked, his acts.

'Amadin, my other companion, was as slow and deep 'of feeling, as Lytton was brilliant, versatile, and cold. 'His temperament was generally grave, even to appa-'rent dulness; his eye gave little light, but a slow fire 'burned in its depths. His was a character not to be 'revealed to himself, or others, except by the important 'occasions of life. Though every day, no doubt, deep-'ened and enriched him, it brought little that he could 'show or recall. But when his soul, capable of religion, 'capable of love, was moved, all his senses were united 'in the word or action that followed, and the impression 'made on you was entire. I have scarcely known any 'capable of such true manliness as he. His poetry, 'written, or unwritten, was the experience of life. It 'lies in few lines, as yet, but not one of them will ever 'need to be effaced.

'Early that serious eye inspired in me a trust that has 'never been deceived. There was no magnetism in 'him, no lights and shades that could stir the imagina-'tion; no bright ideal suggested by him stood between 'the friend and his self. As the years matured that 'self, I loved him more, and knew him as he knew him-'self, always in the present moment; he could never 'occupy my mind in absence.'

Another of her early friends, Rev. F. H. Hedge, has sketched his acquaintance with her in the following paper, communicated by him for these memoirs. Somewhat older than Margaret, and having enjoyed an education at a German university, his conversation was full of interest and excitement to her. He opened to her a whole world of thoughts and speculations which gave movement to her mind in a congenial direction.

"My acquaintance with Margaret commenced in the year 1823, at Cambridge, my native place and hers. I was then a member of Harvard College, in which my father held one of the offices of instruction, and I used frequently to meet her in the social circles of which the families connected with the college formed the nucleus. Her father, at this time, represented the county of Middlesex in the Congress of the United States.

"Margaret was then about thirteen, — a child in years, but so precocious in her mental and physical developments, that she passed for eighteen or twenty. Agreeably to this estimate, she had her place in society, as a lady full-grown.

"When I recall her personal appearance, as it was then and for ten or twelve years subsequent to this, I have the idea of a blooming girl of a florid complexion and vigorous health, with a tendency to robustness, of which she was painfully conscious, and which, with little regard to hygienic principles, she endeavored to suppress or conceal, thereby preparing for herself much future suffering. With no pretensions to beauty then, or at any time, her face was one that attracted, that awakened a lively interest, that made one desirous of a nearer acquaintance. It was a face that fascinated, without satisfying. Never seen in repose, never allowing a steady perusal of its features, it baffled every attempt to judge the character by physiognomical induction. You saw the evidence of a mighty force, but what direction that force would assume, — whether it would determine itself to social triumphs, or to triumphs of art, — it was impossible to divine. Her moral tendencies, her sentiments, her true and prevailing character, did not appear in the lines of her face. She seemed equal to anything, but might not choose to put forth her strength. You felt that a great possibility lay behind that brow, but you felt, also, that the talent that was in her might miscarry through indifference or caprice.

"I said she had no pretensions to beauty. Yet she was not plain. She escaped the reproach of positive plainness, by her blond and abundant hair, by her excellent teeth, by her sparkling, dancing, busy eyes, which, though usually half closed from near-sightedness, shot piercing glances at those with whom she conversed, and, most of all, by the very peculiar and graceful carriage of her head and neck, which all who knew her will remember as the most characteristic trait in her personal appearance.

"In conversation she had already, at that early age, begun to distinguish herself, and made much the same impression in society that she did in after years, with the exception, that, as she advanced in life, she learned to control that tendency to sarcasm, — that disposition to 'quiz,' — which was then somewhat excessive. It frightened shy young people from her presence, and made her, for a while, notoriously unpopular with the ladies of her circle.

"This propensity seems to have been aggravated by unpleasant encounters in her school-girl experience. She was a pupil of Dr. Park, of Boston, whose seminary for young ladies was then at the height of a well-earned reputation, and whose faithful and successful endeavors in this department have done much to raise the standard of female education among us. Here the inexperienced country girl was exposed to petty persecutions from the dashing misses of the city, who pleased themselves with giggling criticisms not inaudible, nor meant to be inaudible to their subject, on whatsoever in dress and manner fell short of the city mark.

Then it was first revealed to her young heart, and laid up for future reflection, how large a place in woman's world is given to fashion and frivolity. Her mind reacted on these attacks with indiscriminate sarcasms. She made herself formidable by her wit, and, of course, unpopular. A root of bitterness sprung up in her which years of moral culture were needed to eradicate.

"Partly to evade the temporary unpopularity into which she had fallen, and partly to pursue her studies secure from those social avocations which were found unavoidable in the vicinity of Cambridge and Boston, in 1824 or 5 she was sent to Groton, where she remained two years in quiet seclusion.]

"On her return to Cambridge, in 1826, I renewed my acquaintance, and an intimacy was then formed, which continued until her death. The next seven years, which were spent in Cambridge, were years of steady growth, with little variety of incident, and little that was noteworthy of outward experience, but with great intensity of the inner life. It was with her, as with most young women, and with most young men, too, between the ages of sixteen and twenty-five, a period of preponderating sentimentality, a period of romance and of dreams, of yearning and of passion. She pursued at this time, I think, no systematic study, but she read with the heart, and was learning more from social experience than from books.

"I remember noting at this time a trait which continued to be a prominent one through life, — I mean a passionate love for the beautiful, which comprehended all the kingdoms of nature and art. I have never known one who seemed to derive such satisfaction from the contemplation of lovely forms.

"Her intercourse with girls of her own age and standing was frank and excellent. Personal attractions, and the homage which they received, awakened in her no jealousy. She envied not their success, though vividly aware of the worth of beauty, and inclined to exaggerate her own deficiencies in that kind. On the contrary, she loved to draw these fair girls to herself, and to make them her guests, and was never so happy as when surrounded, in company, with such a bevy. This attraction was mutual, as, according to Goethe, every attraction is. Where she felt an interest, she awakened an interest. Without flattery or art, by the truth and nobleness of her nature, she won the confidence, and made herself the friend and intimate, of a large number of young ladies, — the belles of their day, — with most of whom she remained in correspondence during the greater part of her life.

"In our evening reünions she was always conspicuous by the brilliancy of her wit, which needed but little provocation to break forth in exuberant sallies, that drew around her a knot of listeners, and made her the central attraction of the hour. Rarely did she enter a company in which she was not a prominent object.

"I have spoken of her conversational talent. It continued to develop itself in these years, and was certainly her most decided gift. One could form no adequate idea of her ability without hearing her converse. She did many things well, but nothing so well as she talked. It is the opinion of all her friends, that her writings do her very imperfect justice. For some reason or other, she could never deliver herself in print as she did with her lips. She required the stimulus of attentive ears and answering eyes, to bring out all her power. She must have her auditory about her.

"Her conversation, as it was then, I have seldom heard equalled. It was not so much attractive as commanding. Though remarkably fluent and select, it was neither fluency, nor choice diction, nor wit, nor sentiment, that gave it its peculiar power, but accuracy of statement, keen discrimination, and a certain weight of judgment, which contrasted strongly and charmingly with the youth and sex of the speaker. I do not remember that the vulgar charge of talking 'like a book' was ever fastened upon her, although, by her precision, she might seem to have incurred it. The fact was, her speech, though finished and true as the most deliberate rhetoric of the pen, had always an air of spontaneity which made it seem the grace of the moment,—the result of some organic provision that made finished sentences as natural to her as blundering and hesitation are to most of us. With a little more imagination, she would have made an excellent improvisatrice.

"Here let me say a word respecting the character of Margaret's mind. It was what in woman is generally called a masculine mind; that is, its action was determined by ideas rather than by sentiments. And yet, with this masculine trait, she combined a woman's appreciation of the beautiful in sentiment and the beautiful in action. Her intellect was rather solid than graceful, yet no one was more alive to grace. She was no artist,—she would never have written an epic, or romance, or drama,—yet no one knew better the qualities which go to the making of these; and though catholic as to kind, no one was more rigorously exacting as to quality. Nothing short of the best in each kind would content her.

"She wanted imagination, and she wanted productiveness. She wrote with difficulty. Without external pressure, perhaps, she would never have written at all. She was dogmatic, and not creative. Her strength was in characterization and in criticism. Her *critique* on Goethe, in the second volume of the Dial, is, in my estimation, one of the best things she has written. And, as far as it goes, it is one of the best criticisms extant of Goethe.

"What I especially admired in her was her intellectual sincerity. Her judgments took no bribe from her sex or her sphere, nor from custom nor tradition, nor caprice. She valued truth supremely, both for herself and others. The question with her was not what should be believed, or what ought to be true, but what *is* true. Her yes and no were never conventional; and she often amazed people by a cool and unexpected dissent from the commonplaces of popular acceptation."

Margaret, we have said, saw in each of her friends the secret interior capability, which might become hereafter developed into some special beauty or power. By means of this penetrating, this prophetic insight, she gave each to himself, acted on each to draw out his best nature, gave him an ideal out of which he could draw strength and liberty hour by hour. Thus her influence was ever ennobling, and each felt that in her society he was truer, wiser, better, and yet more free and happy, than elsewhere. The "dry light" which Lord Bacon loved, she never knew; her light was life, was love, was warm with sympathy and a boundless energy of affection and hope. Though her love flattered and charmed her friends, it did not spoil them, for they knew her perfect truth. They knew that she loved them, not for what she imagined, but for what she saw, though she saw it only in the germ. But as the Greeks beheld a Persephone and Athene in the passing stranger, and ennobled humanity into ideal beauty, Margaret saw all her friends thus idealized. She was a balloon of sufficient power to take us all up with her into the serene depth of heaven, where she loved to float, far above the low details of earthly life. Earth lay beneath us as a lovely picture, — its sounds came up mellowed into music.

Margaret was, to persons younger than herself, a Makaria and Natalia. She was wisdom and intellectual beauty, filling life with a charm and glory "known to neither sea nor land." To those of her own age she was sibyl and seer, — a prophetess, revealing the future, pointing the path, opening their eyes to the great aims only worthy of pursuit in life. To those older than herself she was like the Euphorion in Goethe's drama, child of Faust and Helen, — a wonderful union of exuberance and judgment, born of romantic fulness and classic limitation. They saw with surprise her clear good-sense balancing her flow of sentiment and ardent courage. They saw her comprehension of both sides of every question, and gave her their confidence, as to one of equal age, because of so ripe a judgment.

But it was curious to see with what care and conscience she kept her friendships distinct. Her fine practical understanding, teaching her always the value of limits, enabled her to hold apart all her intimacies, nor did one ever encroach on the province of the other. Like a moral Paganini, she played always on a single string, drawing from each its peculiar music, — bringing wild beauty from the slender wire, no less than from the deep-sounding harp-string. Some of her friends had little to give her when compared with others; but I never noticed that she sacrificed in any respect the smaller faculty to the greater. She fully realized that the Divine Being makes each part of this creation divine, and that He dwells in the blade of grass as really if not as fully as in the majestic oak which has braved the storm for a hundred years. She felt in full the thought of a poem which she once copied for me from Barry Cornwall, which begins thus:—

"She was not fair, nor full of grace,
Nor crowned with thought, nor aught beside
No wealth had she of mind or face,
To win our love, or gain our pride,—
No lover's thought her heart could touch,—
No poet's dream was round her thrown;
And yet we miss her — ah, so much!
Now — she has flown."

I will close this section of Cambridge Friendship with the two following passages, the second of which was written to some one unknown to me:

'Your letter was of cordial sweetness to me, as is 'ever the thought of our friendship, — that sober-suited 'friendship, of which the web was so deliberately and 'well woven, and which wears so well.

* * * * * *

'I want words to express the singularity of all my 'past relations; yet let me try.

'From a very early age I have felt that I was not 'born to the common womanly lot. I knew I should 'never find a being who could keep the key of my char- 'acter; that there would be none on whom I could 'always lean, from whom I could always learn; that 'I should be a pilgrim and sojourner on earth, and 'that the birds and foxes would be surer of a place to 'lay the head than I. You understand me, of course; 'such beings can only find their homes in hearts. All 'material luxuries, all the arrangements of society, are 'mere conveniences to them.

'This thought, all whose bearings I did not, indeed, 'understand, affected me sometimes with sadness, some-'times with pride. I mourned that I never should have 'a thorough experience of life, never know the full riches 'of my being; I was proud that I was to test myself in 'the sternest way, that I was always to return to myself, 'to be my own priest, pupil, parent, child, husband, and 'wife. All this I did not understand as I do now; but 'this destiny of the thinker, and (shall I dare to say it?) 'of the poetic priestess, sibylline, dwelling in the cave, 'or amid the Lybian sands, lay yet enfolded in my 'mind. Accordingly, I did not look on any of the per-'sons, brought into relation with me, with common 'womanly eyes.

'Yet, as my character is, after all, still more feminine 'than masculine, it would sometimes happen that I put 'more emotion into a state than I myself knew. I 'really was capable of attachment, though it never 'seemed so till the hour of separation. And if a con-'nexion was torn up by the roots, the soil of my exist-'ence showed an unsightly wound, which long refused 'to clothe itself in verdure.

'With regard to yourself, I was to you all that I 'wished to be. I knew that I reigned in your thoughts 'in my own way. And I also lived with you more truly and freely than with any other person. We were 'truly friends, but it was not friends as men are friends tc 'one another, or as brother and sister. There was, also, 'that pleasure, which may, perhaps, be termed conjugal, 'of finding oneself in an alien nature. Is there any 'tinge of love in this? Possibly! At least, in compar- 'ing it with my relation to ——, I find *that* was strictly 'fraternal. I valued him for himself. I did not care 'for an influence over him, and was perfectly willing to 'have one or fifty rivals in his heart. * *

* * 'I think I may say, I never loved. I but see 'my possible life reflected on the clouds. As in a glass 'darkly, I have seen what I might feel as child, wife, 'mother, but I have never really approached the close 'relations of life. A sister I have truly been to many, — 'a brother to more, — a fostering nurse to, oh how 'many! The bridal hour of many a spirit, when first 'it was wed, I have shared, but said adieu before the 'wine was poured out at the banquet. And there is one 'I always love in my poetic hour, as the lily looks up to 'the star from amid the waters; and another whom I 'visit as the bee visits the flower, when I crave sympa- 'thy. Yet those who live would scarcely consider that 'I am among the living,—and I am isolated, as you say.

'My dear ——, all is well; all has helped me to deci- 'pher the great poem of the universe. I can hardly 'describe to you the happiness which floods my solitary 'hours. My actual life is yet much clogged and im- 'peded, but I have at last got me an oratory, where I 'can retire and pray. With your letter, vanished a last 'regret. You did not act or think unworthily. It is 'enough. As to the cessation of our confidential inter- 'course, circumstances must have accomplished that 'long ago; my only grief was that you should do it 'with your own free will, and for reasons that I thought 'unworthy. I long to honor you, to be honored by you. 'Now we will have free and noble thoughts of one 'another, and all that is best of our friendship shall 'remain.'

II.

CONVERSATION. — SOCIAL INTERCOURSE.

"Be thou what thou singly art, and personate only thyself. Swim smoothly in the stream of thy nature, and live but one man."

SIR THOMAS BROWNE.

"Ah, how mournful look in letters
Black on white, the words to me,
Which from lips of thine cast fetters
Round the heart, or set it free."

GOETHE, *translated by J. S. Dwight.*

"Zu erfinden, zu beschliessen,
Bleibe, Kunstler, oft allein;
Deines Wirkes zu geniessen
Eile freudig zum Verein,
Hier im Ganzen schau erfahre
Deines eignes Lebenslauf,
Und die Thaten mancher Jahre
Gehn dir in dem Nachbar auf."

GOETHE, *Artist's Song.*

WHEN I first knew Margaret, she was much in society, but in a circle of her own, — of friends whom she had drawn around her, and whom she entertained and delighted by her exuberant talent. Of those belonging to this circle, let me recall a few characters.

The young girls whom Margaret had attracted were very different from herself, and from each other. From Boston, Charlestown, Roxbury, Brookline, they came to her, and the little circle of companions would meet now in one house, and now in another, of these pleasant towns. There was A——, a dark-haired, black-eyed beauty, with clear olive complexion, through which the rich blood flowed. She was bright, beauteous, and cold as a gem, — with clear perceptions of character within a narrow limit, — enjoying society, and always surrounded with admirers, of whose feelings she seemed quite unconscious. While they were just ready to die of unrequited love, she stood untouched as Artemis, scarcely aware of the deadly arrows which had flown from her silver bow. I remember that Margaret said, that Tennyson's little poem of the skipping-rope must have been written for her, — where the lover expressing his admiration of the fairy-like motion and the light grace of the lady, is told —

> "Get off, or else my skipping-rope
> Will hit you in the eye."

Then there was B——, the reverse of all this,— tender, susceptible, with soft blue eyes, and mouth of trembling sensibility. How sweet were her songs, in which a single strain of pure feeling ever reminded me of those angel symphonies, —

> "In all whose music, the pathetic minor
> Our ears will cross — "

and when she sang or spoke, her eyes had often the expression of one looking *in* at her thought, not *out* at her companion.

Then there was C——, all animated and radiant with joyful interest in life, — seeing with ready eye the beauty of Nature and of Thought, — entering with quick sympathy into all human interest, taking readily everything which belonged to her, and dropping with sure instinct whatever suited her not. Unknown to her was struggle, conflict, crisis; she grew up harmonious as the flower, drawing nutriment from earth and air, — from "common things which round us lie," and equally from the highest thoughts and inspirations.

Shall I also speak of D——, whose beauty had a half-voluptuous character, from those ripe red lips, those ringlets overflowing the well-rounded shoulders, and the hazy softness of those large eyes? Or of E——, her companion, beautiful too, but in a calmer, purer style, — with eye from which looked forth self-possession, truth and fortitude? Others, well worth notice, I must not notice now.

But among the young men who surrounded Margaret, a like variety prevailed. One was to her interesting, on account of his quick, active intellect, and his contempt for shows and pretences; for his inexhaustible wit, his exquisite taste, his infinitely varied stores of information, and the poetic view which he took of life, painting it with Rembrandt depths of shadow and bursts of light. Another she gladly went to for his compact, thoroughly considered views of God and the world, — for his culture, so much more deep and rich than any other we could find here, — for his conversation, opening in systematic form new fields of thought. Yet men of strong native talent, and rich character, she also liked well to know, however deficient in culture, knowledge, or power of utterance. Each was to her a study, and she never rested till she had found the bottom of every mind, — till she had satisfied herself of its capacity and currents, — measuring it with her sure line, as

—"All human wits
Are measured, but a few."

It was by her singular gift of speech that she cast her spells and worked her wonders in this little circle. Full of thoughts and full of words; capable of poetic improvisation, had there not been a slight overweight of a tendency to the tangible and real; capable of clear, complete, philosophic statement, but for the strong tendency to life which melted down evermore in its lava-current the solid blocks of thought; she was yet, by these excesses, better fitted for the arena of conversation. Here she found none adequate for the equal encounter; when she laid her lance in rest, every champion must go down before it. How fluent her wit, which, for hour after hour, would furnish best entertainment, as she described scenes where she had lately been, or persons she had lately seen! Yet she readily changed from gay to grave, and loved better the serious talk which opened the depths of life. Describing a conversation in relation to Christianity, with a friend of strong mind, who told her he had found, in this religion, a home for his best and deepest thoughts, she says—'Ah! what a pleasure 'to meet with such a daring, yet realizing, mind as his!' But her catholic taste found satisfaction in intercourse with persons quite different from herself in opinions and tendencies, as the following letter, written in her twentieth year, will indicate:

* * * * *

'I was very happy, although greatly restrained by 'the apprehension of going a little too far with these 'persons of singular refinement and settled opinions.

'However, I believe I did pretty well, though I did make 'one or two little mistakes, when most interested; but I 'was not so foolish as to try to retrieve them. One occa- 'sion more particularly, when Mr. G——, after going 'more fully into his poetical opinions than I could have 'expected, stated his sentiments: first, that Wordsworth 'had, in truth, guided, or, rather, completely vivified the 'poetry of this age; secondly, that 't was his influence 'which had, in reality, given all his better individuality 'to Byron. He recurred again and again to this opinion, '*con amore*, and seemed to wish much for an answer; but 'I would not venture, though 't was hard for me to for- 'bear, I knew so well what I thought. Mr. G——'s 'Wordsworthianism, however, is excellent; his beauti- 'ful simplicity of taste, and love of truth, have preserved 'him from any touch of that vague and imbecile enthu- 'siasm, which has enervated almost all the exclusive and 'determined admirers of the great poet whom I have 'known in these parts. His reverence, his feeling, are 'thoroughly intelligent. Everything in his mind is well 'defined; and his horror of the vague, and false, nay, even '(suppose another horror here, for grammar's sake) 'of the startling and paradoxical, have their beauty. I 'think I could know Mr. G—— long, and see him per- 'petually, without any touch of satiety; such variety is 'made by the very absence of pretension, and the love 'of truth. I found much amusement in leading him to 'sketch the scenes and persons which Lockhart portrays 'in such glowing colors, and which he, too, has seen 'with the *eye of taste*, but how different!'

* * * * *

Our friend was well aware that her *forte* was in conversation. Here she felt at home, here she felt her power, and the excitement which the presence of living persons brought, gave all her faculties full activity 'After all,' she says, in a letter, 'this writing is mighty 'dead. Oh, for my dear old Greeks, who talked every-'thing — not to shine as in the Parisian saloons, but to 'learn, to teach, to vent the heart, to clear the mind!'

Again, in 1832: —

'Conversation is my natural element. I need to be 'called out, and never think alone, without imagining 'some companion. Whether this be nature or the force 'of circumstances, I know not; it is my habit, and be-'speaks a second-rate mind.'

I am disposed to think, much as she excelled in general conversation, that her greatest mental efforts were made in intercourse with individuals. All her friends will unite in the testimony, that whatever they may have known of wit and eloquence in others, they have never seen one who, like her, by the conversation of an hour or two, could not merely entertain and inform, but make an epoch in one's life. We all dated back to this or that conversation with Margaret, in which we took a complete survey of great subjects, came to some clear view of a difficult question, saw our way open before us to a higher plane of life, and were led to some definite resolution or purpose which has had a bearing on all our subsequent career. For Margaret's conversation turned, at such times, to life, — its destiny, its duty, its prospect. With comprehensive glance she would survey the past, and sum up, in a few brief words, its results; she would then turn to the future, and, by a natural order, sweep through its chances and alternatives,—passing ever into a more earnest tone, into a more serious view,—and then bring all to bear on the present, till its duties grew plain, and its opportunities attractive. Happy he who can lift conversation, without loss of its cheer, to the highest uses! Happy he who has such a gift as this, an original faculty thus accomplished by culture, by which he can make our common life rich, significant and fair,—can give to the hour a beauty and brilliancy which shall make it eminent long after, amid dreary years of level routine!

I recall many such conversations. I remember one summer's day, in which we rode together, on horseback, from Cambridge to Newton,—a day all of a piece, in which my eloquent companion helped me to understand my past life, and her own,—a day which left me in that calm repose which comes to us, when we clearly apprehend what we ought to do, and are ready to attempt it. I recall other mornings when, not having seen her for a week or two, I would walk with her for hours, beneath the lindens or in the garden, while we related to each other what we had read in our German studies. And I always left her astonished at the progress of her mind, at the amount of new thoughts she had garnered, and filled with a new sense of the worth of knowledge, and the value of life.

There were other conversations, in which, impelled by the strong instinct of utterance, she would state, in words of tragical pathos, her own needs and longings,—her demands on life,—the struggles of mind, and of heart,—her conflicts with self, with nature, with the limitations of circumstances, with insoluble problems, with an unattainable desire. She seemed to feel relief from the expression of these thoughts, though she gained no light from her companion. Many such conversations I remember, while she lived in Cambridge, and one such in Groton; but afterwards, when I met her, I found her mind risen above these struggles, and in a self-possessed state which needed no such outlet for its ferment.

It is impossible to give any account of *these* conversations; but I add a few scraps, to indicate, however slightly, something of her ordinary manner.

'Rev. Mr. —— preached a sermon on TIME. But 'what business had he to talk about time? We should 'like well to hear the opinions of a great man, who had 'made good use of time; but not of a little man, who 'had not used it to any purpose. I wished to get up and 'tell him to speak of something which he knew and felt.'

'The best criticism on those sermons which proclaim 'so loudly the dignity of human nature was from our 'friend E. S. She said, coming out from Dr. Chan-'ning's church, that she felt fatigued by the demands 'the sermon made on her, and would go home and read 'what Jesus said, — "*Ye are of more value than many* '"*sparrows.*" *That* she could bear; it did not seem 'exaggerated praise.'

'The Swedenborgians say, "that is *Correspondence*," 'and the phrenologists, "that it is *Approbativeness*," and 'so think they know all about it. It would not be so, if 'we could be like the birds, — make one method, and 'then desert it, and make a new one, — as they build 'their nests.'

'As regards crime, we cannot understand what we 'have not *already* felt; — thus, all crimes have formed 'part of our minds. We do but recognize one part of 'ourselves in the worst actions of others. When you 'take the subject in this light, do you not incline to 'consider the capacity for action as something widely 'differing from the experience of a feeling?'

'How beautiful the life of Benvenuto Cellini! How 'his occupations perpetually impelled to thought, — to 'gushings of thought naturally excited!'

'Father lectured me for looking satirical when the 'man of Words spake, and so attentive to the man of 'Truth,— that is, of God.'

Margaret used often to talk about the books which she and I were reading.

Godwin. 'I think you will be more and more satisfied 'with Godwin. He has fully lived the double existence 'of man, and he casts the reflexes on his magic mirror 'from a height where no object in life's panorama can 'cause one throb of delirious hope or grasping ambition. 'At any rate, if you study him, you may know all he 'has to tell. He is quite free from vanity, and conceals 'not miserly any of his treasures from the knowledge of 'posterity.

M'lle. D'Espinasse. 'I am swallowing by gasps 'that *cauldrony* beverage of selfish passion and mor- 'bid taste, the letters of M'lle D'Espinasse. It is 'good for me. How odious is the abandonment of pas- 'sion, such as this, unshaded by pride or delicacy, unhal-

'lowed by religion, — a selfish craving only; every 'source of enjoyment stifled to cherish this burning 'thirst. Yet the picture, so minute in its touches, is true 'as death. I should not like Delphine now.'

Events in life, apparently trivial, often seemed to her full of mystic significance, and it was her pleasure to turn such to poetry. On one occasion, the sight of a passion-flower, given by one lady to another, and then lost, appeared to her so significant of the character, relation, and destiny of the two, that it drew from her lines of which two or three seem worth preserving, as indicating her feeling of social relations.

'Dear friend, my heart grew pensive when I saw
'The flower, for thee so sweetly set apart,
'By one whose passionless though tender heart
'Is worthy to bestow, as angels are,
'By an unheeding hand conveyed away,
'To close, in unsoothed night, the promise of its day.

* * * * *

'The mystic flower read in thy soul-filled eye
'To its life's question the desired reply,
'But came no nearer. On thy gentle breast
'It hoped to find the haven of its rest;
'But in cold night, hurried afar from thee,
'It closed its once half-smiling destiny.

'Yet thus, methinks, it utters as it dies, —
'"By the pure truth of those calm, gentle eyes
'"Which saw my life should find its aim in thine,
'"I see a clime where no strait laws confine.
'"In that blest land where *twos* ne'er know a *three*,
'"Save as the accord of their fine sympathy,
'"O, best-loved, I will wait for thee!"'

III.

STUDIES.

"Nur durch das Morgenthor des Schönen
Drangst du in der Erkenntniss Land;
An hohen Glanz sich zu gewöhnen
Uebt sich am Reize der Verstand.
Was bei dem Saitenklang der Musen
Mit süssem Beben dich durchdrang,
Erzog die Kraft in deinem Busen,
Die sich dereinst zum Weltgeist schwang."

SCHILLER.

"To work, with heart resigned and spirit strong;
Subdue, with patient toil, life's bitter wrong,
Through Nature's dullest, as her brightest ways,
We will march onward, singing to thy praise."

E. S., *in the Dial.*

"The peculiar nature of the scholar's occupation consists in this,—that science, and especially that side of it from which he conceives of the whole, shall continually burst forth before him in new and fairer forms. Let this fresh spiritual youth never grow old within him; let no form become fixed and rigid; let each sunrise bring him new joy and love in his vocation, and larger views of its significance."

FICHTE.

Of Margaret's studies while at Cambridge, I knew personally only of the German. She already, when I first became acquainted with her, had become familiar with the masterpieces of French, Italian and Spanish literature. But all this amount of reading had not made her "deep-learned in books and shallow in herself;"

for she brought to the study of most writers "a spirit and genius equal or superior,"—so far, at least, as the analytic understanding was concerned. Every writer whom she studied, as every person whom she knew, she placed in his own class, knew his relation to other writers, to the world, to life, to nature, to herself. Much as they might delight her, they never swept her away. She breasted the current of their genius, as a stately swan moves up a stream, enjoying the rushing water the more because she resists it. In a passionate love-struggle she wrestled thus with the genius of De Staël, of Rousseau, of Alfieri, of Petrarch.

The first and most striking element in the genius of Margaret was the clear, sharp understanding, which keenly distinguished between things different, and kept every thought, opinion, person, character, in its own place, not to be confounded with any other. The god Terminus presided over her intellect. She knew her thoughts as we know each other's faces; and opinions, with most of us so vague, shadowy, and shifting, were in her mind substantial and distinct realities. Some persons see distinctions, others resemblances; but she saw both. No sophist could pass on her a counterfeit piece of intellectual money; but also she recognized the one pure metallic basis in coins of different epochs, and when mixed with a very ruinous alloy. This gave a comprehensive quality to her mind most imposing and convincing, as it enabled her to show the one Truth, or the one Law, manifesting itself in such various phenomena. Add to this her profound faith in truth, which made her a Realist of that order that thoughts to her were things. The world of her thoughts rose around her mind as a panorama,—the sun in the sky, the flowers distinct in the foreground, the pale mountain sharply, though faintly, cutting the sky with its outline in the distance, — and all in pure light and shade, all in perfect perspective.

Margaret began to study German early in 1832. Both she and I were attracted towards this literature, at the same time, by the wild bugle-call of Thomas Carlyle, in his romantic articles on Richter, Schiller, and Goethe, which appeared in the old Foreign Review, the Edinburgh Review, and afterwards in the Foreign Quarterly. I believe that in about three months from the time that Margaret commenced German, she was reading with ease the masterpieces of its literature. Within the year, she had read Goethe's Faust, Tasso, Iphigenia, Hermann and Dorothea, Elective Affinities, and Memoirs; Tieck's William-Lovel, Prince Zerbino, and other works; Körner, Novalis, and something of Richter; all of Schiller's principal dramas, and his lyric poetry. Almost every evening I saw her, and heard an account of her studies. Her mind opened under this influence, as the apple-blossom at the end of a warm week in May. The thought and the beauty of this rich literature equally filled her mind and fascinated her imagination.

But if she studied books thus earnestly, still more frequently did she turn to the study of men. Authors and their personages were not ideal beings merely, but full of human blood and life. So living men and women were idealized again, and transfigured by her rapid fancy, — every trait intensified, developed, ennobled. Lessing says that "The true portrait painter will paint his subject, flattering him as art ought to flatter, — painting the face not as it actually is, but as creation designed, omitting the imperfections arising from the resistance of the material worked in." Margaret's portrait-painting intellect treated persons in this way. She saw them as God designed them, — omitting the loss from wear and tear, from false position, from friction of untoward circumstances. If we may be permitted to take a somewhat transcendental distinction, she saw them not as they *actually* were, but as they *really* were. This accounts for her high estimate of her friends, — too high, too flattering, indeed, but justified to her mind by her knowledge of their interior capabilities.

The following extract illustrates her power, even at the age of nineteen, of comprehending the relations of two things lying far apart from each other, and of rising to a point of view which could overlook both: —

'I have had, — while staying a day or two in Bos-'ton, — some of Shirley's, Ford's, and Heywood's plays 'from the Athenæum. There are some noble strains 'of proud rage, and intellectual, but most poetical, all-'absorbing, passion. One of the finest fictions I recol-'lect in those specimens of the Italian novelists, — 'which you, I think, read when I did, — noble, where it 'illustrated the Italian national spirit, is ruined by the 'English novelist, who has transplanted it to an uncon-'genial soil; yet he has given it beauties which an 'Italian eye could not see, by investing the actors with 'deep, continuing, truly English affections.'

* * * * *

The following criticism on some of the dialogues of Plato, (dated June 3d, 1833,) in a letter returning the book, illustrates her downright way of asking world-revered authors to accept the test of plain common sense. As a finished or deliberate opinion, it ought not to be read; for it was not intended as such, but as a first impression hastily sketched. But read it as an illustration of the method in which her mind worked, and you will see that she meets the great Plato modestly, but boldly, on human ground, asking him for satisfactory proof of all that he says, and treating him as a human being, speaking to human beings.

'*June* 3, 1833.—I part with Plato with regret. I 'could have wished to "enchant myself," as Socrates 'would say, with him some days longer. Eutyphron is 'excellent. 'Tis the best specimen I have ever seen of 'that mode of convincing. There is one passage in 'which Socrates, as if it were *aside*,—since the remark 'is quite away from the consciousness of Eutyphron,— 'declares, "qu'il aimerait incomparablement mieux des '"principes fixes et inébranlables à l'habilité de Dédale '"avec les tresors de Tantale." I delight to hear such 'things from those whose lives have given the right to 'say them. For 't is not always true what Lessing says, and I, myself, once thought,—

"F.—Von was fur Tugenden spricht er denn?
MINNA.—Er spricht von keiner; denn ihn fehlt keine."

'For the mouth sometimes talketh virtue from the 'overflowing of the heart, as well as love, anger, &c.

'"Crito" I have read only once, but like it. I have 'not got it in my heart though, so clearly as the others.
'The "Apology" I deem only remarkable for the

'noble tone of sentiment, and beautiful calmness. I 'was much affected by Phædo, but think the argu- 'ment weak in many respects. The nature of abstract 'ideas is clearly set forth; but there is no justice in rea- 'soning, from their existence, that our souls have lived 'previous to our present state, since it was as easy for 'the Deity to create at once the idea of beauty within 'us, as the sense which brings to the soul intelligence 'that it exists in some outward shape. He does not 'clearly show his opinion of what the soul is; whether 'eternal *as* the Deity, created *by* the Deity, or how. In 'his answer to Simmias, he takes advantage of the gen- 'eral meaning of the words harmony, discord, &c. The 'soul might be a result, without being a harmony. But 'I think too many things to write, and some I have not 'had time to examine. Meanwhile I can think over 'parts, and say to myself, "beautiful," "noble," and use 'this as one of my enchantments.'

'I send two of your German books. It pains me to 'part with Ottilia. I wish we could learn books, as we 'do pieces of music, and repeat them, in the author's 'order, when taking a solitary walk. But, now, if I 'set out with an Ottilia, this wicked fairy associa- 'tion conjures up such crowds of less lovely compan- 'ions, that I often cease to feel the influence of the elect 'one. I don't like Goethe so well as Schiller now. I 'mean, I am not so happy in reading him. That per- 'fect wisdom and *merciless* nature seems cold, after 'those seducing pictures of forms more beautiful than 'truth. Nathless, I should like to read the second part 'of Goethe's Memoirs, if you do not use it now.'

'1832.—I am thinking how I omitted to talk a vol-'ume to you about the "Elective Affinities." Now I 'shall never say half of it, for which I, on my own 'account, am sorry. But two or three things I would 'ask:—

'What do you think of Charlotte's proposition, that 'the accomplished pedagogue must be tiresome in soci-'ety?

'Of Ottilia's, that the afflicted, and ill-educated, are 'oftentimes singled out by fate to instruct others, and 'her beautiful reasons why?

'And what have you thought of the discussion touch-'ing graves and monuments?

'I am now going to dream of your sermon, and of 'Ottilia's china-asters. Both shall be driven from my 'head to-morrow, for I go to town, allured by de-'spatches from thence, promising much entertainment. 'Woe unto them if they disappoint me!

'Consider it, I pray you, as the "nearest duty" to 'answer my questions, and not act as you did about the 'sphinx-song.'

'I have not anybody to speak to, that does not 'talk common-place, and I wish to talk about such an 'uncommon person,—about Novalis! a wondrous youth, 'and who has only written one volume. That is pleas-'ant! I feel as though I could pursue my natural 'mode with him, get acquainted, then make my mind 'easy in the belief that I know all that is to be known. 'And he died at twenty-nine, and, as with Körner, your 'feelings may be single; you will never be called upon 'to share his experience, and compare his future feelings 'with his present. And his life was so full and so still.

'Then it is a relief, after feeling the immense superiority 'of Goethe. It seems to me as if the mind of Goethe 'had embraced the universe. I have felt this lately, in 'reading his lyric poems. I am enchanted while I read. 'He comprehends every feeling I have ever had so per-'fectly, expresses it so beautifully; but when I shut the 'book, it seems as if I had lost my personal identity; 'all my feelings linked with such an immense variety 'that belong to beings I had thought so different. What 'can I bring? There is no answer in my mind, except '"It is so," or "It will be so," or "No doubt such and '"such feel so." Yet, while my judgment becomes 'daily more tolerant towards others, the same attracting 'and repelling work is going on in my feelings. But I 'persevere in reading the great sage, some part of every 'day, hoping the time will come, when I shall not feel 'so overwhelmed, and leave off this habit of wishing to 'grasp the whole, and be contented to learn a little every 'day, as becomes a pupil.

'But now the one-sidedness, imperfection, and glow, 'of a mind like that of Novalis, seem refreshingly human 'to me. I have wished fifty times to write some letters 'giving an account, first, of his very pretty life, and 'then of his one volume, as I re-read it, chapter by 'chapter. If you will pretend to be very much inter-'ested, perhaps I will get a better pen, and write them 'to you.' * *

NEED OF COMMUNION.

'*Aug.* 7, 1832.—I feel quite lost; it is so long since I 'have talked myself. To see so many acquaintances, to 'talk so many words, and never tell my mind completely 'on any subject — to say so many things which do not 'seem called out, makes me feel strangely vague and 'movable.

''Tis true, the time is probably near when I must live 'alone, to all intents and purposes, — separate entirely 'my acting from my thinking world, take care of my 'ideas without aid, — except from the illustrious dead, '— answer my own questions, correct my own feelings, 'and do all that hard work for myself. How tiresome ''tis to find out all one's self-delusion! I thought 'myself so very independent, because I could conceal 'some feelings at will, and did not need the same 'excitement as other young characters did. And I am 'not independent, nor never shall be, while I can get 'anybody to minister to me. But I shall go where 'there is never a spirit to come, if I call ever so loudly.

'Perhaps I shall talk to you about Körner, but 'need not write. He charms me, and has become 'a fixed star in the heaven of my thought; but I 'understand all that he excites perfectly. I felt very '*new* about Novalis, — "the good Novalis," as you call 'him after Mr. Carlyle. He is, indeed, *good*, most 'enlightened, yet most pure; every link of his experi-'ence framed — no, *beaten* — from the tried gold.

'I have read, thoroughly, only two of his pieces, "Die '"Lehrlinge zu Sais," and "Heinrich von Ofterdingen." 'From the former I have only brought away piecemeal 'impressions, but the plan and treatment of the latter, 'I believe, I understand. It describes the development 'of poetry in a mind; and with this several other devel-'opments are connected. I think I shall tell you all I 'know about it, some quiet time after your return, but, 'if not, will certainly keep a Novalis-journal for you 'some favorable season, when I live regularly for a fort-'night.'

'*June*, 1833. — I return Lessing. I could hardly get 'through Miss Sampson. E. Galeotti is good in the 'same way as Minna. Well-conceived and sustained 'characters, interesting situations, but never that pro-'found knowledge of human nature, those minute 'beauties, and delicate vivifying traits, which lead on 'so in the writings of some authors, who may be name-'less. I think him easily followed; strong, but not 'deep.'

'*May*, 1833. — *Groton.* — I think you are wrong in 'applying your artistical ideas to occasional poetry. An 'epic, a drama, must have a fixed form in the mind of 'the poet from the first; and copious draughts of ambro-'sia quaffed in the heaven of thought, soft fanning gales 'and bright light from the outward world, give muscle 'and bloom, — that is, give life, — to this skeleton. But 'all occasional poems must be moods, and can a mood 'have a form fixed and perfect, more than a wave of 'the sea?'

'Three or four afternoons I have passed very happily 'at my beloved haunt in the wood, reading Goethe's '"Second Residence in Rome." Your pencil-marks 'show that you have been before me. I shut the 'book each time with an earnest desire to live as he 'did, — always to have some engrossing object of pur-'suit. I sympathize deeply with a mind in that 'state. While mine is being used up by ounces, I wish 'pailfuls might be poured into it. I am dejected and 'uneasy when I see no results from my daily existence, 'but I am suffocated and lost when I have not the bright 'feeling of progression.' * *

'I think I am less happy, in many respects, than you, 'but particularly in this. You can speak freely to me 'of all your circumstances and feelings, can you not? 'It is not possible for me to be so profoundly frank with 'any earthly friend. Thus my heart has no proper 'home; it only can prefer some of its visiting-places to 'others; and with deep regret I realize that I have, at 'length, entered on the concentrating stage of life. It 'was not time. I had been too sadly cramped. I had 'not learned enough, and must always remain imper- 'fect. Enough! I am glad I have been able to say so 'much.'

'I have read nothing, — to signify, — except Goethe's '"Campagne in Frankreich." Have you looked through 'it, and do you remember his intercourse with the Wer- 'therian Plessing? That tale pained me exceedingly. 'We cry, "help, help," and there is no help — in man 'at least. How often I have thought, if I could see 'Goethe, and tell him my state of mind, he would sup- 'port and guide me! He would be able to understand; 'he would show me how to rule circumstances, instead 'of being ruled by them; and, above all, he would not 'have been so sure that all would be for the best, with- 'out our making an effort to act out the oracles; he 'would have wished to see me what Nature intended. 'But his conduct to Plessing and Ohlenschlager shows 'that to him, also, an appeal would have been vain.'

'Do you really believe there is anything "all-compre-'"hending" but religion? Are not these distinctions 'imaginary? Must not the philosophy of every mind, 'or set of minds, be a system suited to guide them, and 'give a home where they can bring materials among 'which to accept, reject, and shape at pleasure? Nova-'lis calls those, who harbor these ideas, "unbelievers;" 'but hard names make no difference. He says with 'disdain, "To *such*, philosophy is only a system which '"will spare them the trouble of reflecting." Now this 'is just my case. I *do* want a system which shall suf-'fice to my character, and in whose applications I shall 'have faith. I do not wish to *reflect* always, if reflect-'ing must be always about one's identity, whether '"*ich*" am the true "*ich*," &c. I wish to arrive at 'that point where I can trust myself, and leave off say-'ing, "It seems to me," and boldly feel, It *is* so TO ME. 'My character has got its natural regulator, my heart 'beats, my lips speak truth, I can walk alone, or offer 'my arm to a friend, or if I lean on another, it is not 'the debility of sickness, but only wayside weariness. 'This is the philosophy *I* want; this much would sat-'isfy *me*.

'Then Novalis says, "Philosophy is the art of dis-'"covering the place of truth in every encountered '"event and circumstance, to attune all relations to '"truth."

'Philosophy is peculiarly home-sickness; an over-'mastering desire to be at home.

'I think so; but what is there *all-comprehending*, eternally-conscious, about that?'

'*Sept.*, 1832. — "Not see the use of metaphysics?'

'A moderate portion, taken at stated intervals, I hold to 'be of much use as discipline of the faculties. I only 'object to them as having an absorbing and anti-produc- 'tive tendency. But 't is not always so; may not be so 'with you. Wait till you are two years older, before you 'decide that 't is your vocation. Time enough at six- 'and-twenty to form yourself into a metaphysical phi- 'losopher. The brain does not easily get too dry for *that.* 'Happy you, in these ideas which give you a tendency to 'optimism. May you become a proselyte to that con- 'soling faith. I shall never be able to follow you, but 'shall look after you with longing eyes.'

'*Groton.*—Spring has come, and I shall see you soon. 'If I could pour into your mind all the ideas which 'have passed through mine, you would be well enter- 'tained, I think, for three or four days. But no hour 'will receive aught beyond its own appropriate wealth.

'I am at present engaged in surveying the level on 'which the public mind is poised. I no longer lie in 'wait for the tragedy and comedy of life; the rules of 'its *prose* engage my attention. I talk incessantly with 'common-place people, full of curiosity to ascertain the 'process by which materials, apparently so jarring and 'incapable of classification, get united into that strange 'whole, the American public. I have read all Jefferson's 'letters, the North American, the daily papers, &c., 'without end. H. seems to be weaving his Kantisms 'into the American system in a tolerably happy manner.'

* * 'George Thompson has a voice of uncommon 'compass and beauty; never sharp in its highest, or 'rough and husky in its lowest, tones. A perfect enun-

'ciation, every syllable round and energetic; though his 'manner was the one I love best, very rapid, and full of 'eager climaxes. Earnestness in every part, — sometimes 'impassioned earnestness, — a sort of "Dear friends, be-'"lieve, *pray* believe, I love you, and you MUST believe as '"I do" expression, even in the argumentative parts. I 'felt, as I have so often done before, if I were a man, 'the gift I would choose should be that of eloquence. 'That power of forcing the vital currents of thousands 'of human hearts into ONE current, by the constraining 'power of that most delicate instrument, the voice, is so 'intense, — yes, I would prefer it to a more extensive 'fame, a more permanent influence.'

'Did I describe to you my feelings on hearing Mr. 'Everett's eulogy on Lafayette? No; I did not. 'That was exquisite. The old, hackneyed story; not 'a new anecdote, not a single reflection of any value; 'but the manner, the *manner*, the delicate inflections of 'voice, the elegant and appropriate gesture, the sense 'of beauty produced by the whole, which thrilled us all 'to tears, flowing from a deeper and purer source than 'that which answers to pathos. This was fine; but I 'prefer the Thompson manner. Then there is Mr. Web-'ster's, unlike either; simple grandeur, nobler, more 'impressive, less captivating. I have heard few fine 'speakers; I wish I could hear a thousand.

'Are you vexed by my keeping the six volumes of your 'Goethe? I read him very little either; I have so little 'time, — many things to do at home, — my three children, 'and three pupils besides, whom I instruct.

'By the way, I have always thought all that was 'said about the anti-religious tendency of a classical edu-'cation to be old wives' tales. But their puzzles about

'Virgil's notions of heaven and virtue, and his gracefully-'described gods and goddesses, have led me to alter my 'opinions; and I suspect, from reminiscences of my own 'mental history, that if all governors do not think the 'same 't is from want of that intimate knowledge of their 'pupils' minds which I naturally possess. I really find 'it difficult to keep their *morale* steady, and am inclined 'to think many of my own sceptical sufferings are 'traceable to this source. I well remember what reflec-'tions arose in my childish mind from a comparison of 'the Hebrew history, where every moral obliquity is 'shown out with such naïveté, and the Greek history, 'full of sparkling deeds and brilliant sayings, and their 'gods and goddesses, the types of beauty and power, with 'the dazzling veil of flowery language and poetical im-'agery cast over their vices and failings.'

'My own favorite project, since I began seriously to 'entertain any of that sort, is six historical tragedies; of 'which I have the plans of three quite perfect. How-'over, the attempts I have made on them have served to 'show me the vast difference between conception and 'execution. Yet I am, though abashed, not altogether 'discouraged. My next favorite plan is a series of tales 'illustrative of Hebrew history. The proper junctures 'have occurred to me during my late studies on the his-'torical books of the Old Testament. This task, how-'ever, requires a thorough and imbuing knowledge of 'the Hebrew manners and spirit, with a chastened energy 'of imagination, which I am as yet far from possessing. 'But if I should be permitted peace and time to follow 'out my ideas, I have hopes. Perhaps it is a weakness 'to confide to you embryo designs, which never may 'glow into life, or mock me by their failure.'

'I have long had a suspicion that no mind can sys'tematize its knowledge, and carry on the concentrating 'processes, without some fixed opinion on the subject of 'metaphysics. But that indisposition, or even dread of 'the study, which you may remember, has kept me 'from meddling with it, till lately, in meditating on the 'life of Goethe, I thought I must get some idea of the 'history of philosophical opinion in Germany, that I 'might be able to judge of the influence it exercised upon 'his mind. I think I can comprehend him every other way, 'and probably interpret him satisfactorily to others,—if I 'can get the proper materials. When I was in Cambridge, 'I got Fichte and Jacobi; I was much interrupted, but 'some time and earnest thought I devoted. Fichte I 'could not understand at all; though the treatise which 'I read was one intended to be popular, and which he 'says must compel (*bezwingen*) to conviction. Jacobi I 'could understand in details, but not in system. It 'seemed to me that his mind must have been moulded 'by some other mind, with which I ought to be ac'quainted, in order to know him well,—perhaps Spi'noza's. Since I came home, I have been consulting 'Buhle's and Tennemann's histories of philosophy, and 'dipping into Brown, Stewart, and that class of books.'

'After I had cast the burden of my cares upon you, I 'rested, and read Petrarch for a day or two. But that 'could not last. I had begun to "take an account '"of stock," as Coleridge calls it, and was forced to pro'ceed He says few persons ever did this faithfully, without being dissatisfied with the result, and lowering 'their estimate of their supposed riches. With me it 'has ended in the most humiliating sense of poverty; 'and only just enough pride is left to keep your poor 'friend off the parish. As it is, I have already asked 'items of several besides yourself; but, though they 'have all given what they had, it has by no means an- 'swered my purpose; and I have laid their gifts aside, 'with my other hoards, which gleamed so fairy bright, 'and are now, in the hour of trial, turned into mere 'slate-stones. I am not sure that even if I do find the 'philosopher's stone, I shall be able to transmute them 'into the gold they looked so like formerly. It will be 'long before I can give a distinct, and at the same time 'concise, account of my present state. I believe it is a 'great era. I am thinking now, — really thinking, I 'believe; certainly it seems as if I had never done 'so before. If it does not kill me, something will come 'of it. Never was my mind so active; and the subjects 'are God, the universe, immortality. But shall I be fit 'for anything till I have absolutely re-educated myself? 'Am I, can I make myself, fit to write an account of 'half a century of the existence of one of the master- 'spirits of this world? It seems as if I had been very 'arrogant to dare to think it; yet will I not shrink back 'from what I have undertaken, — even by failure I shall 'learn much.'

'I am shocked to perceive you think I am *writing* the 'life of Goethe. No, indeed! I shall need a great deal 'of preparation before I shall have it clear in my head. 'I have taken a great many notes; but I shall not begin 'to write it, till it all lies mapped out before me. I have no materials for ten years of his life, from the time he 'went to Weimar, up to the Italian journey. Besides, I 'wish to see the books that have been written about him 'in Germany, by friend or foe. I wish to look at the 'matter from all sides. New lights are constantly dawn- 'ing on me; and I think it possible I shall come out from 'the Carlyle view, and perhaps from yours, and distaste 'you, which will trouble me.

* * 'How am I to get the information I want, unless 'I go to Europe? To whom shall I write to choose my 'materials? I have thought of Mr. Carlyle, but still 'more of Goethe's friend, Von Muller. I dare say he 'would be pleased at the idea of a life of G. written 'in this hemisphere, and be very willing to help me. 'If you have anything to tell me, you will, and not 'mince matters. Of course, my impressions of Goethe's 'works cannot be influenced by information I get about 'his *life;* but, as to this latter, I suspect I must have 'been hasty in my inferences. I apply to you without 'scruple. There are subjects on which men and women 'usually talk a great deal, but apart from one another. 'You, however, are well aware that I am very destitute 'of what is commonly *called* modesty. With regard to 'this, how fine the remark of our present subject: '"Courage and modesty are virtues which every sort of '"society reveres, because they are virtues which cannot '"be counterfeited; also, they are known by the *same* '"*hue.*" When that blush does not come naturally to 'my face, I do not drop a veil to make people think it is 'there. All this may be very unlovely, but it is *I.*'

CHANNING ON SLAVERY.

'This is a noble work. So refreshing its calm, benign 'atmosphere, after the pestilence-bringing gales of the 'day. It comes like a breath borne over some solemn 'sea which separates us from an island of righteousness. 'How valuable is it to have among us a man who, 'standing apart from the conflicts of the herd, watches 'the principles that are at work, with a truly paternal 'love for what is human, and may be permanent; ready 'at the proper point to give his casting-vote to the cause 'of Right! The author has amplified on the grounds of 'his faith, to a degree that might seem superfluous, if the 'question had not become so utterly bemazed and be-'darkened of late. After all, it is probable that, in 'addressing the public at large, it is *not* best to express a 'thought in as few words as possible; there is much 'classic authority for diffuseness.'

RICHTER.

Groton.—'Ritcher says, the childish heart vies in the 'height of its surges with the manly, only is not furnished 'with *lead* for sounding them.

'How thoroughly am I converted to the love of Jean 'Paul, and wonder at the indolence or shallowness 'which could resist so long, and call his profuse riches 'want of system! What a mistake! System, plan, 'there is, but on so broad a basis that I did not at first 'comprehend it. In every page I am forced to pencil. I 'will make me a book, or, as he would say, bind me a 'bouquet from his pages, and wear it on my heart of 'hearts, and be ever refreshing my wearied inward sense 'with its exquisite fragrance. I must have improved, to 'love him as I do.'

IV.

CHARACTER. — AIMS AND IDEAS OF LIFE.

"O friend, how flat and tasteless such a life!
Impulse gives birth to impulse, deed to deed,
Still toilsomely ascending step by step,
Into an unknown realm of dark blue clouds.
What crowns the ascent? Speak, or I go no further.
I need a goal, an aim. I cannot toil,
Because the steps are here; in their ascent
Tell me THE END, or I sit still and weep."

"NATURLICHE TOCHTER,"
Translated by Margaret.

"And so he went onward, ever onward, for twenty-seven years — then, indeed, he had gone far enough."

GOETHE'S *words concerning Schiller*

I WOULD say something of Margaret's inward condition, of her aims and views in life, while in Cambridge, before closing this chapter of her story. Her powers, whether of mind, heart, or will, have been sufficiently indicated in what has preceded. In the sketch of her friendships and of her studies, we have seen the affluence of her intellect, and the deep tenderness of her woman's nature. We have seen the energy which she displayed in study and labor.

But to what *aim* were these powers directed? Had she any clear view of the demands and opportunities of life, any definite plan, any high, pure purpose? This is, after all, the test question, which detects the low-born and low-minded wearer of the robe of gold, —

"Touch them inwardly, they smell of copper."

Margaret's life *had an aim*, and she was, therefore, essentially a moral person, and not merely an overflowing genius, in whom "impulse gives birth to impulse, deed to deed." This aim was distinctly apprehended and steadily pursued by her from first to last. It was a high, noble one, wholly religious, almost Christian. It gave dignity to her whole career, and made it heroic.

This aim, from first to last, was SELF-CULTURE. If she ever was ambitious of knowledge and talent, as a means of excelling others, and gaining fame, position, admiration, — this vanity had passed before I knew her, and was replaced by the profound desire for a full development of her whole nature, by means of a full experience of life.

In her description of her own youth, she says, 'VERY 'EARLY I KNEW THAT THE ONLY OBJECT IN LIFE WAS TO 'GROW.' This is the passage: —

'I was now in the hands of teachers, who had not, 'since they came on the earth, put to themselves one 'intelligent question as to their business here. Good 'dispositions and employment for the heart gave a tone 'to all they said, which was pleasing, and not perverting. 'They, no doubt, injured those who accepted the husks 'they proffered for bread, and believed that exercise of 'memory was study, and to know what others knew, 'was the object of study. But to me this was all penetrable. I had known great living minds, — I had seen 'how they took their food and did their exercise, and 'what their objects were. *Very early I knew that the 'only object in life was to grow.* I was often false to 'this knowledge, in idolatries of particular objects, or 'impatient longings for happiness, but I have never lost 'sight of it, have always been controlled by it, and this 'first gift of thought has never been superseded by a 'later love.'

In this she spoke truth. The good and the evil which flow from this great idea of self-development she fully realized. This aim of life, originally self-chosen, was made much more clear to her mind by the study of Goethe, the great master of this school, in whose unequalled eloquence this doctrine acquires an almost irresistible beauty and charm.

"Wholly religious, and almost Christian," I said, was this aim. It was religious, because it recognized something divine, infinite, imperishable in the human soul, — something divine in outward nature and providence, by which the soul is led along its appointed way. It was almost Christian in its superiority to all low, worldly, vulgar thoughts and cares; in its recognition of a high standard of duty, and a great destiny for man. In its strength, Margaret was enabled to do and bear, with patient fortitude, what would have crushed a soul not thus supported. Yet it is not the highest aim, for in all its forms, whether as personal improvement, the salvation of the soul, or ascetic religion, it has at its core a profound selfishness. Margaret's soul was too generous for any low form of selfishness. Too noble to become an Epicurean, too large-minded to become a modern ascetic, the defective nature of her rule of life, showed itself in her case, only in a certain supercilious tone toward "the vulgar herd," in the absence (at this period) of a tender humanity, and in an idolatrous hero-worship of genius and power. Afterward, too, she may have suffered from her desire for a universal human experience, and an unwillingness to see that we must often be content to enter the Kingdom of Heaven halt and maimed, — that a perfect development here must often be wholly renounced.

But how much better to pursue with devotion, like that of Margaret, an imperfect aim, than to worship with lip-service, as most persons do, even though it be in a loftier temple, and before a holier shrine! With Margaret, the doctrine of self-culture was a devotion to which she sacrificed all earthly hopes and joys, — everything but manifest duty. And so her course was "onward, ever onward," like that of Schiller, to her last hour of life.

> Burned in her cheek with ever deepening fire
> The spirit's YOUTH, which never passes by ; —
> The COURAGE which, though worlds in hate conspire,
> Conquers, at last, their dull hostility ; —
> The lofty FAITH, which, ever mounting higher,
> Now presses on, now waiteth patiently, —
> With which the good tends ever to his goal,
> With which day finds, at last, the earnest soul.

But this high idea which governed our friend's life, brought her into sharp conflicts, which constituted the pathos and tragedy of her existence, — first with her circumstances, which seemed so inadequate to the needs of her nature, — afterwards with duties to relatives and friends, — and, finally, with the law of the Great Spirit, whose will she found it so hard to acquiesce in.

The circumstances in which Margaret lived appeared to her life a prison. She had no room for utterance, no sphere adequate; her powers were unemployed. With what eloquence she described this want of a field! Often have I listened with wonder and admiration, satisfied that she exaggerated the evil, and yet unable to combat her rapid statements. Could she have seen in how few years a way would open before her, by which she could emerge into an ample field, — how soon she would find troops of friends, fit society, literary occupation, and the opportunity of studying the great works of art in their own home, — she would have been spared many a sharp pang.

Margaret, like every really earnest and deep nature, felt the necessity of a religious faith as the foundation of character. The first notice which I find of her views on this point is contained in the following letter to one of her youthful friends, when only nineteen: —

* * * * *

'I have hesitated much whether to tell you what you 'ask about my religion. You are mistaken! I have 'not formed an opinion. I have determined not to form 'settled opinions at present. Loving or feeble natures 'need a positive religion, a visible refuge, a protection, 'as much in the passionate season of youth as in those 'stages nearer to the grave. But mine is not such. My 'pride is superior to any feelings I have yet experienced: 'my affection is strong admiration, not the necessity of 'giving or receiving assistance or sympathy. When disappointed, I do not ask or wish consolation, — I wish to 'know and feel my pain, to investigate its nature and 'its source; I will not have my thoughts diverted, or my 'feelings soothed; 't is therefore that my young life is 'so singularly barren of illusions. I know, I feel the 'time must come when this proud and impatient heart 'shall be stilled, and turn from the ardors of Search and 'Action, to lean on something above. But—shall I say 'it?—the thought of that calmer era is to me a thought 'of deepest sadness; so remote from my present being is 'that future existence, which still the mind may conceive. I believe in Eternal Progression. I believe in 'a God, a Beauty and Perfection to which I am to strive 'all my life for assimilation. From these two articles 'of belief, I draw the rules by which I strive to regulate 'my life. But, though I reverence all religions as necessary to the happiness of man, I am yet ignorant of 'the religion of Revelation. Tangible promises! well 'defined hopes! are things of which I do not *now* feel 'the need. At present, my soul is intent on this life, and 'I think of religion as its rule; and, in my opinion, this 'is the natural and proper course from youth to age. 'What I have written is not hastily concocted, it has a 'meaning. I have given you, in this little space, the 'substance of many thoughts, the clues to many cherished opinions. 'T is a subject on which I rarely 'speak. I never said so much but once before. I 'have here given you all I know, or think, on the most 'important of subjects—could you but read understandingly!'

* * * * *

I find, in her journals for 1833, the following passages, expressing the religious purity of her aspirations at that time:—

'Blessed Father, nip every foolish wish in blossom. 'Lead me *any way* to truth and goodness; but if it might 'be, I would not pass from idol to idol. Let no mean 'sculpture deform a mind disorderly, perhaps ill-fur-'nished, but spacious and life-warm. Remember thy 'child, such as thou madest her, and let her understand 'her little troubles, when possible, oh, beautiful Deity!'

'*Sunday morning.* — Mr. —— preached on the nature 'of our duties, social and personal. The sweet dew of 'truth penetrated my heart like balm. He pointed out 'the various means of improvement, whereby the hum-'blest of us may be beneficent at last. How just, how 'nobly true, — how modestly, yet firmly uttered, — his 'opinions of man, — of time, — of God!

'My heart swelled with prayer. I began to feel hope 'that time and toil might strengthen me to despise the '"vulgar parts of felicity," and live as becomes an 'immortal creature. I am sure, quite sure, that I am 'getting into the right road. Oh, lead me, my Father! 'root out false pride and selfishness from my heart; 'inspire me with virtuous energy, and enable me to im-'prove every talent for the eternal good of myself and 'others.'

A friend of Margaret, some years older than herself, gives me the following narrative: —

"I was," says she, in substance, "suffering keenly from a severe trial, and had secluded myself from all my friends, when Margaret, a girl of twenty, forced her way to me. She sat with me, and gave me her sympathy, and, with most affectionate interest, sought to draw me away from my gloom. As far as she was able, she gave me comfort. But as my thoughts were then much led to religious subjects, she sought to learn my religious experience, and listened to it with great interest. I told her how I had sat in darkness for two long years, waiting for the light, and in full faith that it would come; how I had kept my soul patient and quiet, — had surrendered self-will to God's will, — had watched and waited till at last His great mercy came in an infinite peace to my soul. Margaret was never weary of asking me concerning this state, and said, 'I would gladly give all my talents and knowledge for such an experience as this.'

"Several years after," continues this friend, "I was travelling with her, and we sat, one lovely night, looking at the river, as it rolled beneath the yellow moonlight. We spoke again of God's light in the soul, and I said — 'Margaret! has that light dawned on *your* soul?' She answered, 'I think it has. But, oh! it is so glorious that I fear it will not be permanent, and so precious that I dare not speak of it, lest it should be gone.'

"That was the whole of our conversation, and I did not speak to her again concerning it."

Before this time, however, during her residence at Cambridge, she seemed to reach the period of her existence in which she descended lowest into the depths of gloom. She felt keenly, at this time, the want of a home for her heart. Full of a profound tendency toward life, capable of an ardent love, her affections were thrown back on her heart, to become stagnant, and for a while to grow bitter there. Then it was that she felt how empty and worthless were all the attainments and triumphs of the mere intellect; then it was that "she went about to cause her heart to despair of all the labor she had taken under the sun." Had she not emerged from this valley of the shadow of death, and come on to a higher plane of conviction and hope, her life would have been a most painful tragedy. But, when we know how she passed on and up, ever higher and higher, to the mountain-top, leaving one by one these dark ravines and mist-shrouded valleys, and ascending to where a perpetual sunshine lay, above the region of clouds, and was able to overlook with eagle glance the widest panorama, — we can read, with sympathy indeed, but without pain, the following extracts from a journal: —

'It was Thanksgiving day, (Nov., 1831,) and I was 'obliged to go to church, or exceedingly displease my 'father. I almost always suffered much in church from 'a feeling of disunion with the hearers and dissent from 'the preacher; but to-day, more than ever before, the 'services jarred upon me from their grateful and joyful 'tone. I was wearied out with mental conflicts, and in 'a mood of most childish, child-like sadness. I felt 'within myself great power, and generosity, and tender-'ness; but it seemed to me as if they were all unrecog-'nized, and as if it was impossible that they should be 'used in life. I was only one-and-twenty; the past 'was worthless, the future hopeless; yet I could not 'remember ever voluntarily to have done a wrong thing, 'and my aspiration seemed very high. I looked round 'the church, and envied all the little children; for I sup-'posed they had parents who protected them, so that 'they could never know this strange anguish, this dread 'uncertainty. I knew not, then, that none could have 'any father but God. I knew not, that I was not the 'only lonely one, that I was not the selected Œdipus, 'the special victim of an iron law. I was in haste for 'all to be over, that I might get into the free air. * *

'I walked away over the fields as fast as I could walk. 'This was my custom at that time, when I could no 'longer bear the weight of my feelings, and fix my atten- 'tion on any pursuit; for I do believe I never voluntarily 'gave way to these thoughts one moment. The force I 'exerted I think, even now, greater than I ever knew in 'any other character. But when I could bear myself no 'longer, I walked many hours, till the anguish was 'wearied out, and I returned in a state of prayer. To- 'day all seemed to have reached its height. It seemed 'as if I could never return to a world in which I had no 'place,—to the mockery of humanities. I could not act 'a part, nor seem to live any longer. It was a sad and 'sallow day of the late autumn. Slow processions of sad 'clouds were passing over a cold blue sky; the hues of 'earth were dull, and gray, and brown, with sickly strug- 'gles of late green here and there; sometimes a moaning 'gust of wind drove late, reluctant leaves across the 'path;—there was no life else. In the sweetness of my 'present peace, such days seem to me made to tell man 'the worst of his lot; but still that November wind can 'bring a chill of memory.

'I paused beside a little stream, which I had envied in 'the merry fulness of its spring life. It was shrunken, 'voiceless, choked with withered leaves. I marvelled 'that it did not quite lose itself in the earth. There was 'no stay for me, and I went on and on, till I came to 'where the trees were thick about a little pool, dark and 'silent. I sat down there. I did not think; all was dark, and cold, and still. Suddenly the sun shone out with that transparent sweetness, like the last smile of a 'dying lover, which it will use when it has been unkind 'all a cold autumn day. And, even then, passed into 'my thought a beam from its true sun, from its native 'sphere, which has never since departed from me. I 'remembered how, a little child, I had stopped myself 'one day on the stairs, and asked, how came I here? 'How is it that I seem to be this Margaret Fuller? 'What does it mean? What shall I do about it? I 'remembered all the times and ways in which the same 'thought had returned. I saw how long it must be before the soul can learn to act under these limitations of 'time and space, and human nature; but I saw, also, 'that it MUST do it,—that it must make all this false 'true,—and sow new and immortal plants in the garden 'of God, before it could return again. I saw there was no 'self; that selfishness was all folly, and the result of circumstance; that it was only because I thought self real 'that I suffered; that I had only to live in the idea of the 'ALL, and all was mine. This truth came to me, and I 'received it unhesitatingly; so that I was for that hour 'taken up into God. In that true ray most of the relations of earth seemed mere films, phenomena. * *

'My earthly pain at not being recognized never went 'deep after this hour. I had passed the extreme of passionate sorrow; and all check, all failure, all ignorance, 'have seemed temporary ever since. When I consider 'that this will be nine years ago next November, I am 'astonished that I have not gone on faster since; that I 'am not yet sufficiently purified to be taken back to God. 'Still, I did but touch then on the only haven of Insight. 'You know what I would say. I was dwelling in the ineffable, the unutterable. But the sun of earth set, and 'it grew dark around; the moment came for me to go. 'I had never been accustomed to walk alone at night, 'for my father was very strict on that subject, but 'now I had not one fear. When I came back, the moon 'was riding clear above the houses. I went into the 'churchyard, and there offered a prayer as holy, if not 'as deeply true, as any I know now; a prayer, which per-'haps took form as the guardian angel of my life. If that 'word in the Bible, Selah, means what gray-headed old 'men think it does, when they read aloud, it should be 'written here, — Selah!

'Since that day, I have never more been completely 'engaged in self; but the statue has been emerging, 'though slowly, from the block. Others may not see 'the promise even of its pure symmetry, but I do, and 'am learning to be patient. I shall be all human yet; 'and then the hour will come to leave humanity, and 'live always in the pure ray.

'This first day I was taken up; but the second time 'the Holy Ghost descended like a dove. I went out 'again for a day, but this time it was spring. I walked 'in the fields of Groton. But I will not describe that 'day; its music still sounds too sweetly near. Suffice it 'to say, I gave it all into our Father's hands, and was no 'stern-weaving Fate more, but one elected to obey, and 'love, and at last know. Since then I have suffered, as 'I must suffer again, till all the complex be made simple, 'but I have never been in discord with the grand har-'mony.'

GROTON AND PROVIDENCE.

LETTERS AND JOURNALS.

"What hath not man sought out and found,
But his dear God? Who yet his glorious love
Embosoms in us, mellowing the ground
With showers, and frosts, with love and awe."

HERBERT.

"No one need pride himself upon Genius, for it is the free-gift of God; but of honest Industry and true devotion to his destiny any man may well be proud; indeed, this thorough integrity of purpose is itself the Divine Idea in its most common form, and no really honest mind is without communion with God"

FICHTE.

"God did anoint thee with his odorous oil,
To wrestle, not to reign; and he assigns
All thy tears over, like pure crystallines,
For younger fellow-workers of the soil
To wear for amulets. So others shall
Take patience, labor, to their hearts and hands,
From thy hands, and thy heart, and thy brave cheer,
And God's grace fructify through thee to all."

ELIZABETH B. BARRETT.

"While I was restless, nothing satisfied,
Distrustful, most perplexed — yet felt somehow
A mighty power was brooding, taking shape
Within me; and this lasted till one night
When, as I sat revolving it and more,
A still voice from without said, — 'Seest thou not,
Desponding child, whence came defeat and loss?
Even from thy strength.'"

BROWNING.

III.

GROTON AND PROVIDENCE.

'HEAVEN's discipline has been invariable to me. 'The seemingly most pure and noble hopes have 'been blighted; the seemingly most promising con-'nections broken. The lesson has been endlessly 'repeated: "Be humble, patient, self-sustaining; hope '"only for occasional aids; love others, but not engross-'"ingly, for by being much alone your appointed task '"can best be done!" What a weary work is before me, 'ere that lesson shall be fully learned! Who shall 'wonder at the stiff-necked, and rebellious folly of 'young Israel, bowing down to a brute image, though 'the prophet was bringing messages from the holy 'mountain, while one's own youth is so obstinately 'idolatrous! Yet will I try to keep the heart with 'diligence, nor ever fear that the sun is gone out 'because I shiver in the cold and dark!'

Such was the tone of resignation in which Margaret wrote from Groton, Massachusetts, whither, much to her regret, her father removed in the spring of 1833. Extracts from letters and journals will show how stern was her schooling there, and yet how constant was her faith, that

> "God keeps a niche
> In heaven to hold our idols! And albeit
> He breaks them to our faces, and denies
> That our close kisses should impair their white,
> I know we shall behold them raised, complete,
> The dust shook from their beauty, — glorified,
> New Memnons singing in the great God-light."

SAD WELCOME HOME.

'*Groton, April* 25, 1833. — I came hither, summoned 'by the intelligence, that our poor ——— had met with 'a terrible accident. I found the dear child, — who had 'left me so full of joy and eagerness, that I thought 'with a sigh, not of envy, how happy he, at least, would 'be here, — burning with fever. He had expected me 'impatiently, and was very faint lest it should not be '"Margaret" who had driven up. I confess I greeted 'our new home with a flood of bitter tears. He behaves 'with great patience, sweetness, and care for the com-'fort of others. This has been a severe trial for mother, 'fatigued, too, as she was, and full of care; but her con-'duct is angelic. I try to find consolation in all kinds 'of arguments, and to distract my thoughts till the pre-'cise amount of injury is surely known. I am not idle 'a moment. When not with ———, in whose room I 'sit, sewing, and waiting upon him, or reading aloud 'a great part of the day, I solace my soul with Goethe, 'and follow his guidance into realms of the "Wahren '"Guten, and Schönen."'

OCCUPATIONS.

'*May*, 1833. — As to German, I have done less than

'I hoped, so much had the time been necessarily broken 'up. I have with me the works of Goethe which I 'have not yet read, and am now engaged upon '"Kunst and Alterthum," and "Campagne in Frank- 'reich." I still prefer Goethe to any one, and, as I 'proceed, find more and more to learn, and am made 'to feel that my general notion of his mind is most 'imperfect, and needs testing and sifting.

'I brought your beloved Jean Paul with me, too. 'I cannot yet judge well, but think we shall not be 'intimate. His infinitely variegated, and certainly most 'exquisitely colored, web fatigues attention. I prefer, 'too, wit to humor, and daring imagination to the rich- 'est fancy. Besides, his philosophy and religion seem 'to be of the sighing sort, and, having some tendency 'that way myself, I want opposing force in a favorite 'author. Perhaps I have spoken unadvisedly; if so, I 'shall recant on further knowledge.'

And thus recant she did, when familiar acquaintance with the genial and sagacious humorist had won for him her reverent love.

RICHTER.

'Poet of Nature! Gentlest of the wise,
'Most airy of the fanciful, most keen
'Of satirists! — thy thoughts, like butterflies,
'Still near the sweetest scented flowers have been·
'With Titian's colors thou canst sunset paint,
'With Raphael's dignity, celestial love;
'With Hogarth's pencil, each deceit and feint
'Of meanness and hypocrisy reprove;

'Canst to devotion's highest flight sublime
'Exalt the mind, by tenderest pathos' art,
'Dissolve, in purifying tears, the heart,
'Or bid it, shuddering, recoil at crime;
'The fond illusions of the youth and maid,
'At which so many world-formed sages sneer,
'When by thy altar-lighted torch displayed,
'Our natural religion must appear.
'All things in thee tend to one polar star,
'Magnetic all thy influences are!'

'Some murmur at the "want of system" in Richter's 'writings.

'A labyrinth! a flowery wilderness!
'Some in thy "slip-boxes" and "honey-moons"
'Complain of—*want of order*, I confess,
'But not of *system* in its highest sense.
'Who asks a guiding clue through this wide mind,
'In love of Nature such will surely find.
'In tropic climes, live like the tropic bird,
'Whene'er a spice-fraught grove may tempt thy stay;
'Nor be by cares of colder climes disturbed—
'No frost the summer's bloom shall drive away;
'Nature's wide temple and the azure dome
'Have plan enough for the free spirit's home!'

'Your Schiller has already given me great pleas 'ure. I have been reading the "Revolt in the Neth- 'erlands" with intense interest, and have reflected 'much upon it. The volumes are numbered in my 'little book-case, and as the eye runs over them, I 'thank the friendly heart that put all this genius and 'passion within my power.

'I am glad, too, that you thought of lending me '"Bigelow's Elements." I have studied the Archi- 'tecture attentively, till I feel quite mistress of it all.

'But I want more engravings, Vitruvius, Magna Græcia, 'the Ionian Antiquities, &c. Meanwhile, I have got out 'all our tours in Italy. Forsyth, a book I always loved 'much, I have re-read with increased pleasure, by this 'new light. Goethe, too, studied architecture while in 'Italy; so his books are full of interesting information; 'and Madame De Stael, though not deep, is tasteful."

'American History! Seriously, my mind is regener-'ating as to my country, for I am beginning to appre-'ciate the United States and its great men. The violent 'antipathies, — the result of an exaggerated love for, 'shall I call it by so big a name as the "poetry of being?" '— and the natural distrust arising from being forced to 'hear the conversation of half-bred men, all whose petty 'feelings were roused to awkward life by the paltry 'game of local politics, — are yielding to reason and 'calmer knowledge. Had I but been educated in the 'knowledge of such men as Jefferson, Franklin, Rush! 'I have learned now to know them partially. And I 'rejoice, if only because my father and I can have so 'much in common on this topic. All my other pursuits 'have led me away from him; here he has much infor-'mation and ripe judgment. But, better still, I hope to 'feel no more that sometimes despairing, sometimes 'insolently contemptuous, feeling of incongeniality with 'my time and place. Who knows but some proper and 'attainable object of pursuit may present itself to the 'cleared eye? At any rate, wisdom is good, if it brings 'neither bliss nor glory.'

'*March*, 1834. — Four pupils are a serious and fa-tiguing charge for one of my somewhat ardent and 'impatient disposition. Five days in the week I have 'given daily lessons in three languages, in Geography 'and History, besides many other exercises on alternate 'days. This has consumed often eight, always five 'hours of my day. There has been, also, a great deal 'of needle-work to do, which is now nearly finished, so 'that I shall not be obliged to pass my time about it 'when everything looks beautiful, as I did last summer. 'We have had very poor servants, and, for some time 'past, only one. My mother has been often ill. My 'grandmother, who passed the winter with us, has been 'ill. Thus, you may imagine, as I am the only grown-up 'daughter, that my time has been considerably taxed.

'But as, sad or merry, I must always be learning, I 'laid down a course of study at the beginning of winter, 'comprising certain subjects, about which I had always 'felt deficient. These were the History and Geography 'of modern Europe, beginning the former in the four-'teenth century; the Elements of Architecture; the 'works of Alfieri, with his opinions on them; the his-'torical and critical works of Goethe and Schiller, and 'the outlines of history of our own country.

'I chose this time as one when I should have nothing 'to distract or dissipate my mind. I have nearly com-'pleted this course, in the style I proposed, — not minute 'or thorough, I confess, — though I have had only three 'evenings in the week, and chance hours in the day, 'for it. I am very glad I have undertaken it, and feel 'the good effects already. Occasionally, I try my hand 'at composition, but have not completed anything to my 'own satisfaction. I have sketched a number of plans, 'but if ever accomplished, it must be in a season of more 'joyful energy, when my mind has been renovated, and refreshed by change of scene or circumstance. My translation of Tasso cannot be published at present, if 'it ever is.'

'My object is to examine thoroughly, as far as my 'time and abilities will permit, the evidences of the 'Christian Religion. I have endeavored to get rid of 'this task as much and as long as possible; to be con-'tent with superficial notions, and, if I may so express 'it, to adopt religion as a matter of taste. But I meet 'with infidels very often; two or three of my particular 'friends are deists; and their arguments, with distress-'ing sceptical notions of my own, are haunting me 'forever. I must satisfy myself; and having once be-'gun, I shall go on as far as I can.

'My mind often swells with thoughts on these sub-'jects, which I long to pour out on some person of supe-'rior calmness and strength, and fortunate in more 'accurate knowledge. I should feel such a quieting 'reaction. But, generally, it seems best that I should go 'through these conflicts alone. The process will be 'slower, more irksome, more distressing, but the results 'will be my own, and I shall feel greater confidence in 'them.'

MISS MARTINEAU.

In the summer of 1835, Margaret found a fresh stimulus to self-culture in the society of Miss Martineau, whom she met while on a visit at Cambridge, in the house of her friend, Mrs. Farrar. How animating this intercourse then was to her, appears from her journals.

'Miss Martineau received me so kindly as to banish 'all embarrassment at once. * * We had some talk 'about "Carlyleism," and I was not quite satisfied with 'the ground she took, but there was no opportunity for 'full discussion. * * I wished to give myself wholly 'up to receive an impression of her. * * What shrewd-'ness in detecting various shades of character! Yet, 'what she said of Hannah More and Miss Edgeworth, 'grated upon my feelings.' * *

Again, later:—'I cannot conceive how we chanced 'upon the subject of our conversation, but never shall I 'forget what she said. It has bound me to her. In 'that hour, most unexpectedly to me, we passed the bar-'rier that separates acquaintance from friendship, and 'I saw how greatly her heart is to be valued.'

And again:—'We sat together close to the pulpit. 'I was deeply moved by Mr. ——'s manner of praying 'for "our friends," and I put up this prayer for my com-'panion, which I recorded, as it rose in my heart: "Au-'"thor of good, Source of all beauty and holiness, thanks '"to Thee for the purifying, elevating communion that '"I have enjoyed with this beloved and revered being. '"Grant, that the thoughts she has awakened, and the '"bright image of her existence, may live in my mem-'"ory, inciting my earth-bound spirit to higher words '"and deeds. May her path be guarded and blessed. '"May her noble mind be kept firmly poised in its '"native truth, unsullied by prejudice or error, and "strong to resist whatever outwardly or inwardly shall '"war against its high vocation. May each day bring '"to this generous seeker new riches of true philosophy '"and of Divine Love. And, amidst all trials, give her '"to know and feel that Thou, the All-sufficing, art '"with her, leading her on through eternity to likeness '"of Thyself."'

'I sigh for an intellectual guide. Nothing but the 'sense of what God has done for me, in bringing me 'nearer to himself, saves me from despair. With what 'envy I looked at Flaxman's picture of Hesiod sitting 'at the the feet of the Muse! How blest would it be to 'be thus instructed in one's vocation! Anything would 'I do and suffer, to be sure that, when leaving earth, 'I should not be haunted with recollections of "aims '"unreached, occasions lost." I have hoped some friend 'would do, — what none has ever yet done, — compre-'hend me wholly, mentally, and morally, and enable me 'better to comprehend myself. I have had some hope 'that Miss Martineau might be this friend, but cannot 'yet tell. She has what I want, — vigorous reasoning 'powers, invention, clear views of her objects, — and she 'has been trained to the best means of execution. Add 'to this, that there are no strong intellectual sympathies 'between us, such as would blind her to my defects.'

'A delightful letter from Miss Martineau. I mused 'long upon the noble courage with which she stepped 'forward into life, and the accurate judgment with 'which she has become acquainted with its practical 'details, without letting her fine imagination become 'tamed. I shall be cheered and sustained, amidst all 'fretting and uncongenial circumstances, by remembrance 'of her earnest love of truth and ardent faith.'

ILLNESS.

'A terrible feeling in my head, but kept about my 'usual avocations. Read Ugo Foscolo's Sepolcri, and 'Pindemonti's answer, but could not relish either, so dis-'tressing was the weight on the top of the brain; sewed 'awhile, and then went out to get warm, but could not, 'though I walked to the very end of Hazel-grove, and 'the sun was hot upon me. Sat down, and, though 'seemingly able to think with only the lower part of my 'head, meditated literary plans, with full hope that, if I 'could command leisure, I might do something good. 'It seemed as if I should never reach home, as I was 'obliged to sit down incessantly. * *

'For nine long days and nights, without intermission, 'all was agony, — fever and dreadful pain in my head. 'Mother tended me like an angel all that time, scarcely 'ever leaving me, night or day. My father, too, habitu-'ally so sparing in tokens of affection, was led by his 'anxiety to express what he felt towards me in stronger 'terms than he had ever used in the whole course of my 'life. He thought I might not recover, and one morning, 'coming into my room, after a few moments' conversa-'tion, he said: "My dear, I have been thinking of you '"in the night, and I cannot remember that you have '"any *faults*. You have defects, of course, as all mortals '"have, but I do not know that you have a single fault." 'These words, — so strange from him, who had scarce 'ever in my presence praised me, and who, as I knew, 'abstained from praise as hurtful to his children, — 'affected me to tears at the time, although I could not 'foresee how dear and consolatory this extravagant 'expression of regard would very soon become. The 'family were deeply moved by the fervency of his 'prayer of thanksgiving, on the Sunday morning when I 'was somewhat recovered; and to mother he said, "I '"have no room for a painful thought now that our '"daughter is restored."

'For myself, I thought I should die; but I was calm, 'and looked to God without fear. When I remem- 'bered how much struggle awaited me if I remained, 'and how improbable it was that any of my cherished 'plans would bear fruit, I felt willing to go. But 'Providence did not so will it. A much darker dispen- 'sation for our family was in store.'

DEATH OF HER FATHER.

'On the evening of the 30th of September, 1835, 'my father was seized with cholera, and on the 2d 'of October, was a corpse. For the first two days, my 'grief, under this calamity, was such as I dare not 'speak of. But since my father's head is laid in the 'dust, I feel an awful calm, and am becoming famil- 'iar with the thoughts of being an orphan. I have 'prayed to God that duty may now be the first object, 'and self set aside. May I have light and strength 'to do what is right, in the highest sense, for my 'mother, brothers, and sister. * *

'It has been a gloomy week, indeed. The children 'have all been ill, and dearest mother is overpowered 'with sorrow, fatigue, and anxiety. I suppose she must 'be ill too, when the children recover. I shall endeavor 'to keep my mind steady, by remembering that there is 'a God, and that grief is but for a season. Grant, oh 'Father, that neither the joys nor sorrows of this past 'year shall have visited my heart in vain! Make me 'wise and strong for the performance of immediate 'duties, and ripen me, by what means Thou seest best, 'for those which lie beyond. * *

'My father's image follows me constantly. Whenever 'I am in my room, he seems to open the door, and to 'look on me with a complacent, tender smile. What 'would I not give to have it in my power, to make that 'heart once more beat with joy! The saddest feeling 'is the remembrance of little things, in which I have 'fallen short of love and duty. I never sympathized in 'his liking for this farm, and secretly wondered how a 'mind which had, for thirty years, been so widely 'engaged in the affairs of men, could care so much for 'trees and crops. But now, amidst the beautiful autumn 'days, I walk over the grounds, and look with painful 'emotions at every little improvement. He had selected 'a spot to place a seat where I might go to read alone, 'and had asked me to visit it. I contented myself with '"When you please, father;" but we never went! What 'would I not now give, if I had fixed a time, and shown 'more interest! A day or two since, I went there. The 'tops of the distant blue hills were veiled in delicate 'autumn haze; soft silence brooded over the landscape; 'on one side, a brook gave to the gently sloping meadow 'spring-like verdure; on the other, a grove, — which he 'had named for me, — lay softly glowing in the gor- 'geous hues of October. It was very sad. May this 'sorrow give me a higher sense of duty in the relation- 'ships which remain.

'Dearest mother is worn to a shadow. Sometimes, 'when I look on her pale face, and think of all her grief, 'and the cares and anxieties which now beset her, I am 'appalled by the thought that she may not continue 'with us long. Nothing sustains me now but the 'thought that God, who saw fit to restore me to life 'when I was so very willing to leave it, — more so, per-'haps, than I shall ever be again, — must have some 'good work for me to do.'

'*Nov.* 3, 1835. — I thought I should be able to write ere now, how our affairs were settled, but that time has not come yet. 'My father left no will, and, in conse-'quence, our path is hedged in by many petty difficul-'ties. He has left less property than we had antici-'pated, for he was not fortunate in his investments in 'real estate. There will, however, be enough to main-'tain my mother, and educate the children decently. I 'have often had reason to regret being of the softer sex, 'and never more than now. If I were an eldest son, I 'could be guardian to my brothers and sister, adminis-'ter the estate, and really become the head of my family. 'As it is, I am very ignorant of the management and 'value of property, and of practical details. I always 'hated the din of such affairs, and hoped to find a life-'long refuge from them in the serene world of litera-'ture and the arts. But I am now full of desire to learn 'them, that I may be able to advise and act, where it is 'necessary. The same mind which has made other 'attainments, can, in time, compass these, however un-'congenial to its nature and habits.'

'I shall be obliged to give up selfishness in the end. 'May God enable me to see the way clear, and not to 'let down the intellectual, in raising the moral tone of 'my mind. Difficulties and duties became distinct the 'very night after my father's death, and a solemn 'prayer was offered then, that I might combine what is 'due to others with what is due to myself. The spirit 'of that prayer I shall constantly endeavor to maintain. 'What ought to be done for a few months to come is 'plain, and, as I proceed, the view will open'

TRIAL.

The death of her father brought in its train a disappointment as keen as Margaret could well have been called on to bear. For two years and more she had been buoyed up to intense effort by the promise of a visit to Europe, for the end of completing her culture. And as the means of equitably remunerating her parents for the cost of such a tour, she had faithfully devoted herself to the teaching of the younger members of the family. Her honored friends, Professor and Mrs. Farrar, who were about visiting the Old World, had invited her to be their companion; and, as Miss Martineau was to return to England in the ship with them, the prospect before her was as brilliant with generous hopes as her aspiring imagination could conceive. But now, in her journal of January 1, 1836, she writes: —

'The New-year opens upon me under circumstances 'inexpressibly sad. I must make the last great sacri- 'fice, and, apparently, for evil to me and mine. Life, 'as I look forward, presents a scene of struggle and pri- 'vation only. Yet "I bate not a jot of heart," though 'much "of hope." My difficulties are not to be com- 'pared with those over which many strong souls have 'triumphed. Shall I then despair? If I do, I am not a 'strong soul.'

Margaret's family treated her, in this exigency, with the grateful consideration due to her love, and urgently besought her to take the necessary means, and fulfil her father's plan. But she could not make up her mind to forsake them, preferring rather to abandon her long-cherished literary designs. Her struggles and her triumph thus appear in her letters: —

'*January* 30, 1836. — I was a great deal with Miss 'Martineau, while in Cambridge, and love her more than 'ever. She is to stay till August, and go to England 'with Mr. and Mrs. Farrar. If I should accompany them 'I shall be with her while in London, and see the best 'literary society. If I should go, you will be with 'mother the while, will not you?* Oh, dear E——, 'you know not how I fear and tremble to come to a 'decision. My temporal all seems hanging upon it, and 'the prospect is most alluring. A few thousand dollars 'would make all so easy, so safe. As it is, I cannot tell 'what is coming to us, for the estate will not be settled 'when I go. I pray to God ceaselessly that I may decide 'wisely.'

'*April* 17*th*, 1836. — If I am not to go with you I shal 'be obliged to tear my heart, by a violent effort, from its 'present objects and natural desires. But I shall feel the 'necessity, and will do it if the life-blood follows through 'the rent. Probably, I shall not even think it best to 'correspond with you at all while you are in Europe. 'Meanwhile, let us be friends indeed. The generous and 'unfailing love which you have shown me during these 'three years, when I could be so little to you, your indul-

* Her eldest brother.

'gence for my errors and fluctuations, your steady faith 'in my intentions, have done more to shield and sustain 'me than any other earthly influence. If I must now 'learn to dispense with feeling them constantly near 'me, at least their remembrance can never, never be 'less dear. I suppose I ought, instead of grieving that 'we are soon to be separated, now to feel grateful for an 'intimacy of extraordinary permanence, and certainly of 'unstained truth and perfect freedom on both sides.

'As to my feelings, I take no pleasure in speaking of 'them; but I know not that I could give you a truer 'impression of them, than by these lines which I trans-'late from the German of Uhland. They are entitled '"JUSTIFICATION."

" Our youthful fancies, idly fired,
 The fairest visions would embrace ;
These, with impetuous tears desired,
 Float upward into starry space ;
Heaven, upon the suppliant wild,
 Smiles down a gracious *No !* — In vain
The strife ! Yet be consoled, poor child,
 For the wish passes with the pain.

But when from such idolatry
 The heart has turned, and wiser grown,
In earnestness and purity
 Would make a nobler plan its own, —
Yet, after all its zeal and care,
 Must of its chosen aim despair, —
Some bitter tears may be forgiven
 By *Man*, at least, — *we trust, by Heaven.*"'

BIRTH-DAY.

'*May 23d*, 1836. — I have just been reading Goethe's 'Lebensregel. It is easy to say "Do not trouble your-

'"self with useless regrets for the past; enjoy the pres-'"ent, and leave the future to God." But it is *not* easy 'for characters, which are by nature neither *calm* nor '*careless*, to act upon these rules. I am rather of the 'opinion of Novalis, that "Wer sich der hochsten Lieb '"ergeben Genest von ihnen Wunden nie."

'But I will endeavor to profit by the instructions of 'the great philosopher who teaches, I think, what Christ 'did, to use without overvaluing the world.

'Circumstances have decided that I must not go to 'Europe, and shut upon me the door, as I think, forever, 'to the scenes I could have loved. Let me now try to 'forget myself, and act for others' sakes. What I can 'do with my pen, I know not. At present, I feel no con-'fidence or hope. The expectations so many have been 'led to cherish by my conversational powers, I am dis-'posed to deem ill-founded. I do not think I can pro-'duce a valuable work. I do not feel in my bosom that 'confidence necessary to sustain me in such undertakings, '—the confidence of genius. But I am now but just 'recovered from bodily illness, and still heart-broken by 'sorrow and disappointment. I may be renewed again, 'and feel differently. If I do not soon, I will make up 'my mind to teach. I can thus get money, which I will 'use for the benefit of my dear, gentle, suffering mother, '—my brothers and sister. This will be the greatest 'consolation to me, at all events.'

DEATH IN LIFE.

'The moon tempted me out, and I set forth for a house 'at no great distance. The beloved south-west was 'blowing; the heavens were flooded with light, which 'could not diminish the tremulously pure radiance of the 'evening star; the air was full of spring sounds, and 'sweet spring odors came up from the earth. I felt that 'happy sort of feeling, as if the soul's pinions were 'budding. My mind was full of poetic thoughts, and 'nature's song of promise was chanting in my heart.

'But what a change when I entered that human 'dwelling! I will try to give you an impression of what 'you, I fancy, have never come in contact with. The 'little room — they have but one — contains a bed, a 'table, and some old chairs. A single stick of wood 'burns in the fire-place. It is not needed now, but those 'who sit near it have long ceased to know what spring 'is. They are all frost. Everything is old and faded, 'but at the same time as clean and carefully mended as 'possible. For all they know of pleasure is to get 'strength to sweep those few boards, and mend those old 'spreads and curtains. That sort of self-respect they 'have, and it is all of pride their many years of poor-'tith has left them.

'And there they sit, — mother and daughter! In the 'mother, ninety years have quenched every thought and 'every feeling, except an imbecile interest about her 'daughter, and the sort of self-respect I just spoke of. 'Husband, sons, strength, health, house and lands, all 'are gone. And yet these losses have not had power to 'bow that palsied head to the grave. Morning by morn-'ing she rises without a hope, night by night she lies 'down vacant or apathetic; and the utmost use she can 'make of the day is to totter three or four times across 'the floor by the assistance of her staff. Yet, though we wonder that she is still permitted to cumber the ground, joyless and weary, "the tomb of her dead self." we 'look at this dry leaf, and think how green it once was, 'and how the birds sung to it in its summer day.

'But can we think of spring, or summer, or anything 'joyous or really life-like, when we look at the daughter? '— that bloodless effigy of humanity, whose care is to 'eke out this miserable existence by means of the occa-'sional doles of those who know how faithful and good 'a child she has been to that decrepit creature; who 'thinks herself happy if she can be well enough, by hours 'of patient toil, to perform those menial services which 'they both require; whose talk is of the price of 'pounds of sugar, and ounces of tea, and yards of flan-'nel; whose only intellectual resource is hearing five or 'six verses of the Bible read every day, — "my poor '"head," she says, "cannot bear any more;" and whose 'only hope is the death to which she has been so slowly 'and wearily advancing, through many years like this.

'The saddest part is, that she does *not wish* for death. 'She clings to this sordid existence. Her soul is now so 'habitually enwrapt in the meanest cares, that if she 'were to be lifted two or three steps upward, she would 'not know what to do with life; how, then, shall she 'soar to the celestial heights? Yet she ought; for she 'has ever been good, and her narrow and crushing duties 'have been performed with a self-sacrificing constancy, 'which I, for one, could never hope to equal.

'While I listened to her, — and I often think it good for 'me to listen to her patiently, — the expressions you 'used in your letter, about "drudgery," occurred to me. 'I remember the time when I, too, deified the "soul's '"impulses." It is a noble worship; but, if we do not 'aid it by a just though limited interpretation of what '"Ought" means, it will degenerate into idolatry. For-

'a time it was so with me, and I am not yet good enough 'to love the *Ought*.

'Then I came again into the open air, and saw those 'resplendent orbs moving so silently, and thought that 'they were perhaps tenanted, not only by beings in whom 'I can see the germ of a possible angel, but by myriads 'like this poor creature, in whom that germ is, so far as 'we can see, blighted entirely, I could not help saying, '"O my Father! Thou, whom we are told art all Power, '"and also all Love, how canst Thou suffer such even '"transient specks on the transparence of Thy creation? '"These grub-like lives, undignified even by passion,— '"these life-long quenchings of the spark divine, — why '"dost Thou suffer them? Is not Thy paternal benevo- '"lence impatient till such films be dissipated?"

'Such questionings once had power to move my spirit 'deeply; now, they but shade my mind for an instant. 'I have faith in a glorious explanation, that shall make 'manifest perfect justice and perfect wisdom.'

LITERATURE.

Cut off from access to the scholars, libraries, lectures, galleries of art, museums of science, antiquities, and historic scenes of Europe, Margaret bent her powers to use such opportunities of culture as she could command in her solitary country-home. Journals and letters thus bear witness to her zeal: —

'I am having one of my "intense" times, devouring 'book after book. I never stop a minute, except to talk 'with mother, having laid all little duties on the shelf 'for a few days. Among other things, I have twice read 'through the life of Sir J. Mackintosh; and it has sug-'gested so much to me, that I am very sorry I did not 'talk it over with you. It is quite gratifying, after my 'late chagrin, to find Sir James, with all his metaphysical 'turn, and ardent desire to penetrate it, puzzling so over 'the German philosophy, and particularly what I was 'myself troubled about, at Cambridge, — Jacobi's letters 'to Fichte.

'Few things have ever been written more discrimi-'nating or more beautiful than his strictures upon 'the Hindoo character, his portrait of Fox, and his 'second letter to Robert Hall, after his recovery from 'derangement. Do you remember what he says of the 'want of brilliancy in Priestley's moral sentiments? 'Those remarks, though slight, seem to me to show the 'quality of his mind more decidedly than anything in 'the book. That so much learning, benevolence, and 'almost unparalleled fairness of mind, should be in a 'great measure lost to the world, for want of earnestness 'of purpose, might impel us to attach to the latter attri-'bute as much importance as does the wise uncle in 'Wilhelm Meister.'

'As to what you say of Shelley, it is true that the un-'happy influences of early education prevented his ever 'attaining clear views of God, life, and the soul. At 'thirty, he was still a seeker, — an experimentalist. But 'then his should not be compared with such a mind as '——'s, which, having no such exuberant fancy to 'tame, nor various faculties to develop, naturally comes 'to maturity sooner. Had Shelley lived twenty years 'longer, I have no doubt he would have become a fervent

'Christian, and thus have attained that mental harmony 'which was necessary to him. It is true, too, as you 'say, that we always feel a melancholy imperfection in 'what he writes. But I love to think of those other 'spheres in which so pure and rich a being shall be per-'fected; and I cannot allow his faults of opinion and 'sentiment to mar my enjoyment of the vast capabilities, 'and exquisite perception of beauty, displayed every-'where in his poems.'

'*March* 17, 1836.—I think Herschel will be very val-'uable to me, from the slight glance I have taken of it, 'and I thank Mr. F.; but do not let him expect any-'thing of me because I have ventured on a book so 'profound as the Novum Organum. I have been ex-'amining myself with severity, intellectually as well as 'morally, and am shocked to find how vague and super-'ficial is all my knowledge. I am no longer surprised 'that I should have appeared harsh and arrogant in my 'strictures to one who, having a better-disciplined mind, 'is more sensible of the difficulties in the way of really 'knowing and doing anything, and who, having more 'Wisdom, has more Reverence too. All that passed at 'your house will prove very useful to me; and I trust 'that I am approximating somewhat to that genuine hu-'mility which is so indispensable to true regeneration. 'But do not speak of this to ——, for I am not yet sure 'of the state of my mind.'

'1836.—I have, for the time, laid aside *De Stael* 'and *Bacon*, for *Martineau* and *Southey*. I find, 'with delight, that the former has written on the very subjects I wished most to talk out with her, and prob-

'ably I shall receive more from her in this way than by 'personal intercourse, — for I think more of her character 'when with her, and am stimulated through my affections. 'As to Southey, I am steeped to the lips in enjoyment. I 'am glad I did not know this poet earlier; for I am now 'just ready to receive his truly exalting influences in some 'degree. I think, in reading, I shall place him next to 'Wordsworth. I have finished Herschel, and really be- 'lieve I am a little wiser. I have read, too, Heyne's 'letters twice, Sartor Resartus once, some of Goethe's 'late diaries, Coleridge's Literary Remains, and drank a 'great deal from Wordsworth. By the way, do you 'know his "Happy Warrior"? I find my insight of 'this sublime poet perpetually deepening.'

'Mr. —— says the Wanderjahre is "*wise.*" It 'must be presumed so; and yet one is not satisfied. 'I was perfectly so with my manner of interpreting the 'Lehrjahre; but this sequel keeps jerking my clue, and 'threatens to break it. I do not know our Goethe yet. 'I have changed my opinion about his religious views 'many times. Sometimes I am tempted to think that it 'is only his wonderful knowledge of human nature 'which has excited in me such reverence for his philoso- 'phy, and that no worthy fabric has been elevated on 'this broad foundation. Yet often, when suspecting that 'I have found a huge gap, the next turning it appears 'that it was but an air-hole, and there is a brick all ready 'to stop it. On the whole, though my enthusiasm for 'the Goetherian philosophy is checked, my admiration 'for the genius of Goethe is in nowise lessened, and I 'stand in a sceptical attitude, ready to try his philosophy, 'and, if needs must, play the Eclectic.'

'Did I write that a kind-hearted neighbor, fearing 'I might be *dull*, sent to offer me the use of a *book-caseful* 'of Souvenirs, Gems, and such-like glittering ware? I 'took a two or three year old "Token," and chanced on 'a story, called the "Gentle Boy," which I remem-'bered to have heard was written by somebody in 'Salem. It is marked by so much grace and delicacy 'of feeling, that I am very desirous to know the author, 'whom I take to be a lady.' * *

'With regard to what you say about the American 'Monthly, my answer is, I would gladly sell some part 'of my mind for lucre, to get the command of time; but 'I will not sell my soul: that is, I am perfectly willing 'to take the trouble of writing for money to pay the 'seamstress; but I am *not* willing to have what I write 'mutilated, or what I ought to say dictated to suit the 'public taste. You speak of my writing about Tieck. 'It is my earnest wish to interpret the German authors 'of whom I am most fond to such Americans as are 'ready to receive. Perhaps some might sneer at the 'notion of my becoming a teacher; but where I love so 'much, surely I might inspire others to love a little; and 'I think this kind of culture would be precisely the 'counterpoise required by the utilitarian tendencies of 'our day and place. My very imperfections may be of 'value. While enthusiasm is yet fresh, while I am still 'a novice, it may be more easy to communicate with 'those quite uninitiated, than when I shall have attained 'to a higher and calmer state of knowledge. I hope a 'periodical may arise, by and by, which may think me 'worthy to furnish a series of articles on German litera-'ture, giving room enough and perfect freedom to say 'what I please. In this case, I should wish to devote at 'least eight numbers to Tieck, and should use the Gar-'den of Poesy, and my other translations.

'I have sometimes thought of translating his Little 'Red Riding Hood, for children. If it could be adorned 'with illustrations, like those in the "Story without an 'End," it would make a beautiful little book; but I do 'not know that this could be done in Boston. There is 'much meaning that children could not take in; but, as 'they would never discover this till able to receive the 'whole, the book corresponds exactly with my notions 'of what a child's book should be.

'I should like to begin the proposed series with a re-'view of Heyne's letters on German Literature, which 'afford excellent opportunity for some preparatory hints. 'My plans are so undecided for several coming months, 'that I cannot yet tell whether I shall have the time and 'tranquillity needed to write out the whole course, though 'much tempted by the promise of perfect liberty. I 'could engage, however, to furnish at least two articles 'on Novalis and Körner. I trust you will be interested 'in my favorite Körner. Great is my love for both of 'them. But I wish to write something which shall not 'only *be* free from exaggeration, but which shall *seem* so, 'to those unacquainted with their works.

'I have so much reading to go through with this 'month, that I have but few hours for correspondents. I 'have already discussed five volumes in German, two in 'French, three in English, and not without thought and 'examination. * *

'Tell —— that I read "Titan" by myself, in the after-'noons and evenings of about three weeks. She need 'not be afraid to undertake it. Difficulties of detail 'may, perhaps, not be entirely conquered without a mas-

15

'ter or a good commentary, but she could enjoy all that 'is most valuable alone. I should be very unwilling to 'read it with a person of narrow or unrefined mind; for 'it is a noble work, and fit to raise a reader into that 'high serene of thought where pedants cannot enter.'

FAREWELL TO GROTON.

'The place is beautiful, in its way, but its scenery is 'too tamely smiling and sleeping. My associations with 'it are most painful. There darkened round us the 'effects of my father's ill-judged exchange, — ill-judged, 'so far at least as regarded himself, mother, and me, — 'all violently rent from the habits of our former life, and 'cast upon toils for which we were unprepared: there 'my mother's health was impaired, and mine destroyed; 'there my father died; there were undergone the miserable 'perplexities of a family that has lost its head; there I 'passed through the conflicts needed to give up all which 'my heart had for years desired, and to tread a path for 'which I had no skill, and no call, except that it must be 'trodden by some one, and I alone was ready. Wachu-'set and the Peterboro' hills are blended in my memory 'with hours of anguish as great as I am capable of suf-'fering. I used to look at them towering to the sky, and 'feel that I, too, from birth, had longed to rise, and, 'though for the moment crushed, was not subdued.

'But if those beautiful hills, and wide, rich fields, saw 'this sad lore well learned, they also saw some precious 'lessons given in faith, fortitude, self-command, and 'unselfish love. There too, in solitude, the mind ac-'quired more power of concentration, and discerned the 'beauty of strict method; there too, more than all, the 'heart was awakened to sympathize with the ignorant, 'to pity the vulgar, to hope for the seemingly worthless, 'and to commune with the Divine Spirit of Creation, 'which cannot err, which never sleeps, which will not 'permit evil to be permanent, nor its aim of beauty in 'the smallest particular eventually to fail.'

WINTER IN BOSTON.

In the autumn of 1836 Margaret went to Boston, with the two-fold design of teaching Latin and French in Mr. Alcott's school, which was then highly prosperous, and of forming classes of young ladies in French, German, and Italian.

Her view of Mr. Alcott's plan of education was thus hinted in a journal, one day, after she had been talking with him, and trying to place herself in his mental position: —

Mr. A. 'O for the safe and natural way of Intuition! 'I cannot grope like a mole in the gloomy passages of 'experience. To the attentive spirit, the revelation con-'tained in books is only so far valuable as it comments 'upon, and corresponds with, the universal revelation. 'Yet to me, a being social and sympathetic by natural im-'pulse, though recluse and contemplative by training and 'philosophy, the character and life of Jesus have spoken 'more forcibly than any fact recorded in human history. 'This story of incarnate Love has given me the key to 'all mysteries, and showed me what path should be 'taken in returning to the Fountain of Spirit. Seeing 'that other redeemers have imperfectly fulfilled their 'tasks, I have sought a new way. They all, it seemed 'to me, had tried to influence the human being at too 'late a day, and had laid their plans too wide. They 'began with men; I will begin with babes. They be-'gan with the world; I will begin with the family. So 'I preach the Gospel of the Nineteenth Century.'

M. 'But, preacher, you make *three* mistakes.

'You do not understand the nature of Genius or cre-'ative power.

'You do not understand the reäction of matter on 'spirit.

'You are too impatient of the complex; and, not en-'joying variety in unity, you become lost in abstractions, 'and cannot illustrate your principles.'

On the other hand, Mr. Alcott's impressions of Margaret were thus noted in his diaries: —

"She is clearly a person given to the boldest speculation, and of liberal and varied acquirements. Not wanting in imaginative power, she has the rarest good sense and discretion. She adopts the Spiritual Philosophy, and has the subtlest perception of its bearings. She takes large and generous views of all subjects, and her disposition is singularly catholic. The blending of sentiment and of wisdom in her is most remarkable; and her taste is as fine as her prudence. I think her the most brilliant talker of the day. She has a quick and comprehensive wit, a firm command of her thoughts, and a speech to win the ear of the most cultivated."

In her own classes Margaret was very successful, and thus in a letter sums up the results: —

'I am still quite unwell, and all my pursuits and pro-'pensities have a tendency to make my head worse. It 'is but a bad head, — as bad as if I were a great man! 'I am not entitled to so bad a head by anything I have 'done; but I flatter myself it is very interesting to suffer 'so much, and a fair excuse for not writing pretty let-'ters, and saying to my friends the good things I think 'about them.

'I was so desirous of doing all I could, that I took a 'great deal more upon myself than I was able to bear. 'Yet now that the twenty-five weeks of incessant toil 'are over, I rejoice in it all, and would not have done 'an iota less. I have fulfilled all my engagements faith-'fully; have acquired more power of attention, self-'command, and fortitude; have acted in life as I thought 'I would in my lonely meditations; and have gained 'some knowledge of means. Above all, — blessed be the 'Father of our spirits! — my aims are the same as they 'were in the happiest flight of youthful fancy. I have 'learned too, at last, to rejoice in all past pain, and to see 'that my spirit has been judiciously tempered for its 'work. In future I may sorrow, but can I ever despair?

'The beginning of the winter was forlorn. I was 'always ill; and often thought I might not live, though 'the work was but just begun. The usual disappoint-'ments, too, were about me. Those from whom aid 'was expected failed, and others who aided did not un-'derstand my aims. Enthusiasm for the things loved 'best fled when I seemed to be buying and selling them. 'I could not get the proper point of view, and could not 'keep a healthful state of mind. Mysteriously a gulf 'seemed to have opened between me and most intimate 'friends, and for the first time for many years I was 'entirely, absolutely, alone. Finally, my own character 'and designs lost all romantic interest, and I felt vulgar-

'ized, profaned, forsaken,—though obliged to smile 'brightly and talk wisely all the while. But these 'clouds at length passed away.

'And now let me try to tell you what has been done. 'To one class I taught the German language, and 'thought it good success, when, at the end of three 'months, they could read twenty pages of German at a 'lesson, and very well. This class, of course, was not 'interesting, except in the way of observation and 'analysis of language.

'With more advanced pupils I read, in twenty-four 'weeks, Schiller's Don Carlos, Artists, and Song of the 'Bell, besides giving a sort of general lecture on Schiller; 'Goethe's Hermann and Dorothea, Goetz von Berlich-'ingen, Iphigenia, first part of Faust,—three weeks of 'thorough study this, as valuable to me as to them,—'and Clavigo,—thus comprehending samples of all his 'efforts in poetry, and bringing forward some of his 'prominent opinions; Lessing's Nathan, Minna, Emilia 'Galeotti; parts of Tieck's Phantasus, and nearly the 'whole first volume of Richter's Titan.

'With the Italian class, I read parts of Tasso, Pe-'trarch,—whom they came to almost adore,—Ariosto, 'Alfieri, and the whole hundred cantos of the Divina 'Commedia, with the aid of the fine Athenæum copy, 'Flaxman's designs, and all the best commentaries. 'This last piece of work was and will be truly valuable 'to myself.

'I had, besides, three private pupils, Mrs. ——, who 'became very attractive to me, ——, and little ——, 'who had not the use of his eyes. I taught him Latin 'orally, and read the History of England and Shaks-'peare's historical plays in connection. This lesson was 'given every day for ten weeks, and was very interesting, 'though very fatiguing. The labor in Mr. Alcott's school 'was also quite exhausting. I, however, loved the 'children, and had many valuable thoughts suggested, 'and Mr. A.'s society was much to me.

'As you may imagine, the Life of Goethe is not yet 'written; but I have studied and thought about it much. 'It grows in my mind with everything that does grow 'there. My friends in Europe have sent me the needed 'books on the subject, and I am now beginning to work 'in good earnest. It is very possible that the task may 'be taken from me by somebody in England, or that in 'doing it I may find myself incompetent; but I go on in 'hope, secure, at all events, that it will be the means of 'the highest culture.'

In addition to other labors, Margaret translated, one evening every week, German authors into English, for the gratification of Dr. Channing; their chief reading being in De Wette and Herder.

'It was not very pleasant,' she writes, 'for Dr. C. 'takes in subjects more deliberately than is conceivable 'to us feminine people, with our habits of ducking, 'diving, or flying for truth. Doubtless, however, he 'makes better use of what he gets, and if his sympathies 'were livelier he would not view certain truths in so 'steady a light. But there is much more talking than 'reading; and I like talking with him. I do not feel that 'constraint which some persons complain of, but am 'perfectly free, though less called out than by other in-'tellects of inferior power. I get too much food for 'thought from him, and am not bound to any tiresome 'formality of respect on account of his age and rank in 'the world of intellect. He seems desirous to meet even 'one young and obscure as myself on equal terms, and 'trusts to the elevation of his thoughts to keep him in 'his place.'

She found higher satisfaction still in his preaching: —

'A discourse from Dr. C. on the spirituality of man's 'nature. This was delightful! I came away in the 'most happy, hopeful, and heroic mood. The tone of 'the discourse was so dignified, his manner was so be-'nignant and solemnly earnest, in his voice there was 'such a concentration of all his force, physical and 'moral, to give utterance to divine truth, that I felt 'purged as by fire. If some speakers feed intellect more, 'Dr. C. feeds the whole spirit. O for a more calm, 'more pervading faith in the divinity of my own nature! 'I am so far from being thoroughly tempered and 'seasoned, and am sometimes so presumptuous, at others 'so depressed. Why cannot I lay more to heart the text, '"God is never in a hurry: let man be patient and con-'"fident"?'

PROVIDENCE.

In the spring of 1837, Margaret received a very favorable offer to become a principal teacher in the Greene Street School, at Providence, R. I.

'The proposal is, that I shall teach the elder girls my 'favorite branches, for four hours a day, — choosing my 'own hours, and arranging the course, — for a thousand 'dollars a year, if, upon trial, I am well enough pleased 'to stay. This would be independence, and would 'enable me to do many slight services for my family. 'But, on the other hand, I am not sure that I shall like 'the situation, and am sanguine that, by perseverance, 'the plan of classes in Boston might be carried into full 'effect. Moreover, Mr. Ripley, — who is about publish-'ing a series of works on Foreign Literature, — has 'invited me to prepare the "Life of Goethe," on very 'advantageous terms. This I should much prefer. Yet 'when the thousand petty difficulties which surround 'us are considered, it seems unwise to relinquish imme-'diate independence.'

She accepted, therefore, the offer which promised certain means of aiding her family, and reluctantly gave up the precarious, though congenial, literary project.

SCHOOL EXPERIENCES.

'The new institution of which I am to be "Lady '"Superior" was dedicated last Saturday. People talk 'to me of the good I am to do; but the last fortnight has 'been so occupied in the task of arranging many scholars 'of various ages and unequal training, that I cannot 'yet realize this new era. * *

'The gulf is vast, wider than I could have conceived 'possible, between me and my pupils; but the sight of 'such deplorable ignorance, such absolute burial of the 'best powers, as I find in some instances, makes me com-'prehend, better than before, how such a man as Mr. 'Alcott could devote his life to renovate elementary edu-'cation. I have pleasant feelings when I see that a new 'world has already been opened to them. * *

'Nothing of the vulgar feeling towards teachers, too 'often to be observed in schools, exists towards me.

'The pupils seem to reverence my tastes and opinions 'in all things; they are docile, decorous, and try hard to 'please; they are in awe of my displeasure, but delighted 'whenever permitted to associate with me on familiar 'terms. As I treat them like ladies, they are anxious to 'prove that they deserve to be so treated. * *

'There is room here for a great move in the cause of 'education, and if I could resolve on devoting five or six 'years to this school, a good work might, doubtless, be 'done. Plans are becoming complete in my mind, ways 'and means continually offer, and, so far as I have tried 'them, they succeed. I am left almost as much at lib-'erty as if no other person was concerned. Some sixty 'scholars are more or less under my care, and many of 'them begin to walk in the new paths pointed out. 'General activity of mind, accuracy in processes, con-'stant looking for principles, and search after the good 'and the beautiful, are the habits I strive to develop. * *

'I will write a short record of the last day at school. 'For a week past I have given the classes in philosophy, 'rhetoric, history, poetry, and moral science, short lec-'tures on the true objects of study, with advice as to their 'future course; and to-day, after recitation, I expressed 'my gratification that the minds of so many had been 'opened to the love of good and beauty.

'Then came the time for last words First, I called 'into the recitation room the boys who had been under 'my care. They are nearly all interesting, and have 'showed a chivalric feeling in their treatment of me. Peo-'ple talk of women not being able to govern boys; but I 'have always found it a very easy task. He must be a 'coarse boy, indeed, who, when addressed in a resolute, 'yet gentle manner, by a lady, will not try to merit hei 'esteem. These boys have always rivalled one another 'in respectful behavior. I spoke a few appropriate 'words to each, mentioning his peculiar errors and good 'deeds, mingling some advice with more love, which 'will, I hope, make it remembered. We took a sweet 'farewell. With the younger girls I had a similar inter-'view.

'Then I summoned the elder girls, who have been my 'especial charge. I reminded them of the ignorance in 'which some of them were found, and showed them 'how all my efforts had necessarily been directed to 'stimulating their minds, — leaving undone much which, 'under other circumstances, would have been deemed 'indispensable. I thanked them for the favorable opin-'ion of my government which they had so generally 'expressed, but specified three instances in which I had 'been unjust. I thanked them, also, for the moral 'beauty of their conduct, bore witness that an appeal to 'conscience had never failed, and told them of my hap-'piness in having the faith thus confirmed, that young 'persons can be best guided by addressing their highest 'nature. I declared my consciousness of having com-'bined, not only in speech but in heart, tolerance and 'delicate regard for the convictions of their parents, with 'fidelity to my own, frankly uttered. I assured them of 'my true friendship, proved by my never having cajoled 'or caressed them into good. Every word of praise had 'been earned; all my influence over them was rooted 'in reality; I had never softened nor palliated their 'faults; I had appealed, not to their weakness, but to 'their strength; I had offered to them, always, the lofti-'est motives, and had made every other end subordinate 'to that of spiritual growth. With a heartfelt blessing,

'I dismissed them; but none stirred, and we all sat for 'some moments, weeping. Then I went round the circle 'and bade each, separately, farewell.'

PERSONS.

Margaret's Providence journals are made extremely piquant and entertaining, by her life-like portraiture of people and events; and every page attests the scrupulous justice with which she sought to penetrate through surfaces to reality, and, forgetting personal prejudices, to apply universally the test of truth. A few sketches of public characters may suffice to show with what sagacious, all-observing eyes, she looked about her.

'At the whig caucus, I heard TRISTAM BURGESS,—"The 'old bald Eagle!" His baldness increases the fine 'effect of his appearance, for it seems as if the locks 'had retreated, that the contour of his very strongly 'marked head might be revealed to every eye. His *per-'sonnel*, as well as I could see, was fitted to command 'respect rather than admiration. He is a venerable, not 'a beautiful old man.

'He is a rhetorician,—if I could judge from this 'sample; style inwoven and somewhat ornate, matter 'frequently wrought up to a climax, manner rather 'declamatory, though strictly that of a gentleman and a 'scholar. One art in his oratory was, no doubt, very 'effective, before he lost force and distinctness of voice. 'I allude to his way,—after having reasoned a while, 'till he has reached the desired conclusion,—of leaning 'forward, with hands reposing but figure very earnest, 'and communicating, confidentially as it were, the result 'to the audience. The impression produced in former 'days, when those low, emphatic passages could be dis-

'tinctly heard, must have been very strong. Yet there 'is too much apparent trickery in this, to bear frequent 'repetition. His manner is well adapted for argument, 'and for the expression either of satire or of chivalric 'sentiment.'

'Mr. JOHN NEAL addressed my girls on the destiny and 'vocation of Woman in this country. He gave, truly, a '*manly* view, though not the view of common men, and 'it was pleasing to watch his countenance, where energy 'is animated by genius. He then spoke to the boys, in 'the most noble and liberal spirit, on the exercise of 'political rights. If there is one among them who has 'the germ of a truly independent man, too generous to 'become a party tool, and with soul enough to think, as 'well as feel, for himself, those words were not spoken 'in vain. He was warmed up into giving a sketch of 'his boyhood. It was an eloquent narrative, and is inef-'faceably impressed on my memory, with every look 'and gesture of the speaker. What gave chief charm to 'this history was its fearless ingenuousness. It was 'delightful to note the impression produced by his mag-'netic genius and independent character.

'In the evening we had a long conversation upon 'Woman, Whigism, modern English Poets, Shaks-'peare, — and, in particular, Richard the Third, — about 'which we had actually a fight. Mr. Neal does not 'argue quite fairly, for he uses reason while it lasts, and 'then helps himself out with wit, sentiment and asser-'tion. I should quarrel with his definitions upon almost 'every subject, but his fervid eloquence, brilliancy, end-'less resource, and ready tact, give him great advan-'tage. There was a sort of exaggeration and coxcombry 'in his talk; but his lion-heart, and keen sense of the 'ludicrous, alike in himself as in others, redeem them. 'I should not like to have my motives scrutinized as he 'would scrutinize them, for I prefer rather to disclose 'them myself than to be found out; but I was dis-'satisfied in parting from this remarkable man before 'having seen him more thoroughly.'

'Mr. Whipple addressed the meeting at length. His 'presence is not imposing, though his face is intellectual. 'It is difficult to look at him, for you cannot be taken 'prisoner by his eye, while, *en revanche*, he can look 'at you as long as he pleases; and, as usual, with one 'who can get the better of his auditors, he does not call 'out the best in them. His gestures are remarkably 'fine, free, graceful, and expressive. He has no natural 'advantages of voice, — for it is without compass, depth, 'sweetness, — and has none of the winning tones which 'reach the inmost soul, and none of the tones of passion-'ate energy, which raise you out of your own world into 'the speaker's. But his modulation is smooth, measured, 'dignified, though occasionally injured by too elaborate 'a swell, and his enunciation is admirable.

'His theme was one which has been so thoroughly 'discussed that novelty was not to be looked for; but 'his method and arrangement were excellent, though 'parts were too much expanded, and the whole might 'well have been condensed. There were many felicitous 'popular hits. The humorous touches were skilful, and 'the illustrations on a broad scale good, though in single 'images he failed. Altogether, there was a pervading 'air of ease and mastery, which showed him fit to be a leader of the flock. Though not a man of the Webster 'class, he is among the first of the second class of men 'who apply their powers to practical purposes,—and 'that is saying much.'

'I went to hear JOSEPH JOHN GURNEY, one of the most 'distinguished and influential, it is said, of the English 'Quakers. He is a thick-set, beetle-browed man, with a 'well-to-do-in-the-world air of pious stolidity. I was 'grievously disappointed; for Quakerism has at times 'looked lovely to me, and I had expected at least a spir-'itual exposition of its doctrines from the brother of Mrs. 'Fry. But his manner was as wooden as his matter, 'and had no merit but that of distinct elocution. His 'sermon was a tissue of texts, illy selected, and worse 'patched together, in proof of the assertion that a belief 'in the Trinity is the one thing needful, and that reason, 'unless manacled by a creed, is the one thing dangerous. 'His figures were paltry, his thoughts narrowed down, 'and his very sincerity made corrupt by spiritual pride. 'One could not but pity his notions of the Holy Ghost, 'and his bat-like fear of light. His Man-God seemed to 'be the keeper of a mad-house, rather than the informing 'Spirit of all spirits. After finishing his discourse, Mr. 'G. sang a prayer, in a tone of mingled shout and whine, 'and then requested his audience to sit a while in devout 'meditation. For one, I passed the interval in praying 'for him, that the thick film of self-complacency might 'be removed from the eyes of his spirit, so that he might 'no more degrade religion.'

'Mr. HAGUE is of the Baptist persuasion, and is very 'popular with his own sect. He is small, and carries 'his head erect; he has a high and intellectual, though 'not majestic, forehead; his brows are lowering 'and, when knit in indignant denunciation, give a thun-'derous look to the countenance, and beneath them flash, 'sparkle, and flame, — for all that may be said of light 'in rapid motion is true of them, — his dark eyes. Hazel 'and blue eyes with their purity, steadfastness, subtle 'penetration and radiant hope, may persuade and win, 'but black is the color to command. His mouth has an 'equivocal expression, but as an orator perhaps he gains 'power by the air of mystery this gives.

'He has a very active intellect, sagacity and elevated 'sentiment; and, feeling strongly that God is love, can 'never preach without earnestness. His power comes 'first from his glowing vitality of temperament. While 'speaking, his every muscle is in action, and all his 'action is towards one object. There is perfect *abandon.* 'He is permeated, overborne, by his thought. This 'lends a charm above grace, though incessant nervous-'ness and heat injure his manner. He is never violent, 'though often vehement; pleading tones in his voice 'redeem him from coarseness, even when most eager; 'and he throws himself into the hearts of his hearers, 'not in weak need of sympathy, but in the confidence of 'generous emotion. His second attraction is his individ-'uality. He speaks direct from the conviction of his 'spirit, without temporizing, or artificial method. His is 'the "unpremeditated art," and therefore successful. He 'is full of intellectual life; his mind has not been fettered 'by dogmas, and the worship of beauty finds a place 'there. I am much interested in this truly animated 'being.'

'Mr. R. H. Dana has been giving us readings in the

'English dramatists, beginning with Shakspeare. The 'introductory was beautiful. After assigning to literature 'its high place in the education of the human soul, he 'announced his own view in giving these readings: that 'he should never pander to a popular love of excitement, 'but quietly, without regard to brilliancy or effect, would 'tell what had struck him in these poets; that he had no 'belief in artificial processes of acquisition or communica- 'tion, and having never learned anything except through 'love, he had no hope of teaching any but loving spirits, '&c. All this was arrayed in a garb of most delicate 'grace; but a man of such genuine refinement under- 'values the cannon-blasts and rockets which are needed 'to rouse the attention of the vulgar. His naïve gestures, 'the rapt expression of his face, his introverted eye, and 'the almost childlike simplicity of his pathos, carry one 'back into a purer atmosphere, to live over again youth's 'fresh emotions. I greatly enjoyed his readings in 'Hamlet, and have reviewed in connection what Goethe 'and Coleridge have said. Both have successfully 'seized on the main points in the character of Hamlet, 'and Mr. D. took nearly the same range. His views of 'Ophelia, however, are unspeakably more just than are 'those of Serlo in Wilhelm Meister. I regret that the 'whole course is not to be on Shakspeare, for I should 'like to read with him all the plays.

'I never have met with a person of finer perceptions. 'He leaves out nothing; though he over-refines on some 'passages. He has the most exquisite taste, and freshens 'the souls of his hearers with ever new beauty. He is 'greatly indebted to the delicacy of his physical organ- 'ization for the delicacy of his mental appreciation. But 'when he has told you what *he* likes, the pleasure of 'intercourse is over; for he is a man of prejudice more 'than of reason, and though he can make a lively '*exposé* of his thoughts and feelings, he does not jus- 'tify them. In a word, Mr. Dana has the charms and 'the defects of one whose object in life has been to pre- 'serve his individuality unprofaned.'

ART.

While residing at Providence, and during her visits to Boston, in her vacations, Margaret's mind was opening more and more to the charms of art.

'The Ton-Kunst, the Ton-Welt, give me now more 'stimulus than the written Word; for music seems to 'contain everything in nature, unfolded into perfect har- 'mony. In it the *all* and *each* are manifested in most 'rapid transition; the spiral and undulatory movement 'of beautiful creation is felt throughout, and, as we listen, 'thought is most clearly, because most mystically, per- 'ceived. * *

'I have been to hear Neukomm's Oratorio of David. 'It is to music what Barry Cornwall's verses and Tal- 'fourd's Ion are to poetry. It is completely modern, 'and befits an age of consciousness. Nothing can be 'better arranged as a drama; the parts are in excellent 'gradation, the choruses are grand and effective, the 'composition, as a whole, brilliantly imposing. Yet it 'was dictated by taste and science only. Where are 'the enrapturing visions from the celestial world which 'shone down upon Haydn and Mozart; where the 'revelations from the depths of man's nature, which 'impart such passion to the symphonies of Beethoven; 'where, even, the fascinating fairy land, gay with 'delight, of Rossini? O, Genius! none but thee shall 'make our hearts and heads throb, our cheeks crimson, 'our eyes overflow, or fill our whole being with the 'serene joy of faith.' * *

'I went to see Vandenhoff twice, in Brutus and Vir-'ginius. Another fine specimen of the conscious school; 'no inspiration, yet much taste. Spite of the thread-'paper Tituses, the chambermaid Virginias, the wash-'erwoman Tullias, and the people, made up of half a 'dozen chimney-sweeps, in carters' frocks and red night-'caps, this man had power to recall a thought of the old 'stately Roman, with his unity of will and deed. He 'was an admirable *father*, that fairest, noblest part, — 'with a happy mixture of dignity and tenderness, blend-'ing the delicate sympathy of the companion with the 'calm wisdom of the teacher, and showing beneath the 'zone of duty a heart that has not forgot to throb with 'youthful love. This character, — which did actual 'fathers know how to be, they would fulfil the order of 'nature, and image Deity to their children, — Vandenhoff 'represented sufficiently, at least, to call up the beauti-'ful ideal.'

FANNY KEMBLE.

'When in Boston, I saw the Kembles twice, — in '"Much ado about Nothing," and "The Stranger." 'The first night I felt much disappointed in Miss K. 'In the gay parts a coquettish, courtly manner marred 'the wild mirth and wanton wit of Beatrice. Yet, in 'everything else, I liked her conception of the part; and 'where she urges Benedict to fight with Claudio, and 'where she reads Benedict's sonnet, she was admira-'ble. But I received no more pleasure from Miss K.'s acting out the part than I have done in reading it, and 'this disappointed me. Neither did I laugh, but thought 'all the while of Miss K., — how very graceful she was, 'and whether this and that way of rendering the part 'was just. I do not believe she has comic power within 'herself, though tasteful enough to comprehend any 'part. So I went home, vexed because my "heart was '"not full," and my "brain not on fire" with enthu-'siasm. I drank my milk, and went to sleep, as on 'other dreary occasions, and dreamed not of Miss 'Kemble.

'Next night, however, I went expectant, and all my 'soul was satisfied. I saw her at a favorable distance, 'and she looked beautiful. And as the scene rose in 'interest, her attitudes, her gestures, had the expres-'sion which an Angelo could give to sculpture. 'After she tells her story, — and I was almost suffo-'cated by the effort she made to divulge her sin and 'fall, — she sunk to the earth, her head bowed upon 'her knee, her white drapery falling in large, graceful 'folds about this broken piece of beautiful humanity, '*crushed* in the very manner so well described by Scott 'when speaking of a far different person, "not as '"one who intentionally stoops, kneels, or prostrates '"himself to excite compassion, but like a man borne '"down on all sides by the pressure of some invisible '"force, which crushes him to the earth without power '"of resistance." A movement of abhorrence from me, 'as her insipid confidante turned away, attested the 'triumph of the poet-actress. Had not all been over in 'a moment, I believe I could not have refrained from 'rushing forward to raise the fair frail being, who seemed 'so prematurely humbled in her parent dust. I burst 'into tears; and, with the stifled, hopeless feeling of a 'real sorrow, continued to weep till the very end; nor 'could I recover till I left the house.

'That is genius, which could give such life to this 'play; for, if I may judge from other parts, it is defaced 'by inflated sentiments, and verified by few natural 'touches. I wish I had it to read, for I should like to 'recall her every tone and look.'

'I have been studying Flaxman and Retzsch. How 'pure, how immortal, the language of Form! Fools 'cannot fancy they fathom its meaning; witless *dillet-* '*tanti* cannot degrade it by hackneyed usage; none but 'genius can create or reproduce it. Unlike the colorist, 'he who expresses his thought in form is secure as man 'can be against the ravages of time.'

'I went to the Athenæum in an agonizing conflict of 'mind, when some high influence was needed to rouse 'me from the state of sickly sensitiveness, which, much 'as I despise, I cannot wholly conquer. How soothing 'it was to feel the blessed power of the Ideal world, to 'be surrounded once more with the records of lives 'poured out in embodying thought in beauty! I seemed 'to breathe my native atmosphere, and smoothed my 'ruffled pinions.'

'No wonder God made a world to express his thought. 'Who, that has a soul for beauty, does not feel the need 'of creating, and that the power of creation alone can 'satisfy the spirit? When I thus reflect, the Artist seems 'the only fortunate man. Had I but as much creative genius as I have apprehensiveness!'

'How transcendently lovely was the face of one young 'angel by Raphael! It was the perfection of physical, 'moral, and mental life. Variegated wings, of pinkish-'purple touched with green, like the breasts of doves, 'and in perfect harmony with the complexion, spring 'from the shoulders upwards, and against them leans the 'divine head. The eye seems fixed on the centre of 'being, and the lips are gently parted, as if uttering 'strains of celestial melody.'

'The head of Aspasia was instinct with the volup-'tuousness of intellect. From the eyes, the cheek, 'the divine lip, one might hive honey. Both the 'Loves were exquisite: one, that zephyr sentiment 'which visits all the roses of life; the other, the Amore 'Greco, may be fitly described in these words of Landor: '"There is a gloom in deep love, as in deep water; '"there is a silence in it which suspends the foot, and '"the folded arms and the dejected head are the images '"it reflects. No voice shakes its surface; the Muses '"themselves approach it with a tardy and a timid step, '"with a low and tremulous and melancholy song."'

'The Sibyl I understood. What grace in that beau-'tiful oval! what apprehensiveness in the eye! Such 'is female Genius; it alone understands the God. 'The Muses only sang the praises of Apollo; the Sibyls 'interpreted his will. Nay, she to whom it was offered, 'refused the divine union, and preferred remaining a 'satellite to being absorbed into the sun. You read 'in the eye of this one, and the observation is 'confirmed by the low forehead, that the secret of her 'inspiration lay in the passionate enthusiasm of her nature, rather than in the ideal perfection of any 'faculty.

'A Christ, by Raphael, that I saw the other night, brought Christianity more home to my heart, made me 'more long to be like Jesus, than ever did sermon. It is 'from one of the Vatican frescoes. The Deity, — a stern, 'strong, wise man, of about forty-five, in a square velvet 'cap, truly the Jewish God, inflexibly just, yet jealous 'and wrathful, — is at the top of the picture, looking with 'a gaze of almost frowning scrutiny down into his world. 'A step below is the Son. Stately angelic shapes kneel 'near him in dignified adoration, — brothers, but not peers. 'A cloud of more ecstatic seraphs floats behind the Father. 'At the feet of the Son is the Holy Ghost, the Heavenly 'Dove. In the description, by a connoisseur, of this pic'ture, read to me while I was looking at it, it is spoken 'of as in Raphael's first manner, cold, hard, trammeled. 'But to me how did that face proclaim the Infinite Love! 'His head is bent back, as if seeking to behold the 'Father. His attitude expresses the need of adoring 'something higher, in order to keep him at his highest. 'What sweetness, what purity, in the eyes! I can never 'express it; but I felt, when looking at it, the beauty of 'reverence, of self-sacrifice, to a degree that stripped the 'Apollo of his beams.'

MAGNANIMITY.

Immediately after reading Miss Martineau's book on America, Margaret felt bound in honor to write her a letter, the magnanimity of which is brought out in full relief, by contrast with the expressions already given of her affectionate regard. Extracts from this letter, recorded in her journals, come here rightfully in place: —

'On its first appearance, the book was greeted by a 'volley of coarse and outrageous abuse, and the nine 'days' wonder was followed by a nine days' hue-and-'cry. It was garbled, misrepresented, scandalously ill-'treated. This was all of no consequence. The opin-'ion of the majority you will find expressed in a late 'number of the North American Review. I should think 'the article, though ungenerous, not more so than great 'part of the critiques upon your book.

'The minority may be divided into two classes: 'The one, consisting of those who knew you but slightly, 'either personally, or in your writings. These have now 'read your book; and, seeing in it your high ideal 'standard, genuine independence, noble tone of senti-'ment, vigor of mind and powers of picturesque descrip-'tion, they value your book very much, and rate you 'higher for it.

'The other comprises those who were previously aware 'of these high qualities, and who, seeing in a book to 'which they had looked for a lasting monument to your 'fame, a degree of presumptuousness, irreverence, inac-'curacy, hasty generalization, and ultraism on many 'points, which they did not expect, lament the haste in 'which you have written, and the injustice which you 'have consequently done to so important a task, and to 'your own powers of being and doing. To this class I 'belong.

'I got the book as soon as it came out, — long before I 'received the copy endeared by your handwriting, — and 'devoted myself to reading it. I gave myself up to my 'natural impressions, without seeking to ascertain those of 'others. Frequently I felt pleasure and admiration, but 'more frequently disappointment, sometimes positive dis-'taste.

'There are many topics treated of in this book of 'which I am not a judge; but I do pretend, even where 'I cannot criticize in detail, to have an opinion as to the 'general tone of thought. When Herschel writes his 'Introduction to Natural Philosophy, I cannot test all he 'says, but I cannot err about his fairness, his manliness, 'and wide range of knowledge. When Jouffroy writes 'his lectures, I am not conversant with all his topics of 'thought, but I can appreciate his lucid style and 'admirable method. When Webster speaks on the cur-'rency, I do not understand the subject, but I do under-'stand his mode of treating it, and can see what a blaze of 'light streams from his torch. When Harriet Martineau 'writes about America, I often cannot test that rashness 'and inaccuracy of which I hear so much, but I can feel 'that they exist. A want of soundness, of habits of 'patient investigation, of completeness, of arrangement, 'are felt throughout the book; and, for all its fine de-'scriptions of scenery, breadth of reasoning, and generous 'daring, I cannot be happy in it, because it is not worthy 'of my friend, and I think a few months given to ripen 'it, to balance, compare, and mellow, would have made 'it so. * *

'Certainly you show no spirit of harshness towards 'this country in general. I think your tone most kindly. 'But many passages are deformed by intemperance of 'epithet. * * Would your heart, could you but investi-'gate the matter, approve such overstatement, such a 'crude, intemperate tirade as you have been guilty of 'about Mr. Alcott,—a true and noble man, a philan-'thropist, whom a true and noble woman, also a phi-

17

'lanthropist, should have delighted to honor; whose 'disinterested and resolute efforts, for the redemption of 'poor humanity, all independent and faithful minds 'should sustain, since the "broadcloth" vulgar will be 'sure to assail them; a philosopher, worthy of the palmy 'times of ancient Greece; a man whom Carlyle and 'Berkely, whom you so uphold, would delight to honor; 'a man whom the worldlings of Boston hold in as much 'horror as the worldlings of ancient Athens did Socrates. 'They smile to hear their verdict confirmed from the 'other side of the Atlantic, by their censor, Harriet 'Martineau.

'I do not like that your book should be an abolition 'book. You might have borne your testimony as decid-'edly as you pleased; but why leaven the whole book 'with it? This subject haunts us on almost every page. 'It *is* a great subject, but your book had other purposes 'to fulfil.

'I have thought it right to say all this to you, since I 'felt it. I have shrunk from the effort, for I fear that 'I must lose you. Not that I think all authors are like 'Gil Blas' archbishop. No; if your heart turns from 'me, I shall still love you, still think you noble. I know 'it must be so trying to fail of sympathy, at such a time, 'where we expect it. And, besides, I felt from the book 'that the sympathy between us is less general than I had 'supposed, it was so strong on several points. It is strong 'enough for me to love you ever, and I could no more 'have been happy in your friendship, if I had not spoken 'out now.'

SPIRITUAL LIFE.

'You question me as to the nature of the benefits 'conferred upon me by Mr. E.'s preaching. I answer, that his influence has been more beneficial to me than 'that of any American, and that from him I first learned 'what is meant by an inward life. Many other springs 'have since fed the stream of living waters, but he first 'opened the fountain. That the "mind is its own place," 'was a dead phrase to me, till he cast light upon my 'mind. Several of his sermons stand apart in memory, 'like landmarks of my spiritual history. It would take 'a volume to tell what this one influence did for me 'But perhaps I shall some time see that it was best for 'me to be forced to help myself.'

'Some remarks which I made last night trouble me, 'and I cannot fix my attention upon other things till I 'have qualified them. I suffered myself to speak in too 'unmeasured terms, and my expressions were fitted to 'bring into discredit the religious instruction which has 'been given me, or which I have sought.

'I do not think "all men are born for the purpose of '"unfolding beautiful ideas;" for the vocation of many 'is evidently the culture of affections by deeds of kind-'ness. But I do think that the vocations of men and 'women differ, and that those who are forced to act out 'of their sphere are shorn of inward and outward 'brightness.

'For myself, I wish to say, that, if I am in a mood of 'darkness and despondency, I nevertheless consider such 'a mood unworthy of a Christian, or indeed of any one 'who believes in the immortality of the soul. No one, 'who had steady faith in this and in the goodness of 'God, could be otherwise than cheerful. I reverence the 'serenity of a truly religious mind so much, that I think 'if I live, I may some time attain to it.

'Although I do not believe in a Special Providence 'regulating outward events, and could not reconcile such 'a belief with what I have seen of life, I do not the less 'believe in the paternal government of a Deity. That 'He should visit the souls of those who seek Him seems 'to me the nobler way to conceive of his influence. 'And if there were not some error in my way of seeking, 'I do not believe I should suffer from languor or dead-'ness on spiritual subjects, at the time when I have most 'need to feel myself at home there. To find this error is 'my earnest wish; and perhaps I am now travelling to 'that end, though by a thorny road. It is a mortification 'to find so much yet to do; for at one time the scheme 'of things seemed so clear, that, with Cromwell, I might 'say, "I was once in grace." With my mind I prize 'high objects as much as then: it is my heart which is 'cold. And sometimes I fear that the necessity of urging 'them on those under my care dulls my sense of their 'beauty. It is so hard to prevent one's feelings from 'evaporating in words.'

'"The faint sickness of a wounded heart." How 'frequently do these words of Beckford recur to my 'mind! His prayer, imperfect as it is, says more to me 'than many a purer aspiration. It breathes such an 'experience of impassioned anguish. He had every-'thing,—health, personal advantages, almost boundless 'wealth, genius, exquisite taste, culture; he could, in 'some way, express his whole being. Yet well-nigh he 'sank beneath the sickness of the wounded heart; and 'solitude, "country of the unhappy," was all he craved at last.

'Goethe, too, says he has known, in all his active,

'wise, and honored life, no four weeks of happiness. 'This teaches me on the other side; for, like Goethe, I 'have never given way to my feelings, but have lived 'active, thoughtful, seeking to be wise. Yet I have 'long days and weeks of heartache; and at those 'times, though I am busy every moment, and cultivate 'every pleasant feeling, and look always upwards to the 'pure ideal region, yet this ache is like a bodily wound, 'whose pain haunts even when it is not attended to, and 'disturbs the dreams of the patient who has fallen asleep 'from exhaustion.

'There is a German in Boston, who has a wound in 'his breast, received in battle long ago. It never troubles 'him, except when he sings, and then, if he gives out his 'voice with much expression, it opens, and cannot, for a 'long time, be stanched again. So with me: when I rise 'into one of those rapturous moods of thought, such as I 'had a day or two since, my wound opens again, and all 'I can do is to be patient, and let it take its own time to 'skin over. I see it will never do more. Some time ago 'I thought the barb was fairly out; but no, the frag-'ments rankle there still, and will, while there is any 'earth attached to my spirit. Is it not because, in my 'pride, I held the mantle close, and let the weapon, 'which some friendly physician might have extracted, 'splinter in the wound?'

'*Sunday*, *July*, 1838. — I partook, for the first time, 'of the Lord's Supper. I had often wished to do so, 'but had not been able to find a clergyman, — from whom 'I could be willing to receive it, — willing to admit me on 'my own terms. Mr. H—— did so; and I shall ever 'respect and value him, if only for the liberality he dis-

'played on this occasion. It was the Sunday after the 'death of his wife, a lady whom I truly honored, and 'should, probably, had we known one another longer, 'have also loved. She was the soul of truth and honor; 'her mind was strong, her reverence for the noble and 'beautiful fervent, her energy in promoting the best 'interests of those who came under her influence 'unusual. She was as full of wit and playfulness as 'of goodness. Her union with her husband was really 'one of mind and heart, of mutual respect and tenderness; likeness in unlikeness made it strong. I wished 'particularly to share in this rite on an occasion so suited 'to bring out its due significance.'

FAREWELL TO SUMMER.

'The Sun, the Moon, the Waters, and the Air,
'The hopeful, holy, terrible, and fair,
'All that is ever speaking, never spoken,
'Spells that are ever breaking, never broken,
'Have played upon my soul; and every string
'Confessed the touch, which once could make it ring
'Celestial notes. And still, though changed the tone,
'Though damp and jarring fall the lyre hath known,
'It would, if fitly played, its deep notes wove
'Into one tissue of belief and love,
'Yield melodies for angel audience meet,
'And pæans fit Creative Power to greet.
'O injured lyre! thy golden frame is marred,
'No garlands deck thee, no libations poured
'Tell to the earth the triumphs of thy song;
'No princely halls echo thy strains along.
'But still the strings are there; and, if they break,
'Even in death rare melody will make,
'Might'st thou once more be tuned, and power be given
'To tell in numbers all thou canst of heaven!'

VISITS TO CONCORD.

BY R. W. EMERSON.

Extract from a letter from Madame Arconati to R. W. Emerson.

Je n'ai point rencontré, dans ma vie, de femme plus noble ; ayant autant de sympathie pour ses semblables, et dont l'esprit fut plus vivifiant. Je me suis tout de suite sentie attirée par elle. Quand je fis sa connoissance, j'ignorais que ce fut une femme remarquable.

IV.

VISITS TO CONCORD.

I BECAME acquainted with Margaret in 1835. Perhaps it was a year earlier that Henry Hedge, who had long been her friend, told me of her genius and studies, and loaned me her manuscript translation of Goethe's Tasso. I was afterwards still more interested in her, by the warm praises of Harriet Martineau, who had become acquainted with her at Cambridge, and who, finding Margaret's fancy for seeing me, took a generous interest in bringing us together. I remember, during a week in the winter of 1835–6, in which Miss Martineau was my guest, she returned again and again to the topic of Margaret's excelling genius and conversation, and enjoined it on me to seek her acquaintance; which I willingly promised. I am not sure that it was not in Miss Martineau's company, a little earlier, that I first saw her. And I find a memorandum, in her own journal, of a visit, made by my brother Charles and myself, to Miss Martineau, at Mrs. Farrar's. It was not, however, till the next July, after a little diplomatizing in billets by the ladies, that her first visit to our house was arranged, and she came to spend a fortnight with my wife. I still remember the first half-hour of Margaret's conversation. She was then twenty-six years old. She had a face and frame that would indicate fulness and tenacity of life. She was rather under the middle height; her complexion was fair, with strong fair hair. She was then, as always, carefully and becomingly dressed, and of ladylike self-possession. For the rest, her appearance had nothing prepossessing. Her extreme plainness,—a trick of incessantly opening and shutting her eyelids,—the nasal tone of her voice,—all repelled; and I said to myself, we shall never get far. It is to be said, that Margaret made a disagreeable first impression on most persons, including those who became afterwards her best friends, to such an extreme that they did not wish to be in the same room with her. This was partly the effect of her manners, which expressed an overweening sense of power, and slight esteem of others, and partly the prejudice of her fame. She had a dangerous reputation for satire, in addition to her great scholarship. The men thought she carried too many guns, and the women did not like one who despised them. I believe I fancied her too much interested in personal history; and her talk was a comedy in which dramatic justice was done to everybody's foibles. I remember that she made me laugh more than I liked; for I was, at that time, an eager scholar of ethics, and had tasted the sweets of solitude and stoicism, and I found something profane in the hours of amusing gossip into which she drew me, and, when I returned to my library, had much to think of the crackling of thorns under a pot. Margaret, who had stuffed me out as a philosopher, in her own fancy, was too intent on establishing a good footing between us, to omit any art of winning. She studied my tastes, piqued and amused me, challenged frankness by frankness, and did not conceal the good opinion of me she brought with her, nor her wish to please. She was curious to know my opinions and experiences. Of course, it was impossible long to hold out against such urgent assault. She had an incredible variety of anecdotes, and the readiest wit to give an absurd turn to whatever passed; and the eyes, which were so plain at first, soon swam with fun and drolleries, and the very tides of joy and superabundant life.

This rumor was much spread abroad, that she was sneering, scoffing, critical, disdainful of humble people, and of all but the intellectual. I had heard it whenever she was named. It was a superficial judgment. Her satire was only the pastime and necessity of her talent, the play of superabundant animal spirits. And it will be seen, in the sequel, that her mind presently disclosed many moods and powers, in successive platforms or terraces, each above each, that quite effaced this first impression, in the opulence of the following pictures.

Let us hear what she has herself to say on the subject of tea-table-talk, in a letter to a young lady, to whom she was already much attached:—

'I am repelled by your account of your party. It is 'beneath you to amuse yourself with active satire, with 'what is vulgarly called quizzing. When such a person as —— chooses to throw himself in your way, I sympathize with your keen perception of his ridiculous points. But 'to laugh a whole evening at vulgar nondescripts,—is that 'an employment for one who was born passionately to 'love, to admire, to sustain truth? This would be much 'more excusable in a chameleon like me. Yet, whatever 'may be the vulgar view of my character, I can truly 'say, I know not the hour in which I ever looked for the 'ridiculous. It has always been forced upon me, and is 'the accident of my existence. I would not want the 'sense of it when it comes, for that would show an 'obtuseness of mental organization; but, on peril of my 'soul, I would not move an eyelash to look for it.'

When she came to Concord, she was already rich in friends, rich in experiences, rich in culture. She was well read in French, Italian, and German literature. She had learned Latin and a little Greek. But her English reading was incomplete; and, while she knew Molière, and Rousseau, and any quantity of French letters, memoirs, and novels, and was a dear student of Dante and Petrarca, and knew German books more cordially than any other person, she was little read in Shakspeare; and I believe I had the pleasure of making her acquainted with Chaucer, with Ben Jonson, with Herbert, Chapman, Ford, Beaumont and Fletcher, with Bacon, and Sir Thomas Browne. I was seven years her senior, and had the habit of idle reading in old English books, and, though not much versed, yet quite enough to give me the right to lead her. She fancied that her sympathy and taste had led her to an exclusive culture of southern European books.

She had large experiences. She had been a precocious scholar at Dr. Park's school; good in mathematics and in languages. Her father, whom she had recently lost, had been proud of her, and petted her. She had drawn, at Cambridge, numbers of lively young men about her. She had had a circle of young women who were devoted to her, and who described her as "a wonder of intellect, "who had yet no religion." She had drawn to her every superior young man or young woman she had met, and whole romances of life and love had been confided, counselled, thought, and lived through, in her cognizance and sympathy.

These histories are rapid, so that she had already beheld many times the youth, meridian, and old age of passion. She had, besides, selected, from so many, a few eminent companions, and already felt that she was not likely to see anything more beautiful than her beauties, anything more powerful and generous than her youths. She had found out her own secret by early comparison, and knew what power to draw confidence, what necessity to lead in every circle, belonged of right to her. Her powers were maturing, and nobler sentiments were subliming the first heats and rude experiments. She had outward calmness and dignity. She had come to the ambition to be filled with all nobleness.

Of the friends who surrounded her, at that period, it is neither easy to speak, nor not to speak. A life of Margaret is impossible without them, she mixed herself so inextricably with her company; and when this little book was first projected, it was proposed to entitle it "Margaret and her Friends," the subject persisting to offer itself in the plural number. But, on trial, that form proved impossible, and it only remained that the narrative, like a Greek tragedy, should suppose the chorus always on the stage, sympathizing and sympathized with by the queen of the scene.

Yet I remember these persons as a fair, commanding troop, every one of them adorned by some splendor of beauty, of grace, of talent, or of character, and comprising in their band persons who have since disclosed sterling worth and elevated aims in the conduct of life.

Three beautiful women, — either of whom would have been the fairest ornament of Papanti's Assemblies, but for the presence of the other, — were her friends. One of these early became, and long remained, nearly the central figure in Margaret's brilliant circle, attracting to herself, by her grace and her singular natural eloquence, every feeling of affection, hope, and pride.

Two others I recall, whose rich and cultivated voices in song were,— one a little earlier, the other a little later,— the joy of every house into which they came; and, indeed, Margaret's taste for music was amply gratified in the taste and science which several persons among her intimate friends possessed. She was successively intimate with two sisters, whose taste for music had been opened, by a fine and severe culture, to the knowledge and to the expression of all the wealth of the German masters.

I remember another, whom every muse inspired, skilful alike with the pencil and the pen, and by whom both were almost contemned for their inadequateness, in the height and scope of her aims. 'With her,' said Margaret, 'I can talk of anything. She is like me. She is able to 'look facts in the face. We enjoy the clearest, widest, 'most direct communication. She may be no happier 'than ——, but she will know her own mind too clearly 'to make any great mistake in conduct, and will learn a 'deep meaning from her days.'

'It is not in the way of tenderness that I love ——. 'I prize her always; and this is all the love some 'natures ever know. And I also feel that I may always 'expect she will be with me. I delight to picture to 'myself certain persons translated, illuminated. There 'are a few in whom I see occasionally the future being 'piercing, promising, — whom I can strip of all that masks 'their temporary relations, and elevate to their natural 'position. Sometimes I have not known these persons 'intimately, — oftener I have; for it is only in the deepest 'hours that this light is likely to break out. But some 'of those I have best befriended I cannot thus portray, 'and very few men I can. It does not depend at all 'on the beauty of their forms, at present; it is in the eye 'and the smile, that the hope shines through. I can see 'exactly how —— will look: not like this angel in the 'paper; she will not bring flowers, but a living coal, to 'the lips of the singer; her eyes will not burn as now 'with smothered fires, they will be ever deeper, and glow 'more intensely; her cheek will be smooth, but marble 'pale; her gestures nobly free, but few.'

Another was a lady who was devoted to landscape-painting, and who enjoyed the distinction of being the only pupil of Allston, and who, in her alliance with Margaret, gave as much honor as she received, by the security of her spirit, and by the heroism of her devotion to her friend. Her friends called her "the perpetual peace-offering," and Margaret says of her, — 'She is here, and 'her neighborhood casts the mildness and purity too of 'the moonbeam on the else parti-colored scene.'

There was another lady, more late and reluctantly entering Margaret's circle, with a mind as high, and more mathematically exact, drawn by taste to Greek, as Margaret to Italian genius, tempted to do homage to Margaret's flowing expressive energy, but still more inclined and secured to her side by the good sense and the heroism which Margaret disclosed, perhaps not a little by the sufferings which she addressed herself to alleviate, as long as Margaret lived. Margaret had a courage in her address which it was not easy to resist. She called all her friends by their Christian names. In their early intercourse I suppose this lady's billets were more punctiliously worded than Margaret liked; so she subscribed herself, in reply, 'Your affectionate "Miss Fuller."' When the difficulties were at length surmounted, and the conditions ascertained on which two admirable persons could live together, the best understanding grew up, and subsisted during her life. In her journal is a note: —

'Passed the morning in Sleepy Hollow, with ——. 'What fine, just distinctions she made! Worlds grew 'clearer as we talked. I grieve to see her fine frame 'subject to such rude discipline. But she truly said, '"I am not a failed experiment; for, in the bad hours, I '"do not forget what I thought in the better."'

None interested her more at that time, and for many years after, than a youth with whom she had been acquainted in Cambridge before he left the University, and the unfolding of whose powers she had watched with the warmest sympathy. He was an amateur, and, but for the exactions not to be resisted of an *American*, that is to say, of a commercial, career, — his acceptance of which she never ceased to regard as an apostasy, — himself a high artist. He was her companion, and, though much younger, her guide in the study of art. With him she examined, leaf by leaf, the designs of

Raphael, of Michel Angelo, of Da Vinci, of Guercino, the architecture of the Greeks, the books of Palladio, the Ruins, and Prisons of Piranesi; and long kept up a profuse correspondence on books and studies in which they had a mutual interest. And yet, as happened so often, these literary sympathies, though sincere, were only veils and occasions to beguile the time, so profound was her interest in the character and fortunes of her friend.

There was another youth, whom she found later, of invalid habit, which had infected in some degree the tone of his mind, but of a delicate and pervasive insight, and the highest appreciation for genius in letters, arts, and life. Margaret describes 'his complexion as clear 'in its pallor, and his eye steady.' His turn of mind, and his habits of life, had almost a monastic turn, — a jealousy of the common tendencies of literary men either to display or to philosophy. Margaret was struck with the singular fineness of his perceptions, and the pious tendency of his thoughts, and enjoyed with him his proud reception, not as from above, but almost on equal ground, of Homer and Æschylus, of Dante and Petrarch, of Montaigne, of Calderon, of Goethe. Margaret wished, also, to defend his privacy from the dangerous solicitations to premature authorship: —

'His mind should be approached close by one who 'needs its fragrance. All with him leads rather to 'glimpses and insights, than to broad, comprehensive 'views. Till he needs the public, the public does not 'need him. The lonely lamp, the niche, the dark cathe-'dral grove, befit him best. Let him shroud himself in 'the symbols of his native ritual, till he can issue forth on the wings of song.'

She was at this time, too, much drawn also to a man of poetic sensibility, and of much reading, — which he took the greatest pains to conceal, — studious of the art of poetry, but still more a poet in his conversation than in his poems, — who attracted Margaret by the flowing humor with which he filled the present hour, and the prodigality with which he forgot all the past.

'Unequal and uncertain,' she says, 'but in his good 'moods, of the best for a companion, absolutely aban-'doned to the revelations of the moment, without distrust 'or check of any kind, unlimited and delicate, abundant 'in thought, and free of motion, he enriches life, and fills 'the hour.'

'I wish I could retain ——'s talk last night. It was 'wonderful; it was about all the past experiences frozen 'down in the soul, and the impossibility of being pen-'etrated by anything. "Had I met you," said he, "when '"I was young! — but now nothing can penetrate." 'Absurd as was what he said, on one side, it was the 'finest poetic inspiration on the other, painting the cruel 'process of life, except where genius continually burns 'over the stubble fields.

'"Life," he said, "is continually eating us up." He said, "Mr. E. is quite wrong about books. He wants '"them all good; now I want many bad. Literature is '"not merely a collection of gems, but a great system of '"interpretation." He railed at me as artificial. "It don't '"strike me when you are alone with me," he says; "but '"it does when others are present. You don't follow out '"the fancy of the moment; you converse; you have '"treasured thoughts to tell; you are disciplined, — arti-'"ficial." I pleaded guilty, and observed that I supposed 'that it must be so with one of any continuity of thought, 'or earnestness of character. "As to that," says he, '"I shall not like you the better for your excellence. I '"don't know what is the matter. I feel strongly '"attracted towards you; but there is a drawback in '"my mind,—I don't know exactly what. You will '"always be wanting to grow forward; now I like to '"grow backward, too. You are too ideal. Ideal people '"anticipate their lives; and they make themselves and '"everybody around them restless, by always being '"beforehand with themselves."

'I listened attentively; for what he said was excellent. 'Following up the humor of the moment, he arrests 'admirable thoughts on the wing. But I cannot but see, 'that what they say of my or other obscure lives is true 'of every prophetic, of every tragic character. And then 'I like to have them make me look on that side, and 'reverence the lovely forms of nature, and the shifting 'moods, and the clinging instincts. But I must not let 'them disturb me. There is an only guide, the voice in 'the heart, that asks, "Was thy wish sincere? If so, '"thou canst not stray from nature, nor be so perverted '"but she will make thee true again." I must take my 'own path, and learn from them all, without being par- 'alyzed for the day. We need great energy, faith, and 'self-reliance to endure to-day. My age may not be the 'best, my position may be bad, my character ill-formed; 'but Thou, oh Spirit! hast no regard to aught but the 'seeking heart; and, if I try to walk upright, wilt guide 'me. What despair must he feel, who, after a whole 'life passed in trying to build up himself, resolves that it 'would have been far better if he had kept still as the 'clod of the valley, or yielded easily as the leaf to every 'breeze! A path has been appointed me. I have walked 'in it as steadily as I could. I am what I am; that 'which I am not, teach me in the others. I will bear the 'pain of imperfection, but not of doubt. E. must not 'shake me in my worldliness, nor —— in the fine 'motion that has given me what I have of life, nor this 'child of genius make me lay aside the armor, without 'which I had lain bleeding on the field long since; but, 'if they can keep closer to nature, and learn to interpret 'her as souls, also, let me learn from them what I 'have not.'

And, in connection with this conversation, she has copied the following lines which this gentleman addressed to her: —

"TO MARGARET.

"I mark beneath thy life the virtue shine
That deep within the star's eye opes its day;
I clutch the gorgeous thoughts thou throw'st away
From the profound unfathomable mine,
And with them this mean common hour do twine,
As glassy waters on the dry beach play.
And I were rich as night, them to combine
With my poor store, and warm me with thy ray.
From the fixed answer of those dateless eyes
I meet bold hints of spirit's mystery
As to what 's past, and hungry prophecies
Of deeds to-day, and things which are to be;
Of lofty life that with the eagle flies,
And humble love that clasps humanity."

I have thus vaguely designated, among the numerous group of her friends, only those who were much in her company, in the early years of my acquaintance with her.

She wore this circle of friends, when I first knew her, as a necklace of diamonds about her neck. They were so much to each other, that Margaret seemed to represent them all, and, to know her, was to acquire a place with them. The confidences given her were thei. best, and she held them to them. She was an active, inspiring companion and correspondent, and all the art, the thought, and the nobleness in New England, seemed, at that moment, related to her, and she to it. She was everywhere a welcome guest. The houses of her friends in town and country were open to her, and every hospitable attention eagerly offered. Her arrival was a holiday, and so was her abode. She stayed a few days, often a week, more seldom a month, and all tasks that could be suspended were put aside to catch the favorable hour, in walking, riding, or boating, to talk with this joyful guest, who brought wit, anecdotes, love-stories, tragedies, oracles with her, and, with her broad web of relations to so many fine friends, seemed like the queen of some parliament of love, who carried the key to all confidences, and to whom every question had been finally referred.

Persons were her game, specially, if marked by fortune, or character, or success; — to such was she sent. She addressed them with a hardihood, — almost a haughty assurance, — queen-like. Indeed, they fell in her way, where the access might have seemed difficult, by wonderful casualties; and the inveterate recluse, the coyest maid, the waywardest poet, made no resistance, but yielded at discretion, as if they had been waiting for her, all doors to this imperious dame. She disarmed the suspicion of recluse scholars by the absence of bookishness. The ease with which she entered into conversation made them forget all they had heard of her; and she was infinitely less interested in literature than in life. They saw she valued earnest persons, and Dante, Petrarch, and Goethe, because they thought as she did, and gratified her with high portraits, which she was everywhere seeking. She drew her companions to surprising confessions. She was the wedding-guest, to whom the long-pent story must be told; and they were not less struck, on reflection, at the suddenness of the friendship which had established, in one day, new and permanent covenants. She extorted the secret of life, which cannot be told without setting heart and mind in a glow; and thus had the best of those she saw Whatever romance, whatever virtue, whatever impressive experience, — this came to her; and she lived in a superior circle; for they suppressed all their commonplace in her presence.

She was perfectly true to this confidence. She never confounded relations, but kept a hundred fine threads in her hand, without crossing or entangling any. An entire intimacy, which seemed to make both sharers of the whole horizon of each others' and of all truth, did not yet make her false to any other friend; gave no title to the history that an equal trust of another friend had put in her keeping. In this reticence was no prudery and no effort. For, so rich her mind, that she never was tempted to treachery, by the desire of entertaining. The day was never long enough to exhaust her opulent memory; and I, who knew her intimately for ten years, — from July, 1836, till August, 1846, when she sailed for Europe, — never saw her without surprise at her new powers.

Of the conversations above alluded to, the substance was whatever was suggested by her passionate wish for equal companions, to the end of making life altogether noble. With the firmest tact she led the discourse into the midst of their daily living and working, recognizing the good-will and sincerity which each man has in his aims, and treating so playfully and intellectually all the points, that one seemed to see his life *en beau*, and was flattered by beholding what he had found so tedious in its workday weeds, shining in glorious costume. Each of his friends passed before him in the new light; hope seemed to spring under his feet, and life was worth living. The auditor jumped for joy, and thirsted for unlimited draughts. What! is this the dame, who, I heard, was sneering and critical? this the blue-stocking, of whom I stood in terror and dislike? this wondrous woman, full of counsel, full of tenderness, before whom every mean thing is ashamed, and hides itself; this new Corinne, more variously gifted, wise, sportive, eloquent, who seems to have learned all languages, Heaven knows when or how, — I should think she was born to them, — magnificent, prophetic, reading my life at her will, and puzzling me with riddles like this, 'Yours is an example of a destiny springing from 'character:' and, again, 'I see your destiny hovering 'before you, but it always escapes from you.'

The test of this eloquence was its range. It told on children, and on old people; on men of the world, and on sainted maids. She could hold them all by her honeyed tongue. A lady of the best eminence, whom Margaret occasionally visited, in one of our cities of spindles, speaking one day of her neighbors, said, "I stand in a certain awe of the moneyed men, the manufacturers, and so on, knowing that they will have small interest in Plato, or in Biot; but I saw them approach Margaret, with perfect security, for she could give them bread that they could eat." Some persons are thrown off their balance when in society; others are thrown on to balance; the excitement of company, and the observation of other characters, correct their biases. Margaret always appeared to unexpected advantage in conversation with a large circle. She had more sanity than any other; whilst, in private, her vision was often through colored lenses.

Her talents were so various, and her conversation so rich and entertaining, that one might talk with her many times, by the parlor fire, before he discovered the strength which served as foundation to so much accomplishment and eloquence. But, concealed under flowers and music, was the broadest good sense, very well able to dispose of all this pile of native and foreign ornaments, and quite able to work without them. She could always rally on this, in every circumstance, and in every company, and find herself on a firm footing of equality with any party whatever, and make herself useful, and, if need be, formidable.

The old Anaximenes, seeking, I suppose, for a source sufficiently diffusive, said, that Mind must be *in the air*, which, when all men breathed, they were filled with one intelligence. And when men have larger measures of reason, as Æsop, Cervantes, Franklin, Scott, they gain in universality, or are no longer confined to a few associates, but are good company for all persons, — philosophers, women, men of fashion, tradesmen, and servants. Indeed, an older philosopher than Anaximenes, namely, language itself, had taught to distinguish superior or purer sense as *common* sense.

Margaret had, with certain limitations, or, must we say, *strictures*, these larger lungs, inhaling this universal element, and could speak to Jew and Greek, free and bond, to each in his own tongue. The Concord stage-coachman distinguished her by his respect, and the chambermaid was pretty sure to confide to her, on the second day, her homely romance.

I regret that it is not in my power to give any true report of Margaret's conversation. She soon became an established friend and frequent inmate of our house, and continued, thenceforward, for years, to come, once in three or four months, to spend a week or a fortnight with us. She adopted all the people and all the interests she found here. Your people shall be my people, and yonder darling boy I shall cherish as my own. Her ready sympathies endeared her to my wife and my mother, each of whom highly esteemed her good sense and sincerity. She suited each, and all. Yet, she was not a person to be suspected of complaisance, and her attachments, one might say, were chemical.

She had so many tasks of her own, that she was a very easy guest to entertain, as she could be left to herself, day after day, without apology. According to our usual habit, we seldom met in the forenoon. After dinner, we read something together, or walked, or rode. In the evening, she came to the library, and many and many a conversation was there held, whose details, if they could be preserved, would justify all encomiums. They interested me in every manner; — talent, memory, wit, stern introspection, poetic play, religion, the finest personal feeling, the aspects of the future, each followed each in full activity, and left me, I remember, enriched and sometimes astonished by the gifts of my guest. Her topics were numerous, but the cardinal points of poetry, love, and religion, were never far off. She was a student of art, and, though untravelled, knew, much better than most persons who had been abroad, the conventional reputation of each of the masters. She was familiar with all the field of elegant criticism in literature. Among the problems of the day, these two attracted her chiefly, Mythology and Demonology; then, also, French Socialism, especially as it concerned woman; the whole prolific family of reforms, and, of course, the genius and career of each remarkable person.

She had other friends, in this town, beside those in my house. A lady, already alluded to, lived in the village, who had known her longer than I, and whose prejudices Margaret had resolutely fought down, until she converted her into the firmest and most efficient of friends. In 1842, Nathaniel Hawthorne, already then known to the world by his Twice-Told Tales, came to live in Concord, in the "Old Manse," with his wife, who was herself an artist. With these welcomed persons Margaret formed a strict and happy acquaintance. She liked their old house, and the taste which had filled it with new articles of beautiful form, yet harmonized with the antique furniture left by the former proprietors. She liked, too, the pleasing walks, and rides, and boatings, which that neighborhood commanded.

In 1842, William Ellery Channing, whose wife was

her sister, built a house in Concord, and this circumstance made a new tie and another home for Margaret.

ARCANA.

It was soon evident that there was somewhat a little pagan about her; that she had some faith more or less distinct in a fate, and in a guardian genius; that her fancy, or her pride, had played with her religion. She had a taste for gems, ciphers, talismans, omens, coincidences, and birth-days. She had a special love for the planet Jupiter, and a belief that the month of September was inauspicious to her. She never forgot that her name, Margarita, signified a pearl. 'When I first met 'with the name Leila,' she said, 'I knew, from the very 'look and sound, it was mine; I knew that it meant 'night, — night, which brings out stars, as sorrow brings 'out truths.' Sortilege she valued. She tried *sortes biblicæ*, and her hits were memorable. I think each new book which interested her, she was disposed to put to this test, and know if it had somewhat personal to say to her. As happens to such persons, these guesses were justified by the event. She chose carbuncle for her own stone, and when a dear friend was to give her a gem, this was the one selected. She valued what she had somewhere read, that carbuncles are male and female. The female casts out light, the male has his within himself. 'Mine,' she said, 'is the male.' And she was wont to put on her carbuncle, a bracelet, or some selected gem, to write letters to certain friends. One of her friends she coupled with the onyx, another in a decided way with the amethyst. She learned that the ancients esteemed this gem a talisman to dispel intoxication, to give good thoughts and understanding.

'The Greek meaning is *antidote against drunkenness.*' She characterized her friends by these stones, and wrote to the last mentioned, the following lines: —

'TO ———.

'Slow wandering on a tangled way,
'To their lost child pure spirits say: —
'The diamond marshal thee by day,
'By night, the carbuncle defend,
'Heart's blood of a bosom friend.
'On thy brow, the amethyst,
'Violet of purest earth,
'When by fullest sunlight kissed,
'Best reveals its regal birth;
'And when that haloed moment flies,
'Shall keep thee steadfast, chaste, and wise.'

Coincidences, good and bad, *contretemps*, seals, ciphers, mottoes, omens, anniversaries, names, dreams, are all of a certain importance to her. Her letters are often dated on some marked anniversary of her own, or of her correspondent's calendar. She signalized saints' days, "All-Souls," and "All-Saints," by poems, which had for her a mystical value. She remarked a preëstablished harmony of the names of her personal friends, as well as of her historical favorites; that of Emanuel, for Swedenborg; and Rosencrantz, for the head of the Rosicrucians. 'If Christian Rosencrantz,' she said, 'is not a 'made name, the genius of the age interfered in the 'baptismal rite, as in the cases of the archangels of art, 'Michael and Raphael, and in giving the name of Eman-'uel to the captain of the New Jerusalem. *Sub rosa* '*crux*, I think, is the true derivation, and not the chemical one, generation, corruption, &c.' In this spirit, she soon surrounded herself with a little mythology of her own. She had a series of anniversaries, which she kept. Her seal-ring of the flying Mercury had its legend. She chose the *Sistrum* for her emblem, and had it carefully drawn with a view to its being engraved on a gem. And I know not how many verses and legends came recommended to her by this symbolism. Her dreams, of course, partook of this symmetry. The same dream returns to her periodically, annually, and punctual to its night. One dream she marks in her journal as repeated for the fourth time: —

'In C., I at last distinctly recognized the figure of the 'early vision, whom I found after I had left A., who led 'me, on the bridge, towards the city, glittering in sunset, 'but, midway, the bridge went under water. I have 'often seen in her face that it was she, but refused to 'believe it.'

She valued, of course, the significance of flowers, and chose emblems for her friends from her garden.

'TO ———, WITH HEARTSEASE.

'Content, in purple lustre clad,
'Kingly serene, and golden glad,
'No demi-hues of sad contrition,
'No pallors of enforced submission; —
'Give me such content as this,
'And keep awhile the rosy bliss.'

DÆMONOLOGY.

This catching at straws of coincidence, where all is geometrical, seems the necessity of certain natures. It is true, that, in every good work, the particulars are right, and, that every spot of light on the ground, under the trees, is a perfect image of the sun. Yet, for astronomical purposes, an observatory is better than an orchard; and in a universe which is nothing but generations, or an unbroken suite of cause and effect, to infer Providence, because a man happens to find a shilling on the pavement just when he wants one to spend, is puerile, and much as if each of us should date his letters and notes of hand from his own birthday, instead of from Christ's or the king's reign, or the current Congress. These, to be sure, are also, at first, petty and private beginnings, but, by the world of men, clothed with a social and cosmical character.

It will be seen, however, that this propensity Margaret held with certain tenets of fate, which always swayed her, and which Goethe, who had found room and fine names for all this in his system, had encouraged; and, I may add, which her own experiences, early and late, seemed strangely to justify.

Some extracts, from her letters to different persons, will show how this matter lay in her mind.

'*December* 17, 1829. — The following instance of 'beautiful credulity, in Rousseau, has taken my mind 'greatly. This remote seeking for the decrees of fate, 'this feeling of a destiny, casting its shadows from the 'very morning of thought, is the most beautiful species 'of idealism in our day. 'Tis finely manifested in 'Wallenstein, where the two common men sum up their 'superficial observations on the life and doings of Wal-'lenstein, and show that, not until this agitating crisis, 'have they caught any idea of the deep thoughts which 'shaped that hero, who has, without their feeling it, 'moulded *their* existence.

'"Tasso," says Rousseau, "has predicted my misfor-'"tunes. Have you remarked that Tasso has this '"peculiarity, that you cannot take from his work a '"single strophe, nor from any strophe a single line, '"nor from any line a single word, without disarrang-'"ing the whole poem? Very well! take away the '"strophe I speak of, the stanza has no connection '"with those that precede or follow it; it is absolutely '"useless. *Tasso probably wrote it involuntarily, and* '"*without comprehending it himself.*"

'As to the impossibility of taking from Tasso with-'out disarranging the poem, &c., I dare say 'tis not one 'whit more justly said of his, than of any other narrative 'poem. *Mais, n' importe,* 'tis sufficient if Rousseau 'believed this. I found the stanza in question; admire 'its meaning beauty.

'I hope you have Italian enough to appreciate the sin-'gular perfection in expression. If not, look to Fairfax's 'Jerusalem Delivered, Canto 12, Stanza 77; but Rous-'seau says these lines have no connection with what goes 'before, or after; *they are preceded,* stanza 76, by these 'three lines, which he does not think fit to mention.'

* * * * *

"Misero mostro d'infelice amore ;
Misero mostro a cui sol pena è degna
Dell' immensa impietà, la vita indegna."

"Vivrò fra i miei tormenti e fra le cure,
Mie giuste furie, forsennato errante.
Paventerò l'ombre solinghe e scure,
Che l'primo error mi recheranno avante :

E del sol che scoprì le mie sventure,
A schivo ed in orrore avrò il sembiante.
Temerò me medesmo ; e da me stesso
Sempre fuggendo, avrò me sempre appresso."
LA GERUSALEMME LIBERATA, C. XII. 76, 77.

TO R. W. E.

'*Dec.* 12, 1843. — When Goethe received a letter from 'Zelter, with a handsome superscription, he said, "Lay '"that aside; it is Zelter's true hand-writing. Every '"man has a dæmon, who is busy to confuse and limit '"his life. No way is the action of this power more '"clearly shown, than in the hand-writing. On this '"occasion, the evil influences have been evaded; the '"mood, the hand, the pen and paper have conspired to '"let our friend write truly himself."

'You may perceive, I quote from memory, as the sen- 'tences are anything but Goethean; but I think often of 'this little passage. With me, for weeks and months, 'the dæmon works his will. Nothing succeeds with me. 'I fall ill, or am otherwise interrupted. At these times, 'whether of frost, or sultry weather, I would gladly 'neither plant nor reap,— wait for the better times, which 'sometimes come, when I forget that sickness is ever 'possible; when all interruptions are upborne like 'straws on the full stream of my life, and the words 'that accompany it are as much in harmony as sedges 'murmuring near the bank. Not all, yet not unlike. 'But it often happens, that something presents itself, 'and must be done, in the bad time; nothing presents 'itself in the good: so I, like the others, seem worse 'and poorer than I am.'

In another letter to an earlier friend, she expatiates a little.

'As to the Dæmoniacal, I know not that I can say to 'you anything more precise than you find from Goethe. 'There are no precise terms for such thoughts. The 'word *instinctive* indicates their existence. I intimated 'it in the little piece on the Drachenfels. It may be 'best understood, perhaps, by a symbol. As the sun 'shines from the serene heavens, dispelling noxious 'exhalations, and calling forth exquisite thoughts on the 'surface of earth in the shape of shrub or flower, so 'gnome-like works the fire within the hidden caverns 'and secret veins of earth, fashioning existences which 'have a longer share in time, perhaps, because they are 'not immortal in thought. Love, beauty, wisdom, good-'ness are intelligent, but this power moves only to seize 'its prey. It is not necessarily either malignant or the 'reverse, but it has no scope beyond demonstrating its 'existence. When conscious, self-asserting, it becomes '(as power working for its own sake, unwilling to 'acknowledge love for its superior, must) the devil. 'That is the legend of Lucifer, the star that would 'not own its centre. Yet, while it is unconscious, it is 'not devilish, only dæmoniac. In nature, we trace it in 'all volcanic workings, in a boding position of lights, in 'whispers of the wind, which has no pedigree; in 'deceitful invitations of the water, in the sullen rock, 'which never shall find a voice, and in the shapes of 'all those beings who go about seeking what they may 'devour. We speak of a mystery, a dread; we shud-'der, but we approach still nearer, and a part of our 'nature listens, sometimes answers to this influence, 'which, if not indestructible, is at least indissolubly 'linked with the existence of matter.

'In genius, and in character, it works, as you say,

'instinctively; it refuses to be analyzed by the understanding, and is most of all inaccessible to the person 'who possesses it. We can only say, I have it, he has 'it. You have seen it often in the eyes of those Italian 'faces you like. It is most obvious in the eye. As we 'look on such eyes, we think on the tiger, the serpent, 'beings who lurk, glide, fascinate, mysteriously control. 'For it is occult by its nature, and if it could meet you 'on the highway, and be familiarly known as an 'acquaintance, could not exist. The angels of light 'do not love, yet they do not insist on exterminating it.

'It has given rise to the fables of wizard, enchantress, 'and the like; these beings are scarcely good, yet not 'necessarily bad. Power tempts them. They draw 'their skills from the dead, because their being is 'coeval with that of matter, and matter is the mother 'of death.'

In later days, she allowed herself sometimes to dwell sadly on the resistances which she called her fate, and remarked, that 'all life that has been or could 'be natural to me, is invariably denied.'

She wrote long afterwards: —

'My days at Milan were not unmarked. I have 'known some happy hours, but they all lead to sorrow, 'and not only the cups of wine, but of milk, seem 'drugged with poison, for me. It does not seem to be 'my fault, this destiny. I do not court these things, — 'they come. I am a poor magnet, with power to be 'wounded by the bodies I attract.'

TEMPERAMENT.

I said that Margaret had a broad good sense, which brought her near to all people. I am to say that she had also a strong temperament, which is that counter force which makes individuality, by driving all the powers in the direction of the ruling thought or feeling, and, when it is allowed full sway, isolating them. These two tendencies were always invading each other, and now one and now the other carried the day. This alternation perplexes the biographer, as it did the observer. We contradict on the second page what we affirm on the first: and I remember how often I was compelled to correct my impressions of her character when living; for after I had settled it once for all that she wanted this or that perception, at our next interview she would say with emphasis the very word.

I think, in her case, there was something abnormal in those obscure habits and necessities which we denote by the word Temperament. In the first days of our acquaintance, I felt her to be a foreigner, — that, with her, one would always be sensible of some barrier, as if in making up a friendship with a cultivated Spaniard or Turk. She had a strong constitution, and of course its reäctions were strong; and this is the reason why in all her life she has so much to say of her *fate*. She was in jubilant spirits in the morning, and ended the day with nervous headache, whose spasms, my wife told me, produced total prostration. She had great energy of speech and action, and seemed formed for high emergencies.

Her life concentrated itself on certain happy days,

happy hours, happy moments. The rest was a void. She had read that a man of letters must lose many days, to work well in one. Much more must a Sappho or a sibyl. The capacity of pleasure was balanced by the capacity of pain. 'If I had wist! —' she writes, 'I am a 'worse self-tormentor than Rousseau, and all my riches 'are fuel to the fire. My beautiful lore, like the tropic 'clime, hatches scorpions to sting me. There is a verse, 'which Annie of Lochroyan sings about her ring, that 'torments my memory, 't is so true of myself.'

When I found she lived at a rate so much faster than mine, and which was violent compared with mine, I foreboded rash and painful crises, and had a feeling as if a voice cried, *Stand from under!* — as if, a little further on, this destiny was threatened with jars and reverses, which no friendship could avert or console. This feeling partly wore off, on better acquaintance, but remained latent; and I had always an impression that her energy was too much a force of blood, and therefore never felt the security for her peace which belongs to more purely intellectual natures. She seemed more vulnerable. For the same reason, she remained inscrutable to me; her strength was not my strength, — her powers were a surprise. She passed into new states of great advance, but I understood these no better. It were long to tell her peculiarities. Her childhood was full of presentiments. She was then a somnambulist. She was subject to attacks of delirium, and, later, perceived that she had spectral illusions. When she was twelve, she had a determination of blood to the head. 'My parents,' she said, 'were much mortified to see the fineness of my 'complexion destroyed. My own vanity was for a time 'severely wounded; but I recovered, and made up my 'mind to be bright and ugly.'

She was all her lifetime the victim of disease and pain. She read and wrote in bed, and believed that she could understand anything better when she was ill. Pain acted like a girdle, to give tension to her powers. A lady, who was with her one day during a terrible attack of nervous headache, which made Margaret totally helpless, assured me that Margaret was yet in the finest vein of humor, and kept those who were assisting her in a strange, painful excitement, between laughing and crying, by perpetual brilliant sallies. There were other peculiarities of habit and power. When she turned her head on one side, she alleged she had second sight, like St. Francis. These traits or predispositions made her a willing listener to all the uncertain science of mesmerism and its goblin brood, which have been rife in recent years.

She had a feeling that she ought to have been a man, and said of herself, 'A man's ambition with a woman's 'heart, is an evil lot.' In some verses which she wrote 'To the Moon,' occur these lines: —

> 'But if I steadfast gaze upon thy face,
> 'A human secret, like my own, I trace;
> 'For, through the woman's smile looks the male eye.'

And she found something of true portraiture in a disagreeable novel of Balzac's, "*Le Livre Mystique*," in which an equivocal figure exerts alternately a masculine and a feminine influence on the characters of the plot.

Of all this nocturnal element in her nature she was very conscious, and was disposed, of course, to give it

20

as fine names as it would carry, and to draw advantage from it. 'Attica,' she said to a friend, 'is your province, Thessaly is mine: Attica produced the marble 'wonders of the great geniuses; but Thessaly is the 'land of magic.'

'I have a great share of Typhon to the Osiris, wild 'rush and leap, blind force for the sake of force.'

'Dante, thou didst not describe, in all thy apartments 'of Inferno, this tremendous repression of an existence 'half unfolded; this swoon as the soul was ready to be 'born.'

'Every year I live, I dislike routine more and more, 'though I see that society rests on that, and other false'hoods. The more I screw myself down to hours, the 'more I become expert at giving out thought and life 'in regulated rations,—the more I weary of this world, 'and long to move upon the wing, without props and 'sedan chairs.'

TO R. W. E.

'*Dec.* 26, 1839.—If you could look into my mind 'just now, you would send far from you those who love 'and hate. I am on the Drachenfels, and cannot get 'off; it is one of my naughtiest moods. Last Sunday, 'I wrote a long letter, describing it in prose and verse, 'and I had twenty minds to send it you as a literary 'curiosity; then I thought, this might destroy relations, 'and I might not be able to be calm and chip marble 'with you any more, if I talked to you in magnetism 'and music; so I sealed and sent it in the due direction.

'I remember you say, that forlorn seasons often turn out the most profitable. Perhaps I shall find it so. 'I have been reading Plato all the week, because I 'could not write. I hoped to be tuned up thereby. I 'perceive, with gladness, a keener insight in myself, 'day by day; yet, after all, could not make a good 'statement this morning on the subject of beauty.'

She had, indeed, a rude strength, which, if it could have been supported by an equal health, would have given her the efficiency of the strongest men. As it was, she had great power of work. The account of her reading in Groton is at a rate like Gibbon's, and, later, that of her writing, considered with the fact that writing was not grateful to her, is incredible. She often proposed to her friends, in the progress of intimacy, to write every day. 'I think less than a daily offering of 'thought and feeling would not content me, so much 'seems to pass unspoken.' In Italy, she tells Madame Arconati, that she has 'more than a hundred correspondents;" and it was her habit there to devote one day of every week to those distant friends. The facility with which she assumed stints of literary labor, which veteran feeders of the press would shrink from,— assumed and performed, — when her friends were to be served, I have often observed with wonder, and with fear, when I considered the near extremes of ill-health, and the manner in which her life heaped itself in high and happy moments, which were avenged by lassitude and pain.

'As each task comes,' she said, 'I borrow a readiness 'from its aspect, as I always do brightness from the face 'of a friend. Yet, as soon as the hour is past, I sink.

I think most of her friends will remember to have felt, at one time or another, some uneasiness, as if this athletic soul craved a larger atmosphere than it found; as if she were ill-timed and mis-mated, and felt in herself a tide of life, which compared with the slow circulation of others as a torrent with a rill. She found no full expression of it but in music. Beethoven's Symphony was the only right thing the city of the Puritans had for her. Those to whom music has a representative value, affording them a stricter copy of their inward life than any other of the expressive arts, will, perhaps, enter into the spirit which dictated the following letter to her patron saint, on her return, one evening, from the Boston Academy of Music.

'TO BEETHOVEN.

'*Saturday Evening*, 25*th Nov.*, 1843.

'My only friend,

'How shall I thank thee for once more breaking the 'chains of my sorrowful slumber? My heart beats. I 'live again, for I feel that I am worthy audience for 'thee, and that my being would be reason enough for 'thine.

'Master, my eyes are always clear. I see that the 'universe is rich, if I am poor. I see the insignificance 'of my sorrows. In my will, I am not a captive; in my 'intellect, not a slave. Is it then my fault that the palsy 'of my affections benumbs my whole life?

'I know that the curse is but for the time. I know 'what the eternal justice promises. But on this one 'sphere, it is sad. Thou didst say, thou hadst no 'friend but thy art. But that one is enough. I have no art, in which to vent the swell of a soul as deep as thine, Beethoven, and of a kindred frame. Thou wilt not think me presumptuous in this saying, as another might. I have always known that thou wouldst welcome and know me, as would no other who ever 'lived upon the earth since its first creation.

'Thou wouldst forgive me, master, that I have not 'been true to my eventual destiny, and therefore have 'suffered on every side "the pangs of despised love." 'Thou didst the same; but thou didst borrow from 'those errors the inspiration of thy genius. Why is it 'not thus with me? Is it because, as a woman, I am 'bound by a physical law, which prevents the soul from 'manifesting itself? Sometimes the moon seems mock-'ingly to say so,—to say that I, too, shall not shine, 'unless I can find a sun. O, cold and barren moon, 'tell a different tale!

'But thou, oh blessed master! dost answer all my 'questions, and make it my privilege to be. Like a 'humble wife to the sage, or poet, it is my triumph that 'I can understand and cherish thee: like a mistress, I 'arm thee for the fight: like a young daughter, I ten-'derly bind thy wounds. Thou art to me beyond com-'pare, for thou art all I want. No heavenly sweetness 'of saint or martyr, no many-leaved Raphael, no golden 'Plato, is anything to me, compared with thee. The 'infinite Shakspeare, the stern Angelo, Dante,—bitter-'sweet like thee,—are no longer seen in thy presence. 'And, beside these names, there are none that could 'vibrate in thy crystal sphere. Thou hast all of them, 'and that ample surge of life besides, that great winged 'being which they only dreamed of. There is none 'greater than Shakspeare; he, too, is a god; but his 'creations are successive; thy *fiat* comprehends them 'all.

'Last summer, I met thy mood in nature, on those 'wide impassioned plains flower and crag-bestrown. 'There, the tide of emotion had rolled over, and left the 'vision of its smiles and sobs, as I saw to-night from 'thee.

'If thou wouldst take me wholly to thyself——! I am 'lost in this world, where I sometimes meet angels, but 'of a different star from mine. Even so does thy spirit 'plead with all spirits. But thou dost triumph and bring 'them all in.

'Master, I have this summer envied the oriole which 'had even a swinging nest in the high bough. I have 'envied the least flower that came to seed, though that 'seed were strown to the wind. But I envy none when 'I am with thee.'

SELF-ESTEEM.

Margaret at first astonished and repelled us by a complacency that seemed the most assured since the days of Scaliger. She spoke, in the quietest manner, of the girls she had formed, the young men who owed everything to her, the fine companions she had long ago exhausted In the coolest way, she said to her friends, 'I now know 'all the people worth knowing in America, and I find no 'intellect comparable to my own.' In vain, on one occasion, I professed my reverence for a youth of genius, and my curiosity in his future,—'O no, she was intimate 'with his mind,' and I 'spoiled him, by overrating him.' Meantime, we knew that she neither had seen, nor would see, his subtle superiorities.

I have heard, that from the beginning of her life, she idealized herself as a sovereign. She told —— she early saw herself to be intellectually superior to those around her, and that for years she dwelt upon the idea, until she believed that she was not her parents' child, but an European princess confided to their care. She remembered, that, when a little girl, she was walking one day under the apple trees with such an air and step, that her father pointed her out to her sister, saying, *Incedit regina*. And her letters sometimes convey these exultations, as the following, which was written to a lady, and which contained Margaret's translation of Goethe's "Prometheus."

'TO ——.

'1838. — Which of us has not felt the questionings 'expressed in this bold fragment? Does it not seem, 'were we gods, or could steal their fire, we would make 'men not only happier, but free, — glorious? Yes, my 'life is strange; thine is strange. We are, we shall be, 'in this life, mutilated beings, but there is in my bosom a 'faith, that I shall see the reason; a glory, that I can 'endure to be so imperfect; and a feeling, ever elastic, 'that fate and time shall have the shame and the blame, 'if I am mutilated. I will do all I can, — and, if one 'cannot succeed, there is a beauty in martyrdom.

'Your letters are excellent. I did not mean to check 'your writing, only I thought that you might wish a 'confidence that I must anticipate with a protest. But 'I take my natural position always: and the more I see, 'the more I feel that it is regal. Without throne, sceptre, 'or guards, still a queen.'

It is certain that Margaret occasionally let slip, with all the innocence imaginable, some phrase betraying the presence of a rather mountainous ME, in a way to surprise those who knew her good sense. She could say, as if she were stating a scientific fact, in enumerating the merits of somebody, 'He appreciates *me*.' There was something of hereditary organization in this, and something of unfavorable circumstance in the fact, that she had in early life no companion, and few afterwards, in her finer studies; but there was also an ebullient sense of power, which she felt to be in her, which as yet had found no right channels. I remember she once said to me, what I heard as a mere statement of fact, and nowise as unbecoming, that 'no man gave 'such invitation to her mind as to tempt her to a full 'expression; that she felt a power to enrich her thought 'with such wealth and variety of embellishment as 'would, no doubt, be tedious to such as she conversed 'with.'

Her impatience she expressed as she could. 'I feel 'within myself,' she said, 'an immense force, but I can- 'not bring it out. It may sound like a joke, but I do 'feel something corresponding to that tale of the Desti- 'nies falling in love with Hermes.'

In her journal, in the summer of 1844, she writes: — 'Mrs. Ware talked with me about education, — wilful 'education, — in which she is trying to get interested. I 'talk with a Goethean moderation on this subject, which 'rather surprises her and ——, who are nearer the 'entrance of the studio. I am really old on this subject. 'In near eight years' experience, I have learned as much 'as others would in eighty, from my great talent at 'explanation, tact in the use of means, and immediate 'and invariable power over the minds of my pupils. 'My wish has been, to purify my own conscience, when 'near them; give clear views of the aims of this life; 'show them where the magazines of knowledge lie; and 'leave the rest to themselves and the Spirit, who must 'teach and help them to self-impulse. I told Mrs. W. it 'was much if we did not injure them; if they were 'passing the time in a way that was *not bad*, so that 'good influences have a chance. Perhaps people in 'general must expect greater outward results, or they 'would feel no interest.'

Again: 'With the intellect I always have, always 'shall, overcome; but that is not the half of the work. 'The life, the life! O, my God! shall the life never be 'sweet?'

I have inquired diligently of those who saw her often, and in different companies, concerning her habitual tone, and something like this is the report: — In conversation, Margaret seldom, except as a special grace, admitted others upon an equal ground with herself. She was exceedingly tender, when she pleased to be, and most cherishing in her influence; but to elicit this tenderness, it was necessary to submit first to her personally. When a person was overwhelmed by her, and answered not a word, except, "Margaret, be merciful to me, a sinner," then her love and tenderness would come like a seraph's, and often an acknowledgment that she had been too harsh, and even a craving for pardon, with a humility, — which, perhaps, she had caught from the other. But her instinct was not humility, — that was always an afterthought.

This arrogant tone of her conversation, if it came to be the subject of comment, of course, she defended, and with such broad good nature, and on grounds of simple truth, as were not easy to set aside. She quoted from Manzoni's *Carmagnola*, the lines: —

> "Tolga il ciel che alcuno
> Piu altamente di me pensi ch'io stesso."

"God forbid that any one should conceive more highly of me than I myself." Meantime, the tone of her journals is humble, tearful, religious, and rises easily into prayer.

I am obliged to an ingenious correspondent for the substance of the following account of this idiosyncrasy: —

Margaret was one of the few persons who looked upon life as an art, and every person not merely as an artist, but as a work of art. She looked upon herself as a living statue, which should always stand on a polished pedestal, with right accessories, and under the most fitting lights. She would have been glad to have everybody so live and act. She was annoyed when they did not, and when they did not regard her from the point of view which alone did justice to her. No one could be more lenient in her judgments of those whom she saw to be living in this light. Their faults were to be held as "the disproportions of the ungrown giant." But the faults of persons who were unjustified by this ideal, were odious. Unhappily, her constitutional self-esteem sometimes blinded the eyes that should have seen that an idea lay at the bottom of some lives which she did not quite so readily comprehend as beauty; that truth had other manifestations than those which engaged her natural sympathies; that sometimes the soul illuminated only the smallest arc — of a circle so large that it was lost in the clouds of another world.

This apology reminds me of a little speech once made to her, at his own house, by Dr. Channing, who held her in the highest regard: "Miss Fuller, when I consider that you are and have all that Miss —— has so long wished for, and that you scorn her, and that she still admires you, — I think her place in heaven will be very high."

But qualities of this kind can only be truly described by the impression they make on the bystander; and it is certain that her friends excused in her, becaus she had a right to it, a tone which they would have reckoned intolerable in any other. Many years since, one of her earliest and fastest friends quoted Spenser's sonnet as accurately descriptive of Margaret: —

"Rudely thou wrongest my dear heart's desire,
In finding fault with her too portly pride;
The thing which I do most in her admire
Is of the world unworthy most envied.
For, in those lofty looks is close implied
Scorn of base things, disdain of foul dishonor,
Threatening rash eyes which gaze on her so wide
That loosely they ne dare to look upon her:
Such pride is praise, such portliness is honor,
That boldened innocence bears in her eyes;
And her fair countenance, like a goodly banner,
Spreads in defiance of all enemies.
Was never in this world aught worthy tried,
Without a spark of some self-pleasing pride."

BOOKS.

She had been early remarked for her sense and sprightliness, and for her skill in school exercises. Now she had added wide reading, and of the books most grateful to her. She had read the Italian poets by herself, and from sympathy. I said, that, by the leading part she naturally took, she had identified herself with all the elegant culture in this country. Almost every person who had any distinction for wit, or art, or scholarship, was known to her; and she was familiar with the leading books and topics. There is a kind of undulation in the popularity of the great writers, even of the first rank. We have seen a recent importance given to Behmen and Swedenborg; and Shakspeare has unquestionably gained with the present generation. It is distinctive, too, of the taste of the period,—the new vogue given to the genius of Dante. An edition of Cary's translation, reprinted in Boston, many years ago, was rapidly sold; and, for the last twenty years, all studious youths and maidens have been reading the Inferno. Margaret had very early found her way to Dante, and from a certain native preference which she felt or fancied for the Italian genius. The following letter. though of a later date, relates to these studies:—

TO R. W. E.

'*December*, 1842.—When you were here, you seemed 'to think I might perhaps have done something on the '*Vita Nuova;* and the next day I opened the book, and 'considered how I could do it. But you shall not expect 'that, either, for your present occasion. When I first 'mentioned it to you, it was only as a piece of Sunday 'work, which I thought of doing for you alone; and 'because it has never seemed to me you entered enough 'into the genius of the Italian to apprehend the mind, 'which has seemed so great to me, and a star unlike, if 'not higher than all the others in our sky. Else, I should 'have given you the original, rather than any version of 'mine. I intended to translate the poems, with which it 'is interspersed, into plain prose. Milnes and Longfellow 'have tried each their power at doing it in verse, and 'have done better, probably, than I could, yet not well. 'But this would not satisfy me for the public. Besides, 'the translating Dante is a piece of literary presumption, 'and challenges a criticism to which I am not sure that 'I am, as the Germans say, *gewachsen*. Italian, as well 'as German, I learned by myself, unassisted, except as 'to the pronunciation. I have never been brought into 'connection with minds trained to any severity in these 'kinds of elegant culture. I have used all the means 'within my reach, but my not going abroad is an 'insuperable defect in the technical part of my education. 'I was easily capable of attaining excellence, perhaps 'mastery, in the use of some implements. Now I know, 'at least, *what I do not know*, and I get along by never 'voluntarily going beyond my depth, and, when called 'on to do it, stating my incompetency. At moments 'when I feel tempted to regret that I could not follow out 'the plan I had marked for myself, and develop powers 'which are not usual here, I reflect, that if I had 'attained high finish and an easy range in these respects, 'I should not have been thrown back on my own 'resources, or known them as I do. But Lord Brougham 'should not translate Greek orations, nor a maid-of-all-'work attempt such a piece of delicate handling as to 'translate the *Vita Nuova*.'

Here is a letter, without date, to another correspondent:

'To-day, on reading over some of the sonnets of Michel Angelo, I felt them more than usual. I know not why I have not read them thus before, except that the beauty was pointed out to me at first by another, instead of my coming unexpectedly upon it of myself. All the 'great writers, all the persons who have been dear to 'me, I have found and chosen; they have not been pro'posed to me. My intimacy with them came upon me 'as natural eras, unexpected and thrice dear. Thus I 'have appreciated, but not been able to feel, Michel 'Angelo as a poet.

'It is a singular fact in my mental history, that, while 'I understand the principles and construction of language 'much better than formerly, I cannot read so well *les* '*langues méridionales*. I suppose it is that I am less '*méridionale* myself. I understand the genius of the 'north better than I did.'

Dante, Petrarca, Tasso, were her friends among the old poets, — for to Ariosto she assigned a far lower place, — Alfieri and Manzoni, among the new. But what was of still more import to her education, she had read German books, and, for the three years before I knew her, almost exclusively, — Lessing, Schiller, Richter, Tieck, Novalis, and, above all, GOETHE. It was very obvious, at the first intercourse with her, though her rich and busy mind never reproduced undigested reading, that the last writer, — food or poison, — the most powerful of all mental reagents, — the pivotal mind in modern literature, — for all before him are ancients, and all who have read him are moderns, — that this mind had been her teacher, and, of course, the place was filled, nor was there room for any other. She had that symptom which appears in all the students of Goethe,—an ill-dissembled contempt of all criticism on him which they hear from others, as if it were totally irrelevant; and they are themselves always preparing to say the right word, — a *prestige* which is allowed, of course, until they do speak: when they have delivered their volley, they pass, like their foregoers, to the rear.

The effect on Margaret was complete. She was perfectly timed to it. She found her moods met, her topics treated, the liberty of thought she loved, the same climate of mind. Of course, this book superseded all others, for the time, and tinged deeply all her thoughts. The religion, the science, the catholicism, the worship of art, the mysticism and dæmonology, and withal the clear recognition of moral distinctions as final and eternal, all charmed her; and Faust, and Tasso, and Mignon, and Makaria, and Iphigenia, became irresistible names. It was one of those agreeable historical coincidences, perhaps invariable, though not yet registered, the simultaneous appearance of a teacher and of pupils, between whom exists a strict affinity. Nowhere did Goethe find a braver, more intelligent, or more sympathetic reader. About the time I knew her, she was meditating a biography of Goethe, and did set herself to the task in 1837. She spent much time on it, and has left heaps of manuscripts, which are notes, transcripts, and studies in that direction. But she wanted leisure and health to finish it, amid the multitude of projected works with which her brain teemed. She used great discretion on this point, and made no promises. In 1839, she published her translation of Eckermann, a book which makes the basis of the translation of Eckermann since published in London, by Mr. Oxenford. In the Dial, in July, 1841, she wrote an article on Goethe, which is, on many accounts, her best paper.

CRITICISM.

Margaret was in the habit of sending to her correspondents, in lieu of letters, sheets of criticism on her recent readings. From such quite private folios, never intended for the press, and, indeed, containing here and there names and allusions, which it is now necessary to veil or suppress, I select the following notices, chiefly of French books. Most of these were addressed to me, but the three first to an earlier friend.

'Reading Schiller's introduction to the Wars of the 'League, I have been led back to my old friend, the 'Duke of Sully, and his charming king. He was a man, 'that Henri! How gay and graceful seems his unflinch-'ing frankness! He wore life as lightly as the feather 'in his cap. I have become much interested, too, in the 'two Guises, who had seemed to me mere intriguers, and 'not of so splendid abilities, when I was less able to 'appreciate the difficulties they daily and hourly com-'bated. I want to read some more books about them. 'Do you know whether I could get Matthieu, or de 'Thou, or the Memoirs of the House of Nevers?

'I do not think this is a respectable way of passing my 'summer, but I cannot help it.

'I never read any life of Molière. Are the facts very 'interesting? You see clearly in his writing what he 'was: a man not high, not poetic; but firm, wide, gen-'uine, whose clearsightedness only made him more noble. 'I love him well that he could see without showing those 'myriad mean faults of the social man, and yet make 'no nearer approach to misanthropy than his Alceste. 'These witty Frenchmen, Rabelais, Montaigne, Molière, 'are great as were their marshals and *preux chevaliers;* 'when the Frenchman tries to be poetical, he becomes 'theatrical, but he can be romantic, and also dignified, 'maugre shrugs and snuff-boxes.'

'*Thursday Evening.* — Although I have been much 'engaged these two days, I have read Spiridion twice. 'I could have wished to go through it the second time 'more at leisure, but as I am going away, I thought I 'would send it back, lest it should be wanted before my 'return.

'The development of the religious sentiment being 'the same as in Hélene, I at first missed the lyric 'effusion of that work, which seems to me more and 'more beautiful, as I think of it more. This, however, 'was a mere prejudice, of course, as the thought here is 'poured into a quite different mould, and I was not trou-'bled by it on a second reading.

'Again, when I came to look at the work by itself, I 'thought the attempt too bold. A piece of character 'painting does not seem to be the place for a statement 'of these wide and high subjects. For here the philos-'ophy is not merely implied in the poetry and religion, 'but assumes to show a face of its own. And, as none 'should meddle with these matters who are not in ear-'nest, so, such will prefer to find the thought of a teacher 'or fellow-disciple expressed as directly and as bare of 'ornament as possible.

'I was interested in De Wette's Theodor, and that learned and (*on dit*) profound man seemed to me so 'to fail, that I did not finish the book, nor try whether I 'could believe the novice should ever arrive at manly 'stature.

'I am not so clear as to the scope and bearing of this 'book, as of that. I suppose if I were to read Lamen-'nais, or L'Erminier, I should know what they all want 'or intend. And if you meet with *Les paroles d'un 'Croyant*, I will beg you to get it for me, for I am more 'curious than ever. I had supposed the view taken 'by these persons in France, to be the same with that 'of Novalis and the German Catholics, in which I have 'been deeply interested. But from this book, it would 'seem to approach the faith of some of my friends here, 'which has been styled Psychotheism. And the gap in 'the theoretical fabric is the same as with them. I read 'with unutterable interest the despair of Alexis in his 'Eclectic course, his return to the teachings of external 'nature, his new birth, and consequent appreciation of 'poetry and music. But the question of Free Will, — 'how to reconcile its workings with necessity and com-'pensation, — how to reconcile the life of the heart with 'that of the intellect, — how to listen to the whispering 'breeze of Spirit, while breasting, as a man should, the 'surges of the world, — these enigmas Sand and her 'friends seem to have solved no better than M. F. and 'her friends.

'The practical optimism is much the same as ours, 'except that there is more hope for the masses — soon.

'This work is written with great vigor, scarce any 'faltering on the wing. The horrors are disgusting, as 'are those of every writer except Dante. Even genius 'should content itself in dipping the pencil in cloud and mist. The apparitions of Spiridion are managed with great beauty. As in Hélene, as in Novalis, I recog'nized, with delight, the eye that gazed, the ear that 'listened, till the spectres came, as they do to the High'lander on his rocky couch, to the German peasant on 'his mountain. How different from the vulgar eye 'which looks, but never sees! Here the beautiful 'apparition advances from the solar ray, or returns 'to the fountain of light and truth, as it should, when 'eagle eyes are gazing.

'I am astonished at her insight into the life of thought. 'She must know it through some man. Women, under 'any circumstances, can scarce do more than dip the 'foot in this broad and deep river; they have not 'strength to contend with the current. Brave, if they 'do not delicately shrink from the cold water. No 'Sibyls have existed like those of Michel Angelo; those 'of Raphael are the true brides of a God, but not 'themselves divine. It is easy for women to be heroic 'in action, but when it comes to interrogating God, the 'universe, the soul, and, above all, trying to live above 'their own hearts, they dart down to their nests like 'so many larks, and, if they cannot find them, fret 'like the French Corinne. Goethe's Makaria was born 'of the stars. Mr. Flint's Platonic old lady a *lusus* '*naturæ*, and the Dudevant has loved a philosopher.

'I suppose the view of the present state of Catholicism 'no way exaggerated. Alexis is no more persecuted 'than Abelard was, and is so, for the same reasons. From the examinations of the Italian convents in 'Leopold's time, it seems that the grossest materialism 'not only reigns, but is taught and professed in them. 'And Catholicism loads and infects as all dead forms 'do, however beautiful and noble during their lives.' * *

GEORGE SAND, AGAIN.

'1839.—When I first knew George Sand, I thought 'I found tried the experiment I wanted. I did not 'value Bettine so much; she had not pride enough 'for me; only now when I am sure of myself, would 'I pour out my soul at the feet of another. In the 'assured soul it is kingly prodigality; in one which 'cannot forbear, it is mere babyhood. I love *abandon* 'only when natures are capable of the extreme reverse. 'I knew Bettine would end in nothing, when I read her 'book. I knew she could not outlive her love.

'But in *Les Sept Cordes de la Lyre*, which I read first, 'I saw the knowledge of the passions, and of social 'institutions, with the celestial choice which rose above 'them. I loved Hélene, who could so well hear the ter-'rene voices, yet keep her eye fixed on the stars. That 'would be my wish, also, to know all, then choose; I 'ever revered her, for I was not sure that I could have 'resisted the call of the Now, could have left the spirit, 'and gone to God. And, at a more ambitious age, I could 'not have refused the philosopher. But I hoped from 'her steadfastness, and I thought I heard the last tones 'of a purified life:—Gretchen, in the golden cloud, raised 'above all past delusions, worthy to redeem and upbear 'the wise man, who stumbled into the pit of error while 'searching for truth.

'Still, in *André* and in *Jacques*, I traced the same high 'morality of one who had tried the liberty of circum-stance only to learn to appreciate the liberty of law, 'to know that license is the foe of freedom. And, though the sophistry of passion in these books disgusted me, flowers of purest hue seemed to grow upon the 'dank and dirty ground. I thought she had cast aside 'the slough of her past life, and began a new existence 'beneath the sun of a true Ideal.

'But here (in the *Lettres d'un Voyageur*) what do I 'see? An unfortunate bewailing her loneliness, bewailing 'her mistakes, writing for money! She has genius, and 'a manly grasp of mind, but not a manly heart! Will 'there never be a being to combine a man's mind and 'woman's heart, and who yet finds life too rich to weep 'over? Never?

'When I read in *Leone Lioni* the account of the jew-'eller's daughter's life with her mother, passed in dress 'and in learning to be looked at when dressed, *avec un* '*front impassible*, it reminded me exceedingly of ——, 'and her mother. What a heroine she would be for 'Sand! She has the same fearless softness with Juliet, 'and a sportive *naïveté*, a mixture of bird and kitten, 'unknown to the dupe of Lioni.

'If I were a man, and wished a wife, as many do, 'merely as an ornament, or silken toy, I would take '—— as soon as any I know. Her fantastic, impas-'sioned, and mutable nature would yield an inex-'haustible amusement. She is capable of the most 'romantic actions; — wild as the falcon, and voluptuous 'as the tuberose, — yet she has not in her the elements 'of romance, like a deeper and less susceptible nature. 'My cold and reasoning E., with her one love lying, 'perhaps, never to be unfolded, beneath such sheaths 'of pride and reserve, would make a far better heroine.

'Both these characters are natural, while S. and T. are '*naturally factitious*, because so imitative, and her mother 'differs from Juliet and her mother, by the impulse a sin-gle strong character gave them. Even at this distance of time, there is a slight but perceptible taste of iron 'in the water.

'George Sand disappoints me, as almost all beings 'have, especially since I have been brought close to her 'person by the *Lettres d'un Voyageur.* Her remarks 'on Lavater seem really shallow, and hasty, *à la mode* '*du genre feménin.* No self-ruling Aspasia she, but 'a frail woman mourning over a lot. Any peculiarity 'in her destiny seems accidental. She is forced to 'this and that, to earn her bread forsooth!

'Yet her style, — with what a deeply smouldering 'fire it burns! — not vehement, but intense, like Jean 'Jacques.'

ALFRED DE VIGNY.

'*Sept.*, 1839.

'"La harpe tremble encore, et la flûte soupire."

'Sometimes we doubt this, and think the music has 'finally ceased, so sultry still lies the air around us, or 'only disturbed by the fife and drum of talent, calling to 'the parade-ground of social life. The ear grows dull.

'"Faith asks her daily bread,
And Fancy is no longer fed."

'So materialistic is the course of common life, that 'we *ask daily* new Messiahs from literature and art, 'to turn us from the Pharisaic observance of law, to 'the baptism of spirit. But stars arise upon our murky 'sky, and the flute *soupire* from the quarter where we least expect it.

'*La jeune France!* I had not believed in this youth-'ful pretender. I thought she had no pure blood in her 'veins, no aristocratic features in her face, no natural grace in her gait. I thought her an illegitimate child of the generous, but extravagant youth of Ger-'many. I thought she had been left at the foundling 'hospital, as not worth a parent's care, and that now, 'grown up, she was trying to prove at once her parent-'age and her charms by certificates which might be 'headed, Innocent Adultery, Celestial Crime, &c.

'The slight acquaintance I had with Hugo, and com-'pany, did not dispel these impressions. And I thought 'Chateaubriand (far too French for my taste also,) 'belonged to *l'ancien régime,* and that Béranger and 'Courier stood apart. Nodier, Paul de Kock, Sue, Jules 'Janin, I did not know, except through the absurd 'reports of English reviewers; Le Maistre and Lamen-'nais, as little.

'But I have now got a peep at this galaxy. I begin to 'divine the meaning of St. Simonianism, Cousinism, and 'the movement which the same causes have produced in 'belles-lettres. I perceive that *la jeune France* is the 'legitimate, though far younger sister of Germany; 'taught by her, but not born of her, but of a common 'mother. I see, at least begin to see, what she has 'learned from England, and what the bloody rain of the 'revolution has done to fertilize her soil, naturally too 'light.

'Blessed be the early days when I sat at the feet of 'Rousseau, prophet sad and stately as any of Jewry! 'Every onward movement of the age, every downward 'step into the solemn depths of my own soul, recalls thy 'oracles, O Jean Jacques! But as these things only 'glimmer upon me at present, clouds of rose and amber, 'in the perspective of a long, dim woodland glade, which 'I must traverse if I would get a fair look at them from 'the hill-top, — as I cannot, to say sooth, get the works of 'these always working geniuses, but by slow degrees, in 'a country that has no need of them till her railroads 'and canals are finished,—I need not jot down my petty 'impressions of the movement writers. I wish to speak 'of one among them, aided, honored by thēm, but not 'of them. He is to *la jeune France* rather the herald of 'a tourney, or the master of ceremonies at a patriotic 'festival, than a warrior for her battles, or an advocate 'to win her cause.

'The works of M. de Vigny having come in my way, 'I have read quite through this thick volume.

'I read, a year since, in the London and Westminster, 'an admirable sketch of Armand Carrel. The writer 'speaks particularly of the use of which Carrel's expe-'rience of practical life had been to him as an author; 'how it had tempered and sharpened the blade of his 'intellect to the Damascene perfection. It has been of 'like use to de Vigny, though not in equal degree.

'De Vigny *passed*,—but for manly steadfastness, he 'would probably say *wasted*,—his best years in the army. 'He is now about forty; and we have in this book the 'flower of these best years. It is a night-blooming 'Cereus, for his days were passed in the duties of his 'profession. These duties, so tiresome and unprofitable 'in time of peace, were the ground in which the seed 'sprang up, which produced these many-leaved and calm 'night-flowers.

'The first portion of this volume, *Servitude et Gran-'deurs Militaires*, contains an account of the way in 'which he received his false tendency. Cherished on 'the "wounded knees" of his aged father, he listened to tales of the great Frederic, whom the veteran had 'known personally. After an excellent sketch of the king, he says: "I expatiate here, almost in spite of "myself, because this was the first great man whose '"portrait was thus drawn for me at home, — a portrait '"after nature, — and because my admiration of him was '"the first symptom of my useless love of arms, — the '"first cause of one of the most complete delusions of '"my life." This admiration for the great king remained 'so lively in his mind, that even Bonaparte in his ges'tures seemed to him, in later days, a plagiarist.

'At the military school, "the drum stifled the voices '"of our masters, and the mysterious voices of books '"seemed to us cold and pedantic. Tropes and loga'"rithms seemed to us only steps to mount to the star '"of the Legion of Honor, — the fairest star of heaven '"to us children.

'"No meditation could keep long in chains heads made '"constantly giddy by the noise of cannon and bells for '"the *Te Deum*. When one of our former comrades '"returned to pay us a visit in uniform, and his arm in a '"scarf, we blushed at our books, and threw them at the '"heads of our teachers. Our teachers were always '"reading us bulletins from the *grande armée*, and our '"cries of *Vive l'Empereur* interrupted Tacitus and '"Plato. Our preceptors resembled heralds of arms, our '"study halls barracks, and our examinations reviews."

'Thus was he led into the army; and, he says, "It '"was only very late, that I perceived that my services '"were one long mistake, and that I had imported into '"a life altogether active, a nature altogether contem'"plative."

'He entered the army at the time of Napoleon's fall, 'and, like others, wasted life in waiting for war. For 'these young persons could not believe that peace and 'calm were possible to France; could not believe that 'she could lead any life but one of conquest.

'As De Vigny was gradually undeceived, he says: '"Loaded with an ennui which I did not dream of in a '"life I had so ardently desired, it became a necessity to '"me to detach myself by night from the vain and tire- '"some tumult of military days. From these nights, in '"which I enlarged in silence the knowledge I had '"acquired from our public and tumultuous studies, '"proceeded my poems and books. From these days, '"there remain to me these recollections, whose chief '"traits I here assemble around one idea. For, not '"reckoning for the glory of arms, either on the present '"or future, I sought it in the souvenirs of my comrades. '"My own little adventures will not serve, except as '"frame to those pictures of the military life, and of the '"manners of our armies, all whose traits are by no '"means known."

'And thus springs up, in the most natural manner, 'this little book on the army.

'It has the truth, the delicacy, and the healthiness of a 'production native to the soil; the merit of love-letters, 'journals, lyric poems, &c., written without any formal 'intention of turning life into a book, but because the 'writer could not help it. What, more than anything 'else, engaged the attention of De Vigny, was the false 'position of two beings towards a factitious society: 'the soldier, now that standing armies are the mode, 'and the poet, now that Olympic games or pastimes are 'not the mode. He has treated the first best, because 'with profounder *connoissance du fait.* For De Vigny is not a poet; he has only an eye to perceive the existence of these birds of heaven. But in few ways, except 'their own broken harp-tone's thrill, have their peculiar 'sorrows and difficulties been so well illustrated. The 'character of the soldier, with its virtues and faults, is 'portrayed with such delicacy, that to condense would 'ruin. The peculiar reserve, the habit of duty, the 'beauty of a character which cannot look forward, and 'need not look back, are given with distinguished finesse.

'Of the three stories which adorn this part of the book, '*Le Cachet Rouge* is the loveliest, *La Canne au Jonc* 'the noblest. Never was anything more sweetly naïve 'than parts 'of *Le Cachet Rouge. La pauvre petite* '*femme*, she was just such a person as my ——. And 'then the farewell injunctions,— *du pauvre petite maré*, '— the nobleness and the coarseness of the poor captain. 'It is as original as beautiful, *c'est dire beaucoup*. In *La* '*Canne au Jonc*, Collingwood, who embodies the high 'feeling of duty, is taken too raw out of a book,—his 'letters to his daughters. But the effect on the character 'of *le Capitaine Renaud*, and the unfolding of his interior 'life, are done with the spiritual beauty of Manzoni.

'*Cinq-Mars* is a romance in the style of Walter Scott. 'It is well brought out, figures in good relief, lights well 'distributed, sentiment high, but nowhere exaggerated, 'knowledge exact, and the good and bad of human 'nature painted with that impartiality which becomes a 'man, and a man of the world. All right, no failure 'anywhere; also, no wonderful success, no genius, no 'magic. It is one of those works which I should con- 'sider only excusable as the amusement of leisure hours; 'and, though few could write it, chiefly valuable to the 'writer.

'Here he has arranged, as in a bouquet, what he knew, — and a great deal it is,—of the time of Louis XIII., 'as he has of the Regency in "La Marechale d'Ancre," '— a much finer work, indeed one of the best-arranged 'and finished modern dramas. The Leonora Galigai is 'better than anything I have seen in Victor Hugo, and 'as good as Schiller. Stello is a bolder attempt. It is 'the history of three poets, — Gilbert, André Chenier, 'Chatterton. He has also written a drama called Chat-'terton, inferior to the story here. The "marvellous '"boy" seems to have captivated his imagination mar-'vellously. In thought, these productions are worthless; 'for taste, beauty of sentiment, and power of description, 'remarkable. His advocacy of the poets' cause is about 'as effective and well-planned as Don Quixote's tourney 'with the wind-mill. How would you provide for the 'poet *bon homme* De Vigny? — from a joint-stock com-'pany Poet's Fund, or how?

'His translation of Othello, which I glanced at, is good 'for a Frenchman.

'Among his poems, La Frégate, La Sérieuse, Madame 'de Soubise, and Dolorida, please me especially. The 'last has an elegiac sweetness and finish, which are 'rare. It also makes a perfect gem of a cabinet picture. 'Some have a fine strain of natural melody, and give 'you at once the key-note of the situation, as this: —

'"J'aime le son du cor le soir, au fond des bois,
Soit qu'il chante," &c.

And

'"Qu'il est doux, qu'il est doux d'ecouter les histoires
Des histoires du temps passé
Quand les branches des arbres sont noires,
Quand la neige est essaisse, et charge un sol glacé,
Quand seul dans un ciel pâle un peuplier s'élance,
Quand sous le manteau blanc qui vient de le cacher

L'immobile corbeau sur l'arbre se balance
Comme la girouette au bout du long clocher."

'These poems generally are only interesting as the 'leisure hours of an interesting man.

'De Vigny writes in an excellent style; soft, fresh, 'deliberately graceful. Such a style is like fine manners; you think of the words select, appropriate, rather than 'distinguished, or beautiful. De Vigny is a perfect gen-'tleman; and his refinement is rather that of the gentle-'man than that of the poets whom he is so full of. In 'character, he looks naturally at those things which 'interest the man of honor and the man of taste. But 'for literature, he would have known nothing about the 'poets. He should be the elegant and instructive com-'panion of social, not the priest or the minstrel of solitary 'hours.

'Neither has he logic or grasp with his reasoning 'powers, though of this, also, he is ambitious. Observa-'tion is his forte. To see, and to tell with grace, often 'with dignity and pathos, what he sees, is his proper 'vocation. Yet, where he fails, he has too much tact 'and modesty to be despised; and we cannot enough 'admire the absence of faults in a man whose ambition 'soared so much beyond his powers, and in an age and 'a country so full of false taste. He is never seduced 'into sentimentality, paradox, violent contrast, and, above 'all, never makes the mistake of confounding the horri-'ble with the sublime. Above all, he never falls into the 'error, common to merely elegant minds, of painting 'leading minds "*en gigantesque.*" His Richelieu and 'his Bonaparte are treated with great calmness, and 'with dignified ease, almost as beautiful as majestic 'superiority.

'In this volume is contained all that is on record of 'the inner life of a man of forty years. How many 'suns, how many rains and dews, to produce a few buds 'and flowers, some sweet, but not rich fruit! We can-'not help demanding of the man of talent that he should 'be like "the orange tree, that busy plant." But, as 'Landor says, "He who has any thoughts of any worth '"can, and probably will, afford to let the greater part '"lie fallow."

'I have not made a note upon De Vigny's notions of 'abnegation, which he repeats as often as Dr. Channing 'the same watch-word of self-sacrifice. It is that my 'views are not yet matured, and I can have no judg-'ment on the point.'

BÉRANGER.

'*Sept.*, 1839.—I have lately been reading some of 'Béranger's *chansons.* The hour was not propitious. 'I was in a mood the very reverse of Roger Bontemps, 'and beset with circumstances the most unsuited to 'make me sympathize with the prayer—

> '"Pardonnez la gaieté
> De ma philosophie ;"

'yet I am not quite insensible to their wit, high senti-'ment, and spontaneous grace. A wit that sparkles all 'over the ocean of life, a sentiment that never puts the 'best foot forward, but prefers the tone of delicate 'humor, to the mouthings of tragedy; a grace so aerial, 'that it nowhere requires the aid of a thought, for in the light refrains of these productions, the meaning is 'felt as much as in the most pointed lines. Thus, in '"Les Mirmidons," the refrain —

'"Mirmidons, race féconde,
Mirmidons
Enfin nous commandons,
Jupiter livre le monde,
Aux mirmidons, aux mirmidons, (bis,)"

'The swarming of the insects about the dead lion is 'expressed as forcibly as in the most sarcastic passage 'of the chanson. In "La Faridondaine" every sound 'is a witticism, and levels to the ground a bevy of what 'Byron calls "garrison people." "Halte là! ou la sys-'"tème des interpretations" is equally witty, though 'there the form seems to be as much in the saying, 'as in the comic melody of sound.

'In "Adieux à la Campagne," "Souvenirs du Peu-'"ple," "La Déesse de la Liberté," "La Convoi '"de David," a melancholy pathos breathes, which 'touches the heart the more that it is so unpretend-'ing. "Ce n'est plus Lisette," "Mon Habit," "L'In-'"dépendant," "Vous vieillirez, O ma belle Maitresse," a 'gentle graceful sadness wins us. In "Le Dieu des '"Bonnes Gens," "Les Etoiles qui filent," "Les Con-'"seils de Lise," "Treize à Table," a noble dignity is 'admired, while such as "La Fortune" and "La Mé-'"tempsycose" are inimitable in their childlike play-'fulness. "Ma Vocation" I have had and admired for 'many years. He is of the pure ore, a darling fairy 'changling of great mother Nature; the poet of the 'people, and, therefore, of all in the upper classes suffi-ciently intelligent and refined to appreciate the wit and 'sentiment of the people. But his wit is so truly French 'in its lightness and sparkling, feathering vivacity, that 'one like me, accustomed to the bitterness of English 'tonics, suicidal November melancholy, and Byronic 'wrath of satire, cannot appreciate him at once. But 'when used to the gentler stimuli, we like them best, 'and we also would live awhile in the atmosphere of 'music and mirth, content if we have "bread for to-'"day, and hope for to-morrow."

'There are fine lines in his "Cinq Mai;" the sen-'timent is as grand as Manzoni's, though not sustained 'by the same majestic sweep of diction, as, —

'"Ce rocher repousse l'espérance,
L'Aigle n'est plus dans le secret des dieux,
Il fatiguait la victoire à le suivre,
Elle était lasse : il ne l'attendit pas."

'And from "La Gérontocratie, ou les infiniment petits:"

'"Combien d'imperceptibles êtres,
De petits jésuites bilieux!
De milliers d'autres petits prêtres,
Lui portent de petits bons dieux."

'But wit, poet, man of honor, tailor's grandson and 'fairy's favorite, he must speak for himself, and the best 'that can be felt or thought of him cannot be said in 'the way of criticism. I will copy and keep a few of 'his songs. I should like to keep the whole collection 'by me, and take it up when my faith in human nature 'required the gentlest of fortifying draughts.

'How fine his answer to those who asked about the '"de" before his name! —

'"Je suis vilain,
Vilain, vilain," &c.

'"J' honore une race commune,
Car, sensible, quoique malin,
Je n'ai flatté que l'infortune."

'In a note to "Couplets on M. Laisney, *imprimeur à* '"*Peronne*," he says: "It was in his printing-house '"that I was put to prentice; not having been able to '"learn orthography, he imparted to me the taste for '"poetry, gave me lessons in versification, and corrected '"my first essays."'

'Of Bonaparte,—

'"Un conquérant, dans sa fortune altière,
Se fit un jeu des sceptres et des lois,
Et de ses pieds on peut voir la poussière
Empreinte encore sur le bandeau des rois."

'I admire, also, "Le Violon brisé," for its grace and 'sweetness. How fine Béranger on Waterloo!—

'"Its name shall never sadden verse of mine."'

TO R. W. E.

'*Niagara*, 1*st June*, 1843.—I send you a token, made 'by the hands of some Seneca Indian lady. If you use 'it for a watch-pocket, hang it, when you travel, at the 'head of your bed, and you may dream of Niagara. If 'you use it for a purse, you can put in it alms for poets 'and artists, and the subscription-money you receive for 'Mr. Carlyle's book. His book, as it happened, you 'gave me as a birthday gift, and you may take this as 'one to you; for, on yours, was W.'s birthday, J.'s wed-'ding-day, and the day of ——'s death, and we set out 'on this journey. Perhaps there is something about it 'on the purse. The "number five which nature loves," is repeated on it.

'Carlyle's book I have, in some sense, read. It is 'witty, full of pictures, as usual. I would have gone 'through with it, if only for the sketch of Samson, and 'two or three bits of fun which happen to please me. 'No doubt it may be of use to rouse the unthinking to a 'sense of those great dangers and sorrows. But how 'open is he to his own assault. He rails himself out of 'breath at the short-sighted, and yet sees scarce a step 'before him. There is no valuable doctrine in his book, 'except the Goethean, *Do to-day the nearest duty.* Many 'are ready for that, could they but find the way. This 'he does not show. His proposed measures say noth-'ing. Educate the people. That cannot be done by 'books, or voluntary effort, under these paralyzing cir-'cumstances. Emigration! According to his own esti-'mate of the increase of population, relief that way can 'have very slight effect. He ends as he began; as he did 'in Chartism. Everything is very bad. You are fools 'and hypocrites, or you would make it better. I cannot 'but sympathize with him about hero-worship; for I, 'too, have had my fits of rage at the stupid irreverence 'of little minds, which also is made a parade of by the 'pedantic and the worldly. Yet it is a good sign. Democ-'racy is the way to the new aristocracy, as irreligion to 'religion. By and by, if there are great men, they will 'not be brilliant exceptions, redeemers, but favorable 'samples of their kind.

'Mr. C.'s tone is no better than before. He is not 'loving, nor large; but he seems more healthy and 'gay.

'We have had bad weather here, bitterly cold. The place is what I expected: it is too great and beautiful 'to agitate or surprise: it satisfies: it does not excite 'thought, but fully occupies. All is calm; even the rap-'ids do not hurry, as we see them in smaller streams. 'The sound, the sight, fill the senses and the mind.

'At Buffalo, some ladies called on us, who extremely 'regretted they could not witness our emotions, on first 'seeing Niagara. "Many," they said, "burst into tears; '"but with those of most sensibility, the hands become '"cold as ice, and they would not mind if buckets of '"cold water were thrown over them!"'

NATURE.

Margaret's love of beauty made her, of course, a votary of nature, but rather for pleasurable excitement than with a deep poetic feeling. Her imperfect vision and her bad health were serious impediments to intimacy with woods and rivers. She had never paid, — and it is a little remarkable, — any attention to natural sciences. She neither botanized, nor geologized, nor dissected. Still she delighted in short country rambles, in the varieties of landscape, in pastoral country, in mountain outlines, and, above all, in the sea-shore. At Nantasket Beach, and at Newport, she spent a month or two of many successive summers. She paid homage to rocks, woods, flowers, rivers, and the moon. She spent a good deal of time out of doors, sitting, perhaps, with a book in some sheltered recess commanding a landscape. She watched, by day and by night, the skies and the earth, and believed she knew all their expressions. She wrote in her journal, or in her correspondence, a series of "moonlights," in which she seriously attempts to describe the light and scenery of successive nights of the summer moon. Of course, her raptures must appear sickly and superficial to an observer, who, with equal feeling, had better powers of observation.

Nothing is more rare than a talent to describe landscape, and, especially, skyscape, or cloudscape, although a vast number of letters, from correspondents between the ages of twenty and thirty, are filled with experiments in this kind. Margaret, in her turn, made many vain attempts, and, to a lover of nature, who knows that every day has new and inimitable lights and shades, one of these descriptions is as vapid as the raptures of a citizen arrived at his first meadow. Of course, he is charmed, but, of course, he cannot tell what he sees, or what pleases him. Yet Margaret often speaks with a certain tenderness and beauty of the impressions made upon her.

TO ——.

'*Fishkill*, 25 *Nov.*, 1844.—You would have been 'happy as I have been in the company of the mountains. 'They are companions both bold and calm. They 'exhilarate and they satisfy. To live, too, on the bank 'of the great river so long, has been the realization of a 'dream. Though I have been reading and thinking, yet 'this has been my life.'

'After they were all in bed,' she writes from the "Manse," in Concord, 'I went out, and walked till near 'twelve. The moonlight filled my heart. These embow-'ering elms stood in solemn black, the praying monastics 'of this holy night; full of grace, in every sense; their 'life so full, so hushed; not a leaf stirred.'

'You say that nature does not keep her promise; but, 'surely, she satisfies us now and then for the time. 'The drama is always in progress, but here and there 'she speaks out a sentence, full in its cadence, complete 'in its structure; it occupies, for the time, the sense and 'the thought. We have no care for promises. Will you 'say it is the superficialness of my life, that I have known 'hours with men and nature, that bore their proper fruit, '— all present ate and were filled, and there were taken 'up of the fragments twelve baskets full? Is it because 'of the superficial mind, or the believing heart, that I can 'say this?'

'Only through emotion do we know thee, Nature! We 'lean upon thy breast, and feel its pulses vibrate to our 'own. That is knowledge, for that is love. Thought 'will never reach it.'

ART.

There are persons to whom a gallery is everywhere a nome. In this country, the antique is known only by plaster casts, and by drawings. The BOSTON ATHENÆUM, — on whose sunny roof and beautiful chambers may the benediction of centuries of students rest with mine! — added to its library, in 1823, a small, but excellent museum of the antique sculpture, in plaster; — the selection being dictated, it is said, by no less an adviser than Canova. The Apollo, the Laocoon, the Venuses, Diana, the head of the Phidian Jove, Bacchus, Antinous, the Torso Hercules, the Discobolus, the Gladiator Borghese, the Apollino, — all these, and more, the sumptuous gift of Augustus Thorndike. It is much that one man should have power to confer on so many, who never saw him, a benefit so pure and enduring.

To these were soon added a heroic line of antique

busts, and, at last, by Horatio Greenough, the Night and Day of Michel Angelo. Here was old Greece and old Italy brought bodily to New England, and a verification given to all our dreams and readings. It was easy to collect, from the drawing-rooms of the city, a respectable picture-gallery for a summer exhibition. This was also done, and a new pleasure was invented for the studious, and a new home for the solitary. The Brimmer donation, in 1838, added a costly series of engravings, chiefly of the French and Italian museums, and the drawings of Guercino, Salvator Rosa, and other masters. The separate chamber in which these collections were at first contained, made a favorite place of meeting for Margaret and a few of her friends, who were lovers of these works.

First led perhaps by Goethe, afterwards by the love she herself conceived for them, she read everything that related to Michel Angelo and Raphael. She read, pen in hand, Quatremère de Quincy's lives of those two painters, and I have her transcripts and commentary before me. She read Condivi, Vasari, Benvenuto Cellini, Duppa, Fuseli, and Von Waagen, — great and small. Every design of Michel, the four volumes of Raphael's designs, were in the rich portfolios of her most intimate friend. 'I have been very happy,' she writes, 'with 'four hundred and seventy designs of Raphael in my 'possession for a week.'

These fine entertainments were shared with many admirers, and, as I now remember them, certain months about the years 1839, 1840, seem colored with the genius of these Italians. Our walls were hung with prints of the Sistine frescoes; we were all petty collectors; and prints of Correggio and Guercino took the place, for the time, of epics and philosophy.

In the summer of 1839, Boston was still more rightfully adorned with the Allston Gallery; and the sculptures of our compatriots Greenough, and Crawford, and Powers, were brought hither. The following lines were addressed by Margaret to the Orpheus: —

'CRAWFORD'S ORPHEUS.

'Each Orpheus must to the abyss descend,
'For only thus the poet can be wise, —
'Must make the sad Persephone his friend,
'And buried love to second life arise;
'Again his love must lose, through too much love,
'Must lose his life by living life too true;
'For what he sought below has passed above,
'Already done is all that he would do;
'Must tune all being with his single lyre;
'Must melt all rocks free from their primal pain;
'Must search all nature with his one soul's fire;
'Must bind anew all forms in heavenly chain:
'If he already sees what he must do,
'Well may he shade his eyes from the far-shining view.'

Margaret's love of art, like that of most cultivated persons in this country, was not at all technical, but truly a sympathy with the artist, in the protest which his work pronounced on the deformity of our daily manners; her co-perception with him of the eloquence of form; her aspiration with him to a fairer life. As soon as her conversation ran into the mysteries of manipulation and artistic effect, it was less trustworthy. I remember that in the first times when I chanced to see pictures with her, I listened reverently to her opinions, and endeavored to see what she saw. But, on several occasions, finding myself unable to reach it, I came to suspect my guide, and to believe, at last, that her taste in works of art, though honest, was not on universal, but on idiosyncratic, grounds. As it has proved one of the most difficult problems of the practical astronomer to obtain an achromatic telescope, so an achromatic eye, one of the most needed, is also one of the rarest instruments of criticism.

She was very susceptible to pleasurable stimulus, took delight in details of form, color, and sound. Her fancy and imagination were easily stimulated to genial activity, and she erroneously thanked the artist for the pleasing emotions and thoughts that rose in her mind. So that, though capable of it, she did not always bring that highest tribunal to a work of art, namely, the calm presence of greatness, which only greatness in the object can satisfy. Yet the opinion was often well worth hearing on its own account, though it might be wide of the mark as criticism. Sometimes, too, she certainly brought to beautiful objects a fresh and appreciating love; and her written notes, especially on sculpture, I found always original and interesting. Here are some notes on the Athenæum Gallery of Sculpture, in August, 1840, which she sent me in manuscript: —

'Here are many objects worth study. There is Thorwaldsen's Byron. This is the truly beautiful, the ideal 'Byron. This head is quite free from the got-up, cari'catured air of disdain, which disfigures most likenesses 'of him, as it did himself in real life; yet sultry, stern, 'all-craving, all-commanding. Even the heavy style of 'the hair, too closely curled for grace, is favorable to the 'expression of concentrated life. While looking at this 'head, you learn to account for the grand failure in the 'scheme of his existence. The line of the cheek and chin 'are here, as usual, of unrivalled beauty.

'The bust of Napoleon is here also, and will naturally 'be named, in connection with that of Byron, since the one 'in letters, the other in arms, represented more fully than 'any other the tendency of their time; more than any 'other gave it a chance for reaction. There was another 'point of resemblance in the external being of the two, 'perfectly corresponding with that of the internal, a sense 'of which peculiarity drew on Byron some ridicule. I 'mean that it was the intention of nature, that neither 'should ever grow fat, but remain a Cassius in the com- 'monwealth. And both these heads are taken while they 'were at an early age, and so thin as to be still beautiful. 'This head of Napoleon is of a stern beauty. A head 'must be of a style either very stern or very chaste, to 'make a deep impression on the beholder; there must be 'a great force of will and withholding of resources, giving 'a sense of depth below depth, which we call sternness; 'or else there must be that purity, flowing as from an 'inexhaustible fountain through every lineament, which 'drives far off or converts all baser natures. Napoleon's 'head is of the first description; it is stern, and not only 'so, but ruthless. Yet this ruthlessness excites no aver- 'sion; the artist has caught its true character, and given 'us here the Attila, the instrument of fate to serve a 'purpose not his own. While looking on it, came full to mind the well-known lines, —

'"Speak gently of his crimes:
Who knows, Scourge of God, but in His eyes, those crimes
Were virtues?"

'His brows are tense and damp with the dews of 'thought. In that head you see the great future, careless 'of the black and white stones; and even when you turn 'to the voluptuous beauty of the mouth, the impression 'remains so strong, that Russia's snows, and mountains 'of the slain, seem the tragedy that must naturally follow 'the appearance of such an actor. You turn from him, 'feeling that he is a product not of the day, but of the 'ages, and that the ages must judge him.

'Near him is a head of Ennius, very intellectual; self-'centred and self-fed; but wrung and gnawed by un-'ceasing thoughts.

'Yet, even near the Ennius and Napoleon, our Amer-'ican men look worthy to be perpetuated in marble or 'bronze, if it were only for their air of calm, unpretending 'sagacity. If the young American were to walk up an 'avenue lined with such effigies, he might not feel called 'to such greatness as the strong Roman wrinkles tell of, 'but he must feel that he could not live an idle life, and 'should nerve himself to lift an Atlas weight without 'repining or shrinking.

'The busts of Everett and Allston, though admirable 'as every-day likenesses, deserved a genius of a different 'order from Clevenger. Clevenger gives the man as he 'is at the moment, but does not show the possibilities of 'his existence. Even thus seen, the head of Mr. Everett 'brings back all the age of Pericles, so refined and classic 'is its beauty. The two busts of Mr. Webster, by Clev-'enger and Powers, are the difference between prose,— 'healthy and energetic prose, indeed, but still prose, — and 'poetry. Clevenger's is such as we see Mr. Webster on 'any public occasion, when his genius is not called forth. 'No child could fail to recognize it in a moment. Powers' is not so good as a likeness, but has the higher merit of being an ideal of the orator and statesman at a great moment. It is quite an American Jupiter in its eagle calmness of conscious power.

'A marble copy of the beautiful Diana, not so spirited 'as the Athenæum cast. S. C—— thought the difference 'was one of size. This work may be seen at a glance; 'yet does not tire one after survey. It has the freshness 'of the woods, and of morning dew. I admire those long 'lithe limbs, and that column of a throat. The Diana 'is a woman's ideal of beauty; its elegance, its spirit, its 'graceful, peremptory air, are what we like in our own 'sex: the Venus is for men. The sleeping Cleopatra 'cannot be looked at enough; always her sleep seems 'sweeter and more graceful, always more wonderful 'the drapery. A little Psyche, by a pupil of Bartolini, 'pleases us much thus far. The forlorn sweetness 'with which she sits there, crouched down like a 'bruised butterfly, and the languid tenacity of her 'mood, are very touching. The Mercury and Gany-'mede with the Eagle, by Thorwaldsen, are still as 'fine as on first acquaintance. Thorwaldsen seems the 'grandest and simplest of modern sculptors. There is a 'breadth in his thought, a freedom in his design, we do 'not see elsewhere.

'A spaniel, by Gott, shows great talent, and knowledge 'of the animal. The head is admirable; it is so full of 'playfulness and of doggish knowingness.'

I am tempted, by my recollection of the pleasure it gave her, to insert here a little poem, addressed to Margaret by one of her friends, on the beautiful imaginative picture in the gallery of 1840, called "The Dream."

"A youth, with gentle brow and tender cheek,
Dreams in a place so silent, that no bird,
No rustle of the leaves his slumbers break;
Only soft tinkling from the stream is heard,
As in bright little waves it comes to greet
The beauteous One, and play upon his feet.

"On a low bank, beneath the thick shade thrown,
Soft gleams over his brown hair are flitting,
His golden plumes, bending, all lovely shone;
It seemed an angel's home where he was sitting,
Erect, beside, a silver lily grew,
And over all the shadow its sweet beauty threw.

"Dreams he of life? O, then a noble maid
Toward him floats, with eyes of starry light,
In richest robes all radiantly arrayed,
To be his ladye and his dear delight.
Ah no! the distance shows a winding stream;
No lovely ladye moves, no starry eyes do gleam.

"Cold is the air, and cold the mountains blue;
The banks are brown, and men are lying there,
Meagre and old; O, what have they to do
With joyous visions of a youth so fair?
He must not ever sleep as they are sleeping,
Onward through life he must be ever sweeping.

"Let the pale glimmering distance pass away;
Why in the twilight art thou slumbering there?
Wake, and come forth into triumphant day;
Thy life and deeds must all be great and fair.
Canst thou not from the lily learn true glory,
Pure, lofty, lowly? — such should be thy story.

"But no! thou lovest the deep-eyéd Past,
And thy heart clings to sweet remembrances;
In dim cathedral aisles thou 'lt linger last,
And fill thy mind with flitting fantasies.
But know, dear One, the world is rich to-day,
And the unceasing God gives glory forth alway."

I have said she was never weary of studying Michel Angelo and Raphael; and here are some manuscript "notes," which she sent me one day, containing a clear expression of her feeling toward each of these masters, after she had become tolerably familiar with their designs, as far as prints could carry her: —

'On seeing such works as these of Michel Angelo, we 'feel the need of a genius scarcely inferior to his own, 'which should invent some word, or some music, adequate 'to express our feelings, and relieve us from the Titanic 'oppression.

'"Greatness," "majesty," "strength," — to these 'words we had before thought we attached their proper 'meaning. But now we repent that they ever passed our 'lips. Created anew by the genius of this man, we would 'create language anew, and give him a word of response 'worthy his sublime profession of faith. Could we not 'at least have reserved "godlike" for him? For never 'till now did we appreciate the primeval vigor of creation, 'the instant swiftness with which thought can pass to 'deed; never till now appreciate the passage, "Let '"there be light, and there was light," which, be grateful, 'Michel! was clothed in human word before thee.

'One feels so repelled and humbled, on turning from 'Raphael to his contemporary, that I could have hated 'him as a Gentile Choragus might hate the prophet 'Samuel. Raphael took us to his very bosom, as if we 'had been fit for disciples, —

'"Parting with smiles the hair upon the brow,
And telling me none ever was preferred"

'This man waves his serpent wand over me, and beauty's 'self seems no better than a golden calf!

'I could not bear M. De Quincy for intimating that the 'archangel Michel could be jealous; yet I can easily see 'that he might have given cause, by undervaluing his 'divine contemporary. Raphael was so sensuous, so 'lovely and loving. All undulates to meet the eye, glides 'or floats upon the soul's horizon, as soft as is consist- 'ent with perfectly distinct and filled-out forms. The 'graceful Lionardo might see his pictures in moss; the 'beautiful Raphael on the cloud, or wave, or foliage; 'but thou, Michel, didst look straight upwards to the 'heaven, and grasp and bring thine down from the very 'sun of invention.

'How Raphael revels in the image! His life is all 'reproduced; nothing was abstract or conscious. Pan- 'theism, Polytheism, Greek god of Beauty, Apollo 'Musagetes,—what need of life beyond the divine work? '"I paint," said he, "from an idea that comes into my '"mind."

'But thou, Michel, didst not only feel but see the divine 'Ideal. Thine is the conscious monotheism of Jewry. 'Like thy own Moses, even on the mount of celestial 'converse, thou didst ask thy God to show now his face, 'and didst write his words, not in the alphabet of flowers, 'but on stone tables.

'It is, indeed, the two geniuses of Greece and Jewry, 'which are reproduced in these two men. Thauma- 'turgus nature saw fit to wait but a very few years 'before using these moulds again, in smaller space. 'Would you read the Bible aright? look at Michel; the 'Greek Mythology? look at Raphael. Would you know how the sublime coëxists with the beautiful, or the beautiful with the sublime? would you see power and 'truth regnant on the one side, with beauty and love 'harmonious and ministrant, but subordinate; or would 'you look at the other aspect of Deity?—study here. 'Would you open all the founts of marvel, admiration, 'and tenderness?—study both.

'One is not higher than the other; yet I am conscious 'of a slight rebuke from Michel, for having so poured 'out my soul at the feet of his brother angel. He seems 'to remind of Mr. E.'s view, and ask, "Why did you '"not question whether there was not aught else? why '"not reserve some inaccessible stronghold for me? why '"did you unlock the floodgates of the mind to such '"tides of emotion?" But there is no reality or per-'manence in this; it is only a reminder that the feminine 'part of human nature must not be dominant.

'The prophets of Michel Angelo excite all my admira-'tion at the man capable of giving to such a physique 'an expression which commands it. The soul is worthily 'lodged in these powerful frames; and she has the ease 'and dignity of one accustomed to command, and to 'command servants able to obey her hests. Who else 'could have so animated such forms, that they are im-'posing, but never heavy? The strong man is made so 'majestic by his office, that you scarcely feel how strong 'he is. The wide folds of the drapery, the breadth of 'light and shade, are great as anything in

"the large utterance of the early gods."

'How they read,—these prophets and sibyls! Never did the always-baffled, always reäspiring hope of the 'finite to compass the infinite find such expression, except in the *sehnsucht* of music. They are buried in the 'volume. They cannot believe that it has not some-'where been revealed, the word of enigma, the link 'between the human and divine, matter and spirit. 'Evidently, they hope to find it on the very next page. 'I have always thought, that clearly enough did nature 'and the soul's own consciousness respond to the craving 'for immortality. I have thought it great weakness to 'need the voucher of a miracle, or of any of those direct 'interpositions of a divine power, which, in common par-'lance, are alone styled revelation. When the revelations 'of nature seemed to me so clear, I had thought it was 'the weakness of the heart, or the dogmatism of the under-'standing, which had such need of *a book*. But in these 'figures of Michel, the highest power seizes upon a scroll, 'hoping that some other mind may have dived to the 'depths of eternity for the desired pearl, and enable him, 'without delay, consciously to embrace the Everlasting 'Now.

'How fine the attendant intelligences! So youthful 'and fresh, yet so strong. Some merely docile and 'reverent, others eager for utterance before the thought 'be known,—so firm is the trust in its value, so great 'the desire for sympathy. Others so brilliant in the 'attention of the inquiring eye, so intelligent in every 'feature, that they seem to divine the whole, before they 'hear it.

'Zachariah is much the finer of the two prophets.

'Of the sibyls, the *Cumæa* would be disgusting, from 'her overpowering strength in the feminine form, if genius 'had not made her tremendous. Especially the bosom 'gives me a feeling of faintness and aversion I cannot 'express. The female breast looks made for the temple 'of sweet and chaste thoughts, while this is so formed 'as to remind you of the lioness in her lair, and suggest 'a word which I will not write.

'The *Delphica* is even beautiful, in Michel's fair, calm, 'noble style, like the mother and child asleep in the '*Persica*, and *Night* in the casts I have just seen.

'The *Libica* is also more beautiful than grand. Her 'adjuncts are admirable. The elder figure, in the lowest 'pannel,—with what eyes of deep experience, and still 'unquenched enthusiasm, he sits meditating on the past! 'The figures at top are fiery with genius, especially the 'melancholy one, worthy to lift any weight, if he did 'but know how to set about it. As it is, all his strength 'may be wasted, yet he no whit the less noble.

'But the *Persica* is my favorite above all. She is the 'true sibyl. All the grandeur of that wasted frame 'comes from within. The life of thought has wasted 'the fresh juices of the body, and hardened the sere leaf 'of her cheek to parchment; every lineament is sharp, 'every tint tarnished; her face is seamed with wrinkles, '—usually as repulsive on a woman's face as attractive 'on a man. We usually feel, on looking at a woman, as 'if Nature had given them their best dower, and Expe-'rience could prove little better than a step-dame. But 'here, her high ambition and devotion to the life of 'thought gives her the masculine privilege of beauty in 'advancing years. Read on, hermitess of the world! 'what thou seekest is not there, yet thou dost not seek 'in vain.

'The adjuncts to this figure are worthy of it. On the 'right, below, those two divine sleepers, redeeming human 'nature, and infolding expectation in a robe of pearly 'sheen. Here is the sweetness of strength,—honey to 'the valiant; on the other side, its awfulness,—meat to 'the strong man. His sleep is more powerful than the 'waking of myriads of other men. What will he do 'when he has recruited his strength in this night's 'slumber? What wilt thou sing of it, wild-haired child 'of the lyre?

'I admire the heavy fall of the sleeper's luxuriant hair, 'which reminds one of the final shutting down of night 'upon a sullen twilight.

'The other figures, too, are full of augury, sad but 'life-like, in its poetry. On the shield, how perfectly is 'the expression of being struck home to the heart given! 'I wish I could have that shield, in some shape. Only 'a single blow was needed; the hand was sure, the 'breast shrinking, but unresisting. Die, child of my 'affection, child of my old age! Let the blood follow to 'the hilt, for it is the sword of the Lord!

'In looking again, this shield is on the *Libica*, and that 'of the *Persica* represents conquest, not sacrifice.

'Over all these figures broods the spirit of prophecy. 'You see their sternest deed is under the theocratic 'form. There is pride in action, but no selfism in these 'figures.

'When I first came to Michel, I clung to the beautiful 'Raphael, and feared his Druidical axe. But now, after 'the sibyls of Michel, it is unsafe to look at those of 'Raphael; for they seem weak, which is not so, only 'seems so, beside the sterner ideal.

'The beauty of composition here is great, and you feel 'that Michel's works are looked at fragment-wise in 'comparison. Here the eye glides along so naturally, 'does so easily justice to each part.'

LETTERS.

I fear the remark already made on that susceptibility to details in art and nature which precluded the exercise of Margaret's sound catholic judgment, must be extended to more than her connoisseurship. She *had* a sound judgment, on which, in conversation, she could fall back, and anticipate and speak the best sense of the largest company. But, left to herself, and in her correspondence, she was much the victim of Lord Bacon's *idols of the cave*, or self-deceived by her own phantasms. I have looked over volumes of her letters to me and others. They are full of probity, talent, wit, friendship, charity, and high aspiration. They are tainted with a mysticism, which to me appears so much an affair of constitution, that it claims no more respect than the charity or patriotism of a man who has dined well, and feels better for it. One sometimes talks with a genial *bon vivant*, who looks as if the omelet and turtle have got into his eyes. In our noble Margaret, her personal feeling colors all her judgment of persons, of books, of pictures, and even of the laws of the world. This is easily felt in ordinary women, and a large deduction is civilly made on the spot by whosoever replies to their remark. But when the speaker has such brilliant talent and literature as Margaret, she gives so many fine names to these merely sensuous and subjective phantasms, that the hearer is long imposed upon, and thinks so precise and glittering nomenclature cannot be of mere *muscae volitantes*, phœnixes of the fancy, but must be of some real ornithology, hitherto unknown to him. This mere feeling exaggerates a host of trifles into a dazzling mythology. But when one goes to sift it, and find if there be a real meaning, it eludes search. Whole sheets of warm, florid writing are here, in which the eye is caught by "sapphire," "heliotrope," "dragon," "aloes," "Magna Dea," "limboes," "stars," and "purgatory," but can connect all this, or any part of it, with no universal experience.

In short, Margaret often loses herself in sentimentalism. That dangerous vertigo nature in her case adopted, and was to make respectable. As it sometimes happens that a grandiose style, like that of the Alexandrian Platonists, or like Macpherson's Ossian, is more stimulating to the imagination of nations, than the true Plato, or than the simple poet, so here was a head so creative of new colors, of wonderful gleams, — so iridescent, that it piqued curiosity, and stimulated thought, and communicated mental activity to all who approached her; though her perceptions were not to be compared to her fancy, and she made numerous mistakes. Her integrity was perfect, and she was led and followed by love, and was really bent on truth, but too indulgent to the meteors of her fancy.

FRIENDSHIP.

> "Friends she must have, but in no one could find
> A tally fitted to so large a mind."

It is certain that Margaret, though unattractive in person, and assuming in manners, so that the girls complained that "she put upon them," or, with her burly masculine existence, quite reduced them to satellites, yet inspired an enthusiastic attachment. I hear from one witness, as early as 1829, that "all the girls raved about Margaret Fuller," and the same powerful magnetism wrought, as she went on, from year to year, on all ingenuous natures. The loveliest and the highest endowed women were eager to lay their beauty, their grace, the hospitalities of sumptuous homes, and their costly gifts, at her feet. When I expressed, one day, many years afterwards, to a lady who knew her well, some surprise at the homage paid her by men in Italy, — offers of marriage having there been made her by distinguished parties, — she replied: "There is nothing extraordinary in it. Had she been a man, any one of those fine girls of sixteen, who surrounded her here, would have married her: they were all in love with her, she understood them so well." She had seen many persons, and had entire confidence in her own discrimination of characters. She saw and foresaw all in the first interview. She had certainly made her own selections with great precision, and had not been disappointed. When pressed for a reason, she replied, in one instance, 'I have no good reason to give for what I think of ——. 'It is a dæmoniacal intimation. Everybody at —— 'praised her, but their account of what she said gave 'me the same unfavorable feeling. This is the first 'instance in which I have not had faith, if you liked a 'person. Perhaps I am wrong now; perhaps, if I saw 'her, a look would give me a needed clue to her charac- 'ter, and I should change my feeling. Yet I have never 'been mistaken in these intimations, as far as I recollect. 'I hope I am now.'

I am to add, that she gave herself to her friendships with an entireness not possible to any but a woman, with a depth possible to few women. Her friendships, as a girl with girls, as a woman with women, were not unmingled with passion, and had passages of romantic sacrifice and of ecstatic fusion, which I have heard with the ear, but could not trust my profane pen to report. There were, also, the ebbs and recoils from the other party, — the mortal unequal to converse with an immortal, — ingratitude, which was more truly incapacity, the collapse of overstrained affections and powers. At all events, it is clear that Margaret, later, grew more strict, and values herself with her friends on having the tie now "redeemed from all search after Eros." So much, however, of intellectual aim and activity mixed with her alliances, as to breathe a certain dignity and myrrh through them all. She and her friends are fellow-students with noblest moral aims. She is there for help and for counsel. 'Be to the best thou knowest ever 'true!' is her language to one. And that was the effect of her presence. Whoever conversed with her felt challenged by the strongest personal influence to a bold and generous life. To one she wrote, — 'Could a 'word from me avail you, I would say, that I have 'firm faith that nature cannot be false to her child, who 'has shown such an unalterable faith in her piety 'towards her.'

'These tones of my dear ——'s lyre are of the noblest. 'Will they sound purely through her experiences? Will 'the variations be faithful to the theme? Not always 'do those who most devoutly long for the Infinite, know 'best how to modulate their finite into a fair passage of 'the eternal Harmony.

'How many years was it the cry of my spirit, —

> '"Give, give, ye mighty Gods!
> Why do ye thus hold back?"—

'and, I suppose, all noble young persons think for the

time that they would have been more generous than the Olympians. But when we have learned the high lesson *to deserve*, — that boon of manhood, — we see 'they esteemed us too much, to give what we had not 'earned.'

The following passages from her journal and her letters are sufficiently descriptive, each in its way, of her strong affections.

'At Mr. G.'s we looked over prints, the whole evening, 'in peace. Nothing fixed my attention so much as a 'large engraving of Madame Recamier in her boudoir. 'I have so often thought over the intimacy between her 'and Madame De Stael.

'It is so true that a woman may be in love with a 'woman, and a man with a man. I like to be sure of 'it, for it is the same love which angels feel, where —

' "Sie fragen nicht nach Mann und Weib."

'It is regulated by the same law as that of love 'between persons of different sexes; only it is purely 'intellectual and spiritual. Its law is the desire of the 'spirit to realize a whole, which makes it seek in another 'being what it finds not in itself. Thus the beautiful 'seek the strong, and the strong the beautiful; the 'mute seeks the eloquent, &c.; the butterfly settles 'always on the dark flower. Why did Socrates love 'Alcibiades? Why did Körner love Schneider? How 'natural is the love of Wallenstein for Max; that of De 'Stael for De Recamier; mine for ——. I loved ——, 'for a time, with as much passion as I was then strong 'enough to feel. Her face was always gleaming before 'me; her voice was always echoing in my ear; all 'poetic thoughts clustered round the dear image. This 'love was a key which unlocked for me many a treasure 'which I still possess; it was the carbuncle which cast 'light into many of the darkest caverns of human 'nature. She loved me, too, though not so much, 'because her nature was "less high, less grave, less '"large, less deep." But she loved more tenderly, less 'passionately. She loved me, for I well remember her 'suffering when she first could feel my faults, and knew 'one part of the exquisite veil rent away; how she 'wished to stay apart, and weep the whole day.

* * * * *

'I do not love her now with passion, but I still feel 'towards her as I can to no other woman. I thought 'of all this as I looked at Madame Recamier.'

TO R. W. E.

'*7th Feb.*, 1843. — I saw the letter of your new friend, 'and liked it much; only, at this distance, one could not 'be sure whether it was the nucleus or the train of a 'comet, that lightened afar. The dæmons are not busy 'enough at the births of most men. They do not give 'them individuality deep enough for truth to take root 'in. Such shallow natures cannot resist a strong head; 'its influence goes right through them. It is not stopped 'and fermented long enough. But I do not understand 'this hint of hesitation, because you have many friends 'already. We need not economize, we need not hoard 'these immortal treasures. Love and thought are not 'diminished by diffusion. In the widow's cruse is oil 'enough to furnish light for all the world.'

TO R. W. E.

'*15th March*, 1842.—It is to be hoped, my best one, that the experiences of life will yet correct your vocabulary, and that you will not always answer the burst of frank affection by the use of such a word as "flat-"tery."

'Thou knowest, O all-seeing Truth! whether that 'hour is base or unworthy thee, in which the heart 'turns tenderly towards some beloved object, whether 'stirred by an apprehension of its needs, or of its pres-'ent beauty, or of its great promise; when it would lay 'before it all the flowers of hope and love, would soothe 'its weariness as gently as might the sweet south, and '*flatter* it by as fond an outbreak of pride and devotion 'as is seen on the sunset clouds. Thou knowest 'whether these promptings, whether these longings, be 'not truer than intellectual scrutiny of the details of 'character; than cold distrust of the exaggerations even 'of heart. What we hope, what we think of those 'we love, is true, true as the fondest dream of love and 'friendship that ever shone upon the childish heart.

'The faithful shall yet meet a full-eyed love, ready as 'profound, that never needs turn the key on its retire-'ment, or arrest the stammering of an overweening 'trust.'

TO ——.

'I wish I could write you often, to bring before you 'the varied world-scene you cannot so well go out to 'unfold for yourself. But it was never permitted me, 'even where I wished it most. But the forest leaves fall 'unseen, and make a soil on which shall be reared the 'growths and fabrics of a nobler era. This thought 'rounds off each day. Your letter was a little golden 'key to a whole volume of thoughts and feelings. I 'cannot make the one bright drop, like champagne in 'ice, but must pour a full gush, if I speak at all, and 'not think whether the water is clear either.'

With this great heart, and these attractions, it was easy to add daily to the number of her friends. With her practical talent, her counsel and energy, she was pretty sure to find clients and sufferers enough, who wished to be guided and supported. 'Others,' she said, 'lean on this arm, which I have found so frail. 'Perhaps it is strong enough to have drawn a sword, 'but no better suited to be used as a *bolt*, than that of 'Lady Catharine Douglas, of loyal memory.' She could not make a journey, or go to an evening party, without meeting a new person, who wished presently to impart his history to her. Very early, she had written to ——, 'My museum is so well furnished, that I grow lazy 'about collecting new specimens of human nature.' She had soon enough examples of the historic development of rude intellect under the first rays of culture. But, in a thousand individuals, the process is much the same; and, like a professor too long pent in his college, she rejoiced in encountering persons of untutored grace and strength, and felt no wish to prolong the intercourse when culture began to have its effect. I find in her journal a characteristic note, on receiving a letter on books and speculations, from one whom she had valued for his heroic qualities in a life of adventure: —

'These letters of —— are beautiful, and moved me

'deeply. It looks like the birth of a soul. But I loved '*thee*, fair, rich *earth*,—and all that is gone forever. 'This that comes now, we know in much farther stages. 'Yet there is silver sweet in the tone, generous nobility 'in the impulses.'

'Poor Tasso in the play offered his love and service 'too officiously to all. They all rejected it, and declared 'him mad, because he made statements too emphatic of 'his feelings. If I wanted only ideal figures to think 'about, there are those in literature I like better than any 'of your living ones. But I want far more. I want 'habitual intercourse, cheer, inspiration, tenderness. I 'want these for myself; I want to impart them. I have 'done as Timon did, for these last eight years. My early 'intercourses were more equal, because more natural. 'Since I took on me the vows of renunciation, I have 'acted like a prodigal. Like Timon, I have loved to give, 'perhaps not from beneficence, but from restless love. 'Now, like Fortunatus, I find my mistresses will not 'thank me for fires made of cinnamon; rather they run 'from too rich an odor. What shall I do? not curse, 'like him, (oh base!) nor dig my grave in the marge of 'the salt tide. Give an answer to my questions, dæmon! Give a rock for my feet, a bird of peaceful and sufficient 'song within my breast! I return to thee, my Father, from the husks that have been offered me. But I return as one who meant not to leave Thee.'

Of course, she made large demands on her companions, and would soon come to sound their knowledge, and guess pretty nearly the range of their thoughts. There yet remained to command her constancy, what she valued more, the quality and affection proper to each. But she could rarely find natures sufficiently deep and magnetic. With her sleepless curiosity, her magnanimity, and her diamond-ring, like Annie of Lochroyan's, to exchange for gold or for pewter, she might be pardoned for her impatient questionings. To me, she was uniformly generous; but neither did I escape. Our moods were very different; and I remember, that, at the very time when I, slow and cold, had come fully to admire her genius, and was congratulating myself on the solid good understanding that subsisted between us, I was surprised with hearing it taxed by her with superficiality and halfness. She stigmatized our friendship as commercial. It seemed, her magnanimity was not met, but I prized her only for the thoughts and pictures she brought me; — so many thoughts, so many facts yesterday, — so many to-day; — when there was an end of things to tell, the game was up: that, I did not know, as a friend should know, to prize a silence as much as a discourse, — and hence a forlorn feeling was inevitable; a poor counting of thoughts, and a taking the census of virtues, was the unjust reception so much love found. On one occasion, her grief broke into words like these: 'The religious 'nature remained unknown to you, because it could not 'proclaim itself, but claimed to be divined. The deepest 'soul that approached you was, in your eyes, nothing but 'a magic lantern, always bringing out pretty shows of 'life.'

But as I did not understand the discontent then, — of course, I cannot now. It was a war of temperaments, and could not be reconciled by words; but, after each party had explained to the uttermost, it was necessary to fall back on those grounds of agreement which remained, and leave the differences henceforward in respectful silence. The recital may still serve to show to sympathetic persons the true lines and enlargements of her genius. It is certain that this incongruity never interrupted for a moment the intercourse, such as it was, that existed between us.

I ought to add here, that certain mental changes brought new questions into conversation. In the summer of 1840, she passed into certain religious states, which did not impress me as quite healthy, or likely to be permanent; and I said, "I do not understand your tone; it seems exaggerated. You are one who can afford to speak and to hear the truth. Let us hold hard to the common-sense, and let us speak in the positive degree."

And I find, in later letters from her, sometimes playful, sometimes grave allusions to this explanation.

'Is —— there? Does water meet water? — no need 'of wine, sugar, spice, or even a *soupçon* of lemon to 'remind of a tropical climate? I fear me not. Yet, dear 'positives, believe me superlatively yours, MARGARET.'

The following letter seems to refer, under an Eastern guise, and with something of Eastern exaggeration of compliment too, to some such native sterilities in her correspondent: —

TO R. W. E.

'*23d Feb.*, 1840. — I am like some poor traveller of the 'desert, who saw, at early morning, a distant palm, and 'toiled all day to reach it. All day he toiled. The un'feeling sun shot pains into his temples; the burning air, 'filled with sand, checked his breath; he had no water, 'and no fountain sprung along his path. But his eye 'was bright with courage, for he said, "When I reach '"the lonely palm, I will lie beneath its shade. I will '"refresh myself with its fruit. Allah has reared it to '"such a height, that it may encourage the wandering, '"and bless and sustain the faint and weary." But 'when he reached it, alas! it had grown too high to shade 'the weary man at its foot. On it he saw no clustering 'dates, and its one draught of wine was far beyond his 'reach. He saw at once that it was so. A child, a bird, 'a monkey, might have climbed to reach it. A rude hand 'might have felled the whole tree; but the full-grown 'man, the weary man, the gentle-hearted, religious man, 'was no nearer to its nourishment for being close to the 'root; yet he had not force to drag himself further, and 'leave at once the aim of so many fond hopes, so many 'beautiful thoughts. So he lay down amid the inhospitable sands. The night dews pierced his exhausted 'frame; the hyena laughed, the lion roared, in the distance; the stars smiled upon him satirically from their 'passionless peace; and he knew they were like the sun, 'as unfeeling, only more distant. He could not sleep for 'famine. With the dawn he arose. The palm stood as 'tall, as inaccessible, as ever; its leaves did not so 'much as rustle an answer to his farewell sigh. On 'and on he went, and came, at last, to a living spring. 'The spring was encircled by tender verdure, wild fruits 'ripened near, and the clear waters sparkled up to tempt 'his lip. The pilgrim rested, and refreshed himself, and 'looked back with less pain to the unsympathizing palm, 'which yet towered in the distance.

'But the wanderer had a mission to perform, which

'must have forced him to leave at last both palm and 'fountain. So on and on he went, saying to the palm, '"Thou art for another;" and to the gentle waters, "I '"will return."

'Not far distant was he when the sirocco came, and 'choked with sand the fountain, and uprooted the fruit- 'trees. When years have passed, the waters will have 'forced themselves up again to light, and a new oasis 'will await a new wanderer. Thou, Sohrab, wilt, ere 'that time, have left thy bones at Mecca. Yet the 'remembrance of the fountain cheers thee as a blessing; 'that of the palm haunts thee as a pang.

'So talks the soft spring gale of the Shah Nameh. 'Genuine Sanscrit I cannot write. My Persian and 'Arabic you love not. Why do I write thus to one who 'must ever regard the deepest tones of my nature as those 'of childish fancy or worldly discontent?'

PROBLEMS OF LIFE.

Already, too, at this time, each of the main problems of human life had been closely scanned and interrogated by her, and some of them had been much earlier settled. A worshipper of beauty, why could not she also have been beautiful?—of the most radiant sociality, why should not she have been so placed, and so decorated, as to have led the fairest and highest? In her journal is a bitter sentence, whose meaning I cannot mistake: 'Of a disposition that requires the most refined, the most 'exalted tenderness, without charms to inspire it:—poor 'Mignon! fear not the transition through death; no 'penal fires can have in store worse torments than thou 'art familiar with already.'

In the month of May, she writes:—'When all things

'are blossoming, it seems so strange not to blossom too; 'that the quick thought within cannot remould its tene-'ment. Man is the slowest aloes, and I am such a shabby 'plant, of such coarse tissue. I hate not to be beautiful, 'when all around is so.'

Again, after recording a visit to a family, whose taste and culture, united to the most liberal use of wealth, made the most agreeable of homes, she writes: 'Look-'ing out on the wide view, I felt the blessings of my 'comparative freedom. I stand in no false relations. 'Who else is so happy? Here are these fair, unknowing 'children envying the depth of my mental life. They 'feel withdrawn by sweet duties from reality. Spirit! I 'accept; teach me to prize and use whatsoever is given 'me.'

'At present,' she writes elsewhere, 'it skills not. I am 'able to take the superior view of life, and my place in 'it. But I know the deep yearnings of the heart and 'the bafflings of time will be felt again, and then I shall 'long for some dear hand to hold. But I shall never 'forget that my curse is nothing, compared with that of 'those who have entered into those relations, but not 'made them real; who only *seem* husbands, wives, and 'friends.'

'I remain fixed to be, without churlishness or coldness, 'as much alone as possible. It is best for me. I am not 'fitted to be loved, and it pains me to have close dealings 'with those who do not love, to whom my feelings are '"strange." Kindness and esteem are very well. I am 'willing to receive and bestow them; but these alone are 'not worth feelings such as mine. And I wish I may 'make no more mistakes, but keep chaste for mine own 'people.'

There is perhaps here, as in a passage of the same journal quoted already, an allusion to a verse in the ballad of the Lass of Lochroyan: —

> "O yours was gude, and gude enough,
> But aye the best was mine;
> For yours was o' the gude red gold,
> But mine o' the diamond fine."

'There is no hour of absolute beauty in all my past, 'though some have been made musical by heavenly 'hope, many dignified by intelligence. Long urged by 'the Furies, I rest again in the temple of Apollo. Celes-'tial verities dawn constellated as thoughts in the heaven 'of my mind.

'But, driven from home to home, as a renouncer, I get 'the picture and the poetry of each. Keys of gold, silver, 'iron, and lead, are in my casket. No one loves me; 'but I love many a good deal, and see, more or less, into 'their eventual beauty. Meanwhile, I have no fetter on 'me, no engagement, and, as I look on others, — almost 'every other, — can I fail to feel this a great privilege? 'I have nowise tied my hands or feet; yet the varied 'calls on my sympathy have been such, that I hope not 'to be made partial, cold, or ignorant, by this isolation. 'I have no child; but now, as I look on these lovely 'children of a human birth, what low and neutralizing 'cares they bring with them to the mother! The chil-'dren of the muse come quicker, and have not on them the taint of earthly corruption.'

Practical questions in plenty the days and months

brought her to settle,—questions requiring all her wisdom, and sometimes more than all. None recurs with more frequency, at one period, in her journals, than the debate with herself, whether she shall make literature a profession. Shall it be woman, or shall it be artist?

WOMAN, OR ARTIST?

Margaret resolved, again and again, to devote herself no more to these disappointing forms of men and women, but to the children of the muse. 'The *dramatis per-* '*sonæ*,' she said, 'of my poems shall henceforth be 'chosen from the children of immortal Muse. I fix my 'affections no more on these frail forms.' But it was vain; she rushed back again to persons, with a woman's devotion.

Her pen was a non-conductor. She always took it up with some disdain, thinking it a kind of impiety to attempt to report a life so warm and cordial, and wrote on the fly-leaf of her journal,—

'"*Scrivo sol per sfogar' l'interno.*"'

'Since you went away,' she said, 'I have thought of 'many things I might have told you, but I could not 'bear to be eloquent and poetical. It is a mockery thus to 'play the artist with life, and dip the brush in one's own 'heart's blood. One would fain be no more artist, or 'philosopher, or lover, or critic, but a soul ever rushing 'forth in tides of genial life.'

'26 *Dec.*, 1842.—I have been reading the lives of Lord 'Herbert of Cherbury, and of Sir Kenelm Digby. These splendid, chivalrous, and thoughtful Englishmen are 'meat which my soul loveth, even as much as my Ital-'ians. What I demand of men, — that they could act 'out all their thoughts, — these have. They are lives; '— and of such I do not care if they had as many faults 'as there are days in the year, — there is the energy 'to redeem them. Do you not admire Lord Herbert's 'two poems on life, and the conjectures concerning celes-'tial life? I keep reading them.'

'When I look at my papers, I feel as if I had never 'had a thought that was worthy the attention of any but 'myself; and 't is only when, on talking with people, I 'find I tell them what they did not know, that my con-'fidence at all returns.'

'My verses, — I am ashamed when I think there is 'scarce a line of poetry in them, — all rhetorical and 'impassioned, as Goethe said of De Stael. However, 'such as they are, they have been overflowing drops 'from the somewhat bitter cup of my existence.'

'How can I ever write with this impatience of detail? 'I shall never be an artist; I have no patient love of 'execution; I am delighted with my sketch, but if I try '*to finish* it, I am chilled. Never was there a great 'sculptor who did not love to chip the marble.'

'I have talent and knowledge enough to furnish a 'dwelling for friendship, but not enough to deck with 'golden gifts a Delphi for the world.'

'Then a woman of tact and brilliancy, like me, has an 'undue advantage in conversation with men. They are 'astonished at our instincts. They do not see where we 'got our knowledge; and, while they tramp on in their 'clumsy way, we wheel, and fly, and dart hither and 'thither, and seize with ready eye all the weak points, 'like Saladin in the desert. It is quite another thing 'when we come to write, and, without suggestion from 'another mind, to declare the positive amount of thought 'that is in us. Because we seemed to know all, they 'think we can tell all; and, finding we can tell so little, 'lose faith in their first opinion of us, *which, nathless,* '*was true.*'

And again: 'These gentlemen are surprised that I 'write no better, because I talk so well. But I have 'served a long apprenticeship to the one, none to the 'other. I shall write better, but never, I think, so well 'as I talk; for then I feel inspired. The means are 'pleasant; my voice excites me, my pen never. I shall 'not be discouraged, nor take for final what they say, but 'sift from it the truth, and use it. I feel the strength to 'dispense with all illusions. I will stand steady, and 'rejoice in the severest probations.'

'What a vulgarity there seems in this writing for the 'multitude! We know not yet, have not made ourselves 'known to a single soul, and shall we address those still 'more unknown? Shall we multiply our connections, 'and thus make them still more superficial?

'I would go into the crowd, and meet men for the day, 'to help them for the day, but for that intercourse which 'most becomes us. Pericles, Anaxagoras, Aspasia, 'Cleone, is circle wide enough for me. I should think 'all the resources of my nature, and all the tribute it 'could enforce from external nature, none too much to 'furnish the banquet for this circle.

'But where to find fit, though few, representatives for 'all we value in humanity? Where obtain those golden 'keys to the secret treasure-chambers of the soul? No 'samples are perfect. We must look abroad into the 'wide circle, to seek a little here, and a little there, to 'make up our company. And is not the "prent book" 'a good beacon-light to tell where we wait the bark? — 'a reputation, the means of entering the Olympic game, 'where Pindar may perchance be encountered?

'So it seems the mind must reveal its secret; must 'reproduce. And I have no castle, and no natural circle, 'in which I might live, like the wise Makaria, observing 'my kindred the stars, and gradually enriching my 'archives. Makaria here must go abroad, or the stars 'would hide their light, and the archive remain a blank.

'For all the tides of life that flow within me, I am 'dumb and ineffectual, when it comes to casting my 'thought into a form. No old one suits me. If I could 'invent one, it seems to me the pleasure of creation would 'make it possible for me to write. What shall I do, 'dear friend? I want force to be either a genius or a 'character. One should be either private or public. I 'love best to be a woman; but womanhood is at present 'too straitly-bounded to give me scope. At hours, I live 'truly as a woman; at others, I should stifle; as, on the 'other hand, I should palsy, when I would play the 'artist.'

HEROISM.

These practical problems Margaret had to entertain and to solve the best way she could. She says truly, 'there was none to take up her burden whilst she slept.' But she was formed for action, and addressed herself quite simply to her part. She was a woman, an orphan, without beauty, without money; and these negatives will suggest what difficulties were to be surmounted where the tasks dictated by her talents required the good-will of "good society," in the town where she was to teach and write. But she was even-tempered and erect, and, if her journals are sometimes mournful, her mind was made up, her countenance beamed courage and cheerfulness around her. Of personal influence, speaking strictly,—an efflux, that is, purely of mind and character, excluding all effects of power, wealth, fashion, beauty, or literary fame,— she had an extraordinary degree; I think more than any person I have known. An interview with her was a joyful event. Worthy men and women, who had conversed with her, could not forget her, but worked bravely on in the remembrance that this heroic approver had recognized their aims. She spoke so earnestly, that the depth of the sentiment prevailed, and not the accidental expression, which might chance to be common. Thus I learned, the other day, that, in a copy of Mrs. Jameson's Italian Painters, against a passage describing Correggio as a true servant of God in his art, above sordid ambition, devoted to truth, "one of those superior beings of whom there are so few;" Margaret wrote on the margin, 'And yet all might be 'such.' The book lay long on the table of the owner, in Florence, and chanced to be read there by a young artist of much talent. "These words," said he, months afterwards, "struck out a new strength in me. They revived resolutions long fallen away, and made me set my face like a flint."

But Margaret's courage was thoroughly sweet in its temper. She accused herself in her youth of unamiable traits, but, in all the later years of her life, it is difficult to recall a moment of malevolence. The friends whom her strength of mind drew to her, her good heart held fast; and few persons were ever the objects of more persevering kindness. Many hundreds of her letters remain, and they are alive with proofs of generous friendship given and received.

Among her early friends, Mrs. Farrar, of Cambridge, appears to have discovered, at a critical moment in her career, the extraordinary promise of the young girl, and some false social position into which her pride and petulance, and the mistakes of others, had combined to bring her, and she set herself, with equal kindness and address, to make a second home for Margaret in her own house, and to put her on the best footing in the agreeable society of Cambridge. She busied herself, also, as she could, in removing all superficial blemishes from the gem. In a well-chosen travelling party, made up by Mrs. Farrar, and which turned out to be the beginning of much happiness by the friendships then formed, Margaret visited, in the summer of 1835, Newport, New York, and Trenton Falls; and, in the autumn, made the acquaintance, at Mrs. F.'s house, of Miss Martineau, whose friendship, at that moment, was an important stimulus to her mind.

Mrs. Farrar performed for her, thenceforward, all the offices of an almost maternal friendship. She admired her genius, and wished that all should admire it. She counselled and encouraged her, brought to her side the else unsuppliable aid of a matron and a lady, sheltered her in sickness, forwarded her plans with tenderness and constancy, to the last. I read all this in the tone of uniform gratitude and love with which this lady is mentioned in Margaret's letters. Friendships like this praise both parties; and the security with which people of a noble disposition approached Margaret, indicated the quality of her own infinite tenderness. A very intelligent woman applied to her what Stilling said of Goethe: "Her heart, which few knew, was as great as her mind, which all knew;" and added, that, "in character, Margaret was, of all she had beheld, the largest woman, and not a woman who wished to be a man." Another lady added, "She never disappointed you. To any one whose confidence she had once drawn out, she was thereafter faithful. She could talk of persons, and never gossip; for she had a fine instinct that kept her from any reality, and from any effect of treachery." I was still more struck with the remark that followed. "Her life, since she went abroad, is wholly unknown to me; but I have an unshaken trust that what Margaret did she can defend."

She was a right brave and heroic woman. She shrunk from no duty, because of feeble nerves. Although, after her father died, the disappointment of not going to Europe with Miss Martineau and Mrs. Farrar was extreme, and her mother and sister wished her to take her portion of the estate and go; and, on her refusal, entreated the interference of friends to overcome her objections; Margaret would not hear of it, and devoted herself to the education of her brothers and sisters, and then to the making a home for the family. She was exact and punctual in money matters, and maintained herself, and made her full contribution to the support of her family, by the reward of her labors as a teacher, and in her conversation classes. I have a letter from her at Jamaica Plain, dated November, 1840, which begins, —

'This day I write you from my own hired house, and 'am full of the dignity of citizenship. Really, it is 'almost happiness. I retain, indeed, some cares and 'responsibilities; but these will sit light as feathers, for I 'can take my own time for them. Can it be that this 'peace will be mine for five whole months? At any 'rate, five days have already been enjoyed.'

Here is another, written in the same year: —

'I do not wish to talk to you of my ill-health, 'except that I like you should know when it makes 'me do anything badly, since I wish you to excuse 'and esteem me. But let me say, once for all, in 'reply to your letter, that you are mistaken if you 'think I ever wantonly sacrifice my health. I have 'learned that we cannot injure ourselves without injur-'ing others; and besides, that we have no right; for 'ourselves are all we know of heaven. I do not try to 'domineer over myself. But, unless I were sure of 'dying, I cannot dispense with making some exertion, 'both for the present and the future. There is no mor-'tal, who, if I laid down my burden, would take care 'of it while I slept. Do not think me weakly disinter-'ested, or, indeed, disinterested at all.'

Every one of her friends knew assuredly that her sympathy and aid would not fail them when required. She went, from the most joyful of all bridals, to attend a near relative during a formidable surgical operation.

She was here to help others. As one of her friends writes, 'She helped whoever knew her.' She adopted the interests of humble persons, within her circle, with heart-cheering warmth, and her ardor in the cause of suffering and degraded women, at Sing-Sing, was as irresistible as her love of books. She had, many years afterwards, scope for the exercise of all her love and devotion, in Italy, but she came to it as if it had been her habit and her natural sphere. The friends who knew her in that country, relate, with much surprise, that she, who had all her lifetime drawn people by her wit, should recommend herself so highly, in Italy, by her tenderness and large affection. Yet the tenderness was only a face of the wit; as before, the wit was raised above all other wit by the affection behind it. And, truly, there was an ocean of tears always, in her atmosphere, ready to fall.

There was, at New York, a poor adventurer, half patriot, half author, a miserable man, always in such depths of distress, with such squadrons of enemies, that no charity could relieve, and no intervention save him. He believed Europe banded for his destruction, and America corrupted to connive at it. Margaret listened to these woes with such patience and mercy, that she drew five hundred dollars, which had been invested for her in a safe place, and put them in those hapless hands, where, of course, the money was only the prey of new rapacity, to be bewailed by new reproaches. When one of her friends had occasion to allude to this, long afterwards, she replied: —

'In answer to what you say of ——, I wish, indeed, 'the little effort I made for him had been wiselier 'applied. Yet these are not the things one regrets. It 'will not do to calculate too closely with the affectionate 'human impulse. We must consent to make many mis-'takes, or we should move too slow to help our brothers 'much. I am sure you do not regret what you spent on 'Miani, and other worthless people. As things looked 'then, it would have been wrong not to have risked the 'loss.'

TRUTH.

But Margaret crowned all her talents and virtues with a love of truth, and the power to speak it. In great and in small matters, she was a woman of her word, and gave those who conversed with her the unspeakable comfort that flows from plain dealing. Her nature was frank and transparent, and she had a right to say, as she says in her journal: —

'I have the satisfaction of knowing, that, in my coun-'sels, I have given myself no air of being better than 'I am.'

And again: —

'In the chamber of death, I prayed in very early 'years, "Give me truth; cheat me by no illusion." O, 'the granting of this prayer is sometimes terrible to me! 'I walk over the burning ploughshares, and they sear 'my feet. Yet nothing but truth will do; no love will 'serve that is not eternal, and as large as the universe; 'no philanthropy in executing whose behests I myself 'become unhealthy; no creative genius which bursts 'asunder my life, to leave it a poor black chrysalid 'behind. And yet this last is too true of me.'

She describes a visit made in May, 1844, at the house of some valued friends in West Roxbury, and adds: 'We had a long and deep conversation, happy in its 'candor. Truth, truth, thou art the great preservative! 'Let free air into the mind, and the pestilence cannot 'lurk in any corner.'

And she uses the following language in an earnest letter to another friend: —

'My own entire sincerity, in every passage of life, gives 'me a right to expect that I shall be met by no unmean-'ing phrases or attentions.'

'Reading to-day a few lines of ——, I thought with 'refreshment of such lives as T.'s, and V.'s, and W.'s, so 'private and so true, where each line written is really the 'record of a thought or a feeling. I hate poems which 'are a melancholy monument of culture for the sake of 'being cultivated, not of growing.'

Even in trifles, one might find with her the advantage and the electricity of a little honesty. I have had from an eye-witness a note of a little scene that passed in Boston, at the Academy of Music. A party had gone early, and taken an excellent place to hear one of Beethoven's symphonies. Just behind them were soon seated a young lady and two gentlemen, who made an incessant buzzing, in spite of bitter looks cast on them by the whole neighborhood, and destroyed all the musical comfort. After all was over, Margaret leaned across one seat, and catching the eye of this girl, who was pretty and well-dressed, said, in her blandest, gentlest voice, "May I speak with you one moment?" "Certainly," said the young lady, with a fluttered, pleased look, bending forward. "I only wish to say," said Margaret, "that I trust, that, in the whole course of your life, you will not suffer so great a degree of annoyance as you have inflicted on a large party of lovers of music this evening." This was said with the sweetest air, as if to a little child, and it was as good as a play to see the change of countenançe which the young lady exhibited, who had no replication to make to so Christian a blessing.

On graver occasions, the same habit was only more stimulated; and I cannot remember certain passages which called it into play, without new regrets at the costly loss which our community sustains in the loss of this brave and eloquent soul.

People do not speak the truth, not for the want of not knowing and preferring it, but because they have not the organ to speak it adequately. It requires a clear sight, and, still more, a high spirit, to deal with falsehood in the decisive way. I have known several honest persons who valued truth as much as Peter and John, but, when they tried to speak it, *they* grew red and black in the face instead of Ananias, until, after a few attempts, they decided that aggressive truth was not their vocation, and confined themselves thenceforward to silent honesty, except on rare occasions, when either an extreme outrage, or a happier inspiration, loosened their tongue. But a soul is now and then incarnated, whom indulgent nature has not afflicted with any cramp or frost, but who can speak the right word at the right moment, qualify the selfish and hypocritical act with its real name, and, without any loss of serenity, hold up the offence to the purest daylight. Such a truth-speaker is worth more than the best police, and more than the laws or governors; for these do not always know their own side, but will back the crime for want of this very truth-speaker to expose them. That is the theory of the newspaper,—to supersede official by intellectual influence. But, though the apostles establish the journal, it usually happens that, by some strange oversight, Ananias slips into the editor's chair. If, then, we could be provided with a fair proportion of truth-speakers, we could very materially and usefully contract the legislative and the executive functions. Still, the main sphere for this nobleness is private society, where so many mischiefs go unwhipped, being out of the cognizance of law, and supposed to be nobody's business. And society is, at all times, suffering for want of judges and headsmen, who will mark and lop these malefactors.

Margaret suffered no vice to insult her presence, but called the offender to instant account, when the law of right or of beauty was violated. She needed not, of course, to go out of her way to find the offender, and she never did, but she had the courage and the skill to cut heads off which were not worn with honor in her presence. Others might abet a crime by silence, if they pleased; she chose to clear herself of all complicity, by calling the act by its name.

It was curious to see the mysterious provocation which the mere presence of insight exerts in its neighborhood. Like moths about a lamp, her victims voluntarily came to judgment: conscious persons, encumbered with egotism; vain persons, bent on concealing some mean vice; arrogant reformers, with some halting of their own; the compromisers, who wished to reconcile right and wrong; — all came and held out their palms to the wise woman, to read their fortunes, and they were truly told. Many anecdotes have come to my ear, which show how useful the glare of her lamp proved in private circles, and what dramatic situations it created. But these cannot be told. The valor for dragging the accused spirits among his acquaintance to the stake is not in the heart of the present writer. The reader must be content to learn that she knew how, without loss of temper, to speak with unmistakable plainness to any party, when she felt that the truth or the right was injured. For the same reason, I omit one or two letters, most honorable both to her mind and heart, in which she felt constrained to give the frankest utterance to her displeasure. Yet I incline to quote the testimony of one witness, which is so full and so pointed, that I must give it as I find it.

"I have known her, by the severity of her truth, mow down a crop of evil, like the angel of retribution itself, and could not sufficiently admire her courage. A conversation she had with Mr. ——, just before he went to Europe, was one of these things; and there was not a particle of ill-will in it, but it was truth which she could not help seeing and uttering, nor he refuse to accept.

"My friends told me of a similar verdict, pronounced upon Mr. ——, at Paris, which they said was perfectly tremendous. They themselves sat breathless; Mr. —— was struck dumb; his eyes fixed on her with wonder and amazement, yet gazing too with an attention which seemed like fascination. When she had done, he still looked to see if she was to say more, and when he found she had really finished, he arose, took his hat, said faintly, 'I thank you,' and left the room. He afterwards said to Mr. ——, 'I never shall speak ill of her. She has done me good.' And this was the greater triumph, for this man had no theories of impersonality, and was the most egotistical and irritable of self-lovers, and was so unveracious, that one had to hope in charity that his organ for apprehending truth was deficient."

ECSTASY.

I have alluded to the fact, that, in the summer of 1840, Margaret underwent some change in the tone and the direction of her thoughts, to which she attributed a high importance. I remember, at an earlier period, when in earnest conversation with her, she seemed to have that height and daring, that I saw she was ready to do whatever she thought; and I observed that, with her literary riches, her invention and wit, her boundless fun and drollery, her light satire, and the most entertaining conversation in America, consisted a certain pathos of sentiment, and a march of character, threatening to arrive presently at the shores and plunge into the sea of Buddhism and mystical trances. The literature of asceticism and rapturous piety was familiar to her. The conversation of certain mystics, who had appeared in Boston about this time, had interested her, but in no commanding degree. But in this year, 1840, in which events occurred which combined great happiness and pain for her affections, she remained for some time in a sort of ecstatic solitude. She made many attempts to describe her frame of mind to me, but did not inspire me with confidence that she had now come to any experiences that were profound or permanent. She was vexed at the want of sympathy on my part, and I again felt that this craving for sympathy did not prove the inspiration. There was a certain restlessness and fever, which I did not like should deceive a soul which was capable of greatness. But jets of magnanimity were always natural to her; and her aspiring mind, eager for a higher and still a higher ground, made her gradually familiar with the range of the mystics, and, though never herself laid in the chamber called Peace, never quite authentically and originally speaking from the absolute or prophetic mount, yet she borrowed from her frequent visits to its precincts an occasional enthusiasm, which gave a religious dignity to her thought.

'I have plagues about me, but they don't touch me 'now. I thank nightly the benignant Spirit, for the un-'accustomed serenity in which it enfolds me.

'—— is very wretched; and once I could not have 'helped taking on me all his griefs, and through him the 'griefs of his class; but now I drink only the wormwood 'of the minute, and that has always equal parts,—a 'drop of sweet to a drop of bitter. But I shall never be 'callous, never unable to understand *home-sickness*. Am 'not I, too, one of the band who know not where to lay 'their heads? Am I wise enough to hear such things? 'Perhaps not; but happy enough, surely. For that 'Power which daily makes me understand the value of 'the little wheat amid the field of tares, and shows me 'how the kingdom of heaven is sown in the earth like a 'grain of mustard-seed, is good to me, and bids me call unhappiness happy.'

TO ——.

'*March*, 1842.—My inward life has been more rich

'and deep, and of more calm and musical flow than evei 'before. It seems to me that Heaven, whose course has 'ever been to cross-bias me, as Herbert said, is no niggard 'in its compensations. I have indeed been forced to take 'up old burdens, from which I thought I had learned what 'they could teach; the pen has been snatched from my 'hand just as I most longed to use it; I have been forced 'to dissipate, when I most wished to concentrate; to feel 'the hourly presence of others' mental wants, when, it 'seemed, I was just on the point of satisfying my own. 'But a new page is turned, and an era begun, from 'which I am not yet sufficiently remote to describe it as 'I would. I have lived a life, if only in the music I 'have heard, and one development seemed to follow 'another therein, as if bound together by destiny, and all 'things were done for me. All minds, all scenes, have 'ministered to me. Nature has seemed an ever-open 'secret; the Divine, a sheltering love; truth, an always-'springing fountain; and my soul more alone, and less 'lonely, more hopeful, patient, and, above all, more 'gentle and humble in its living. New minds have 'come to reveal themselves to me, though I do not wish 'it, for I feel myself inadequate to the ties already 'formed. I have not strength or time to meet the thoughts 'of those I love already. But these new have come 'with gifts too fair to be refused, and which have cheered 'my passive mind.'

'*June*, 1844.—Last night, in the boat, I could not 'help thinking, each has something, none has enough. 'I fear to want them all; and, through ages, if not 'forever, promises and beckons the life of reception, 'of renunciation. Passing every seven days from one 'region to the other, the maiden grows weary of *packing* '*the trunk*, yet blesses Thee, O rich God!'

Her letters at this period betray a pathetic alternation of feeling, between her aspiring for a rest in the absolute Centre, and her necessity of a perfect sympathy with her friends. She writes to one of them: —

'What I want, the word I crave, I do not expect 'to hear from the lips of man. I do not wish to be, I 'do not wish to have, a *mediator;* yet I cannot help 'wishing, when I am with you, that some tones of the 'longed-for music could be vibrating in the air around 'us. But I will not be impatient again; for, though I 'am but as I am, I like not to feel the eyes I have loved 'averted.'

CONVERSATION.

I have separated and distributed as I could some of the parts which blended in the rich composite energy which Margaret exerted during the ten years over which my occasional interviews with her were scattered. It remains to say, that all these powers and accomplishments found their best and only adequate channel in her conversation; — a conversation which those who have heard it, unanimously, as far as I know, pronounced to be, in elegance, in range, in flexibility, and adroit transition, in depth, in cordiality, and in moral aim, altogether admirable; surprising and cheerful as a poem, and communicating its own civility and elevation like a charm to all hearers. She was here, among our anxious citizens, and frivolous fashionists, as if sent to refine and polish her countrymen, and announce a better day. She poured a stream of amber over the endless store of private anecdotes, of bosom histories, which her wonderful persuasion drew forth, and transfigured them into fine fables. Whilst she embellished the moment, her conversation had the merit of being solid and true. She put her whole character into it, and had the power to inspire. The companion was made a thinker, and went away quite other than he came. The circle of friends who sat with her were not allowed to remain spectators or players, but she converted them into heroes, if she could. The muse woke the muses, and the day grew bright and eventful. Of course, there must be, in a person of such sincerity, much variety of aspect, according to the character of her company. Only, in Margaret's case, there is almost an agreement in the testimony to an invariable power over the minds of all. I conversed lately with a gentleman who has vivid remembrances of his interviews with her in Boston, many years ago, who described her in these terms: — "No one ever came so near. Her mood applied itself to the mood of her companion, point to point, in the most limber, sinuous, vital way, and drew out the most extraordinary narratives; yet she had a light sort of laugh, when all was said, as if she thought she could live over that revelation. And this sufficient sympathy she had for all persons indifferently, — for lovers, for artists, and beautiful maids, and ambitious young statesmen, and for old aunts, and coach-travellers. Ah! she applied herself to the mood of her companion, as the sponge applies itself to water." The description tallies well enough with my observation. I remember she found, one day, at my house, her old friend Mr. ——, sitting with me. She looked at him attentively, and hardly seemed to know him. In the afternoon, he invited her to go with him to Cambridge. The next day she said to me, 'You fancy that you know ——. It is 'too absurd; you have never seen him. When I found 'him here, sitting like a statue, I was alarmed, and 'thought him ill. You sit with courteous, *un*confiding 'smile, and suppose him to be a mere man of talent. 'He is so with you. But the moment I was alone with 'him, he was another creature; his manner, so glassy 'and elaborate before, was full of soul, and the tones of 'his voice entirely different.' And I have no doubt that she saw expressions, heard tones, and received thoughts from her companions, which no one else ever saw or heard from the same parties, and that her praise of her friends, which seemed exaggerated, was her exact impression. We were all obliged to recall Margaret's testimony, when we found we were sad blockheads to other people.

I find among her letters many proofs of this power of disposing equally the hardest and the most sensitive people to open their hearts, on very short acquaintance. Any casual rencontre, in a walk, in a steamboat, at a concert, became the prelude to unwonted confidences.

1843.—'I believe I told you about one new man, a 'Philistine, at Brook Farm. He reproved me, as such 'people are wont, for my little faith. At the end of the 'first meeting in the hall, he seemed to me perfectly 'hampered in his old ways and technics, and I thought 'he would not open his mind to the views of others for 'years, if ever. After I wrote, we had a second meet-'ing, by request, on personal relations; at the end of 'which, he came to me, and expressed delight, and a 'feeling of new light and life, in terms whose modesty 'might have done honor to the wisest.'

'This afternoon we met Mr. —— in his wood; and 'he sat down and told us the story of his life, his court-'ship, and painted the portraits of his father and mother 'with most amusing naïveté. He says: — "How do you '"think I offered myself? I never had told Miss —— '"that I loved her; never told her she was handsome; '"and I went to her, and said, 'Miss ——, I've come to '"offer myself; but first I'll give you my character. '"I'm very poor; you'll have to work: I'm very '"cross and irascible; you'll have everything to bear: '"and I've liked many other pretty girls. Now what '"do you say?' and she said, 'I'll have you:' and '"she's been everything to me.

'"My mother was a Calvinist, very strict, but she was '"always reading 'Abelard and Eloisa,' and crying over '"it. At sixteen, I said to her: 'Mother, you've brought '"me up well; you've kept me strict. Why don't I feel '"that regeneration they talk of? why an't I one of '"the elect?' And she talked to me about the potter '"using his clay as he pleased; and I said: 'Mother, God '"is not a potter: He's a perfect being; and he can't '"treat the vessels he makes, anyhow, but with perfect '"justice, or he's no God. So I'm no Calvinist.'"'

Here is a very different picture: —

'—— has infinite grace and shading in her character: 'a springing and tender fancy, a Madonna depth of 'meditative softness, and a purity which has been 'unstained, and keeps her dignified even in the most 'unfavorable circumstances. She was born for the love 'and ornament of life. I can scarcely forbear weeping 'sometimes, when I look on her, and think what happi-'ness and beauty she might have conferred. She is as 'yet all unconscious of herself, and she rather dreads 'being with me, because I make her too conscious. She 'was on the point, at ——, of telling me all she knew 'of herself; but I saw she dreaded, while she wished, 'that I should give a local habitation and a name to what 'lay undefined, floating before her, the phantom of her 'destiny; or rather lead her to give it, for she always 'approaches a tragical clearness when talking with me.'

'—— has been to see us. But it serves not to know 'such a person, who perpetually defaces the high by 'such strange mingling with the low. It certainly is 'not pleasant to hear of God and Miss Biddeford in a 'breath. To me, this hasty attempt at skimming from 'the deeps of theosophy is as unpleasant as the rude 'vanity of reformers. Dear Beauty! where, where, 'amid these morasses and pine barrens, shall we make 'thee a temple? where find a Greek to guard it, — clear-'eyed, deep-thoughted, and delicate enough to appreciate 'the relations and gradations which nature always ob-'serves?'

An acute and illuminated woman, who, in this age of indifferentism, holds on with both hands to the creed of the Pilgrims, writes of Margaret, whom she saw but once: — "She looked very sensible, but as if contending with ill health and duties. She lay, all the day and evening, on the sofa, and catechized me, who told my literal traditions, like any old bobbin-woman."

I add the testimony of a man of letters, and most competent observer, who had, for a long time, opportunities of daily intercourse with her: —

"When I knew Margaret, I was so young, and perhaps too much disposed to meet people on my own ground, that I may not be able to do justice to her. Her nature was so large and receptive, so sympathetic with youth and genius, so aspiring, and withal so womanly in her understanding, that she made her companion think more of himself, and of a common life, than of herself. She was a companion as few others, if indeed any one, have been. Her heart was underneath her intellectualness, her mind was reverent, her spirit devout; a thinker without dryness; a scholar without pedantry. She could appreciate the finest thoughts, and knew the rich soil and large fields of beauty that made the little vase of otto. With her unusual wisdom and religious spirit, she seemed like the priestess of the youth, opening to him the fields of nature; but she was more than a priestess, a companion also. As I recall her image, I think she may have been too intellectual, and too conscious of intellectual relation, so that she was not sufficiently self-centred on her own personality; and hence something of a duality: but I may not be correct in this impression."

CONVERSATIONS IN BOSTON.

BY R. W. EMERSON.

"Do not scold me; they are guests of my eyes. Do not frown, — they want no bread; they are guests of my words."

TARTAR ECLOGUES

27*

V.

CONVERSATIONS IN BOSTON.

In the year 1839, Margaret removed from Groton, and, with her mother and family, took a house at Jamaica Plain, five miles from Boston. In November of the next year the family removed to Cambridge, and rented a house there, near their old home. In 1841, Margaret took rooms for the winter in town, retaining still the house in Cambridge. And from the day of leaving Groton, until the autumn of 1844, when she removed to New York, she resided in Boston, or its immediate vicinity. Boston was her social centre. There were the libraries, galleries, and concerts which she loved; there were her pupils and her friends; and there were her tasks, and the openings of a new career.

I have vaguely designated some of the friends with whom she was on terms of intimacy at the time when I was first acquainted with her. But the range of her talents required an equal compass in her society; and she gradually added a multitude of names to the list. She knew already all the active minds at Cambridge; and has left a record of one good interview she had with

Allston. She now became intimate with Doctor Channing, and interested him to that point in some of her studies, that, at his request, she undertook to render some selections of German philosophy into English for him. But I believe this attempt was soon abandoned. She found a valuable friend in the late Miss Mary Rotch, of New Bedford, a woman of great strength of mind, connected with the Quakers not less by temperament than by birth, and possessing the best lights of that once spiritual sect. At Newport, Margaret had made the acquaintance of an elegant scholar, in Mr. Calvert, of Maryland. In Providence, she had won, as by conquest, such a homage of attachment, from young and old, that her arrival there, one day, on her return from a visit to Bristol, was a kind of ovation. In Boston, she knew people of every class,—merchants, politicians, scholars, artists, women, the migratory genius, and the rooted capitalist,—and, amongst all, many excellent people, who were every day passing, by new opportunities, conversations, and kind offices, into the sacred circle of friends. The late Miss Susan Burley had many points of attraction for her, not only in her elegant studies, but also in the deep interest which that lady took in securing the highest culture for women. She was very well read, and, avoiding abstractions, knew how to help herself with examples and facts. A friendship that proved of great importance to the next years was that established with Mr. George Ripley; an accurate scholar, a man of character, and of eminent powers of conversation, and already then deeply engaged in plans of an expansive practical bearing, of which the first fruit was the little community which flourished for a few years at Brook Farm. Margaret presently became connected with him in literary labors, and, as long as she remained in this vicinity, kept up her habits of intimacy with the colonists of Brook Farm. At West-Roxbury, too, she knew and prized the heroic heart, the learning and wit of Theodore Parker, whose literary aid was, subsequently, of the first importance to her. She had an acquaintance, for many years, — subject, no doubt, to alternations of sun and shade, — with Mr. Alcott. There was much antagonism in their habitual views, but each learned to respect the genius of the other. She had more sympathy with Mr. Alcott's English friend, Charles Lane, an ingenious mystic, and bold experimenter in practical reforms, whose dexterity and temper in debate she frankly admired, whilst his asceticism engaged her reverence. Neither could some marked difference of temperament remove her from the beneficent influences of Miss Elizabeth Peabody, who, by her constitutional hospitality to excellence, whether mental or moral, has made her modest abode for so many years the inevitable resort of studious feet, and a private theatre for the exposition of every question of letters, of philosophy, of ethics, and of art.

The events in Margaret's life, up to the year 1840, were few, and not of that dramatic interest which readers love. Of the few events of her bright and blameless years, how many are private, and must remain so. In reciting the story of an affectionate and passionate woman, the voice lowers itself to a whisper, and becomes inaudible. A woman in our society finds her safety and happiness in exclusions and privacies. She congratulates herself when she is not called to the market, to the courts, to the polls, to the stage, or to the orchestra. Only the most extraordinary genius can make the career of an artist secure and agreeable to her. Prescriptions almost invincible the female lecturer or professor of any science must encounter; and, except on points where the charities which are left to women as their legitimate province interpose against the ferocity of laws, with us a female politician is unknown. Perhaps this fact, which so dangerously narrows the career of a woman, accuses the tardiness of our civility, and many signs show that a revolution is already on foot.

Margaret had no love of notoriety, or taste for eccentricity, to goad her, and no weak fear of either. Willingly she was confined to the usual circles and methods of female talent. She had no false shame. Any task that called out her powers was good and desirable. She wished to live by her strength. She could converse, and teach, and write. She took private classes of pupils at her own house. She organized, with great success, a school for young ladies at Providence, and gave four hours a day to it, during two years. She translated Eckermann's Conversations with Goethe, and published in 1839. In 1841, she translated the Letters of Gunderode and Bettine, and published them as far as the sale warranted the work. In 1843, she made a tour to Lake Superior and to Michigan, and published an agreeable narrative of it, called "Summer on the Lakes."

Apparently a more pretending, but really also a private and friendly service, she edited the "Dial," a quarterly journal, for two years from its first publication in 1840. She was eagerly solicited to undertake the charge of this work, which, when it began, concentrated a good deal of hope and affection. It had its origin in a club of speculative students, who found the air in America getting a little close and stagnant; and the agitation had perhaps the fault of being too secondary or bookish in its origin, or caught not from primary instincts, but from English, and still more from German books. The journal was commenced with much hope, and liberal promises of many coöperators. But the workmen of sufficient culture for a poetical and philosophical magazine were too few; and, as the pages were filled by unpaid contributors, each of whom had, according to the usage and necessity of this country, some paying employment, the journal did not get his best work, but his second best. Its scattered writers had not digested their theories into a distinct dogma, still less into a practical measure which the public could grasp; and the magazine was so eclectic and miscellaneous, that each of its readers and writers valued only a small portion of it. For these reasons it never had a large circulation, and it was discontinued after four years. But the Dial betrayed, through all its juvenility, timidity, and conventional rubbish, some sparks of the true love and hope, and of the piety to spiritual law, which had moved its friends and founders, and it was received by its early subscribers with almost a religious welcome. Many years after it was brought to a close, Margaret was surprised in England by very warm testimony to its merits; and, in 1848, the writer of these pages found it holding the same affectionate place in many a private bookshelf in England and Scotland, which it had secured at home. Good or bad, it cost a good deal of precious labor from those who served it, and from Margaret most of all. As editor, she received a compensation for the first years, which was intended to be two hundred dollars *per annum*, but which, I fear, never reached even that amount.

But it made no difference to her exertion. She put so

much heart into it that she bravely undertook to open, in the Dial, the subjects which most attracted her; and she treated, in turn, Goethe, and Beethoven, the Rhine and the Romaic Ballads, the Poems of John Sterling, and several pieces of sentiment, with a spirit which spared no labor; and, when the hard conditions of journalism held her to an inevitable day, she submitted to jeopardizing a long-cherished subject, by treating it in the crude and forced article for the month. I remember, after she had been compelled by ill health to relinquish the journal into my hands, my grateful wonder at the facility with which she assumed the preparation of laborious articles, that might have daunted the most practised scribe.

But in book or journal she found a very imperfect expression of herself, and it was the more vexatious, because she was accustomed to the clearest and fullest. When, therefore, she had to choose an employment that should pay money, she consulted her own genius, as well as the wishes of a multitude of friends, in opening a class for conversation. In the autumn of 1839, she addressed the following letter, intended for circulation, to Mrs. George Ripley, in which her general design was stated: —

'My dear friend: — The advantages of a weekly 'meeting, for conversation, might be great enough to 'repay the trouble of attendance, if they consisted only 'in supplying a point of union to well-educated and 'thinking women, in a city which, with great preten-'sions to mental refinement, boasts, at present, nothing 'of the kind, and where I have heard many, of mature 'age, wish for some such means of stimulus and cheer, 'and those younger, for a place where they could state 'their doubts and difficulties, with a hope of gaining 'aid from the experience or aspirations of others. And, 'if my office were only to suggest topics, which would 'lead to conversation of a better order than is usual at 'social meetings, and to turn back the current when 'digressing into personalities or common-places, so that 'what is valuable in the experience of each might be 'brought to bear upon all, I should think the object not 'unworthy of the effort.

'But my ambition goes much further. It is to pass 'in review the departments of thought and knowl-'edge, and endeavor to place them in due relation to 'one another in our minds. To systematize thought, 'and give a precision and clearness in which our sex 'are so deficient, chiefly, I think, because they have 'so few inducements to test and classify what they 'receive. To ascertain what pursuits are best suited to 'us, in our time and state of society, and how we may 'make best use of our means for building up the life of 'thought upon the life of action.

'Could a circle be assembled in earnest, desirous to 'answer the questions, — What were we born to do? 'and how shall we do it?—which so few ever propose 'to themselves till their best years are gone by, I should 'think the undertaking a noble one, and, if my resources 'should prove sufficient to make me its moving spring, 'I should be willing to give to it a large portion of 'those coming years, which will, as I hope, be my best. 'I look upon it with no blind enthusiasm, nor unlim-'ited faith, but with a confidence that I have attained 'a distinct perception of means, which, if there are per-'sons competent to direct them, can supply a great want, 'and promote really high objects. So far as I have tried 'them yet, they have met with success so much beyond 'my hopes, that my faith will not easily be shaken, nor 'my earnestness chilled. Should I, however, be disap-'pointed in Boston, I could hardly hope that such a 'plan could be brought to bear on general society, in 'any other city of the United States. But I do not 'fear, if a good beginning can be made. I am confi-'dent that twenty persons cannot be brought together 'from better motives than vanity or pedantry, to talk 'upon such subjects as we propose, without finding in 'themselves great deficiencies, which they will be very 'desirous to supply.

'Should the enterprise fail, it will be either from 'incompetence in me, or that sort of vanity in them 'which wears the garb of modesty. On the first of these 'points, I need not speak. I cannot be supposed to have 'felt so much the wants of others, without feeling my 'own still more deeply. And, from the depth of this 'feeling, and the earnestness it gave, such power as I 'have yet exerted has come. Of course, those who are 'inclined to meet me, feel a confidence in me, and 'should they be disappointed, I shall regret it not solely 'or most on my own account. I have not given my 'gauge without measuring my capacity to sustain defeat. 'For the other, I know it is very hard to lay aside the 'shelter of vague generalities, the art of coterie criticism, 'and the "delicate disdains" of *good society*, and fear-'lessly meet the light, even though it flow from the sun 'of truth. Yet, as, without such generous courage, 'nothing of value can be learned or done, I hope to 'see many capable of it; willing that others should 'think their sayings crude, shallow, or tasteless, if, by 'such unpleasant means, they may attain real health and vigor, which need no aid from rouge or candle-light, to brave the light of the world.

'Since I saw you, I have been told of persons who 'are desirous to join the class, "if only they need not '"talk." I am so sure that the success of the whole 'depends on conversation being general, that I do not 'wish any one to come, who does not intend, if possible, 'to take an active part. No one will be forced, but 'those who do not talk will not derive the same advan-'tages with those who openly state their impressions, 'and can consent to have it known that they learn by 'blundering, as is the destiny of man here below. And 'general silence, or side talks, would paralyze me. I 'should feel coarse and misplaced, were I to harangue 'over-much. In former instances, I have been able to 'make it easy and even pleasant, to twenty-five out of 'thirty, to bear their part, to question, to define, to state, 'and examine opinions. If I could not do as much now, 'I should consider myself as unsuccessful, and should 'withdraw. But I shall expect communication to be 'effected by degrees, and to do a great deal myself at 'the first meetings. My method has been to open a 'subject, — for instance, Poetry, as expressed in —

'External Nature;

'The life of man;

'Literature;

'The fine arts;

'or, The history of a nation to be studied in —

'Its religious and civil institutions;

'Its literature and arts;

'The characters of its great men;

'and, after as good a general statement as I know 'how to make, select a branch of the subject, and lead 'others to give their thoughts upon it. When they have 'not been successful in verbal utterance of their thoughts, 'I have asked them to attempt it in writing. At the 'next meeting, I would read these "skarts of pen and '"ink" aloud, and canvass their adequacy, without 'mentioning the names of the writers. I found this less 'necessary, as I proceeded, and my companions attained 'greater command both of thought and language; but 'for a time it was useful, and may be now. Great ad- 'vantage in point of discipline may be derived from even 'this limited use of the pen.

'I do not wish, at present, to pledge myself to any 'course of subjects. Generally, I may say, they will 'be such as literature and the arts present in endless 'profusion. Should a class be brought together, I should 'wish, first, to ascertain our common ground, and, in the 'course of a few meetings, should see whether it be prac- 'ticable to follow out the design in my mind, which, as 'yet, would look too grand on paper.

'Let us see whether there will be any organ, before 'noting down the music to which it may give breath.'

Accordingly, a class of ladies assembled at Miss Peabody's rooms, in West Street, on the 6th November, 1839. Twenty-five were present, and the circle comprised some of the most agreeable and intelligent women to be found in Boston and its neighborhood. The following brief report of this first day's meeting remains: —

"Miss Fuller enlarged, in her introductory conversation, on the topics which she touched in her letter to Mrs. Ripley.

'Women are now taught, at school, all that men are; 'they run over, superficially, even *more* studies, without 'being really taught anything. When they come to the 'business of life, they find themselves inferior, and all 'their studies have not given them that practical good 'sense, and mother wisdom, and wit, which grew up 'with our grandmothers at the spinning-wheel. But, 'with this difference; men are called on, from a very 'early period, to reproduce all that they learn. Their 'college exercises, their political duties, their professional 'studies, the first actions of life in any direction, call on 'them to put to use what they have learned. But 'women learn without any attempt to reproduce. Their 'only reproduction is for purposes of display.

'It is to supply this defect,' Miss Fuller said, 'that 'these conversations have been planned. She was not 'here to teach; but she had had some experience in the 'management of such a conversation as was now pro-'posed; she meant to give her view on each subject, and 'provoke the thoughts of others.

'It would be best to take subjects on which we know 'words, and have vague impressions, and compel our-'selves to define those words. We should have, proba-'bly, mortifications to suffer; but we should be encour-'aged by the rapid gain that comes from making a 'simple and earnest effort for expression.'

Miss Fuller had proposed the Grecian Mythology as the subject of the first conversations, and now gave her reasons for the choice. 'It is quite separated from all 'exciting local subjects. It is serious, without being sol-'emn, and without excluding any mode of intellectual 'action; it is playful, as well as deep. It is sufficiently 'wide, for it is a complete expression of the cultivation 'of a nation. It is objective and tangible. It is, also, 'generally known, and associated with all our ideas of 'the arts.

'It originated in the eye of the Greek. He lived 'out of doors: his climate was genial, his senses were 'adapted to it. He was vivacious and intellectual, and 'personified all he beheld. He *saw* the oreads, naiads, 'nereids. Their forms, as poets and painters give them, 'are the very lines of nature humanized, as the child's 'eye sees faces in the embers or in the clouds.

'Other forms of the mythology, as Jupiter, Juno, 'Apollo, are great instincts, or ideas, or facts of the 'internal constitution, separated and personified.'

After exhibiting their enviable mental health, and rebutting the cavils of some of the speakers, — who could not bear, in Christian times, by Christian ladies, that heathen Greeks should be envied, — Miss Fuller declared, 'that she had no desire to go back, and believed 'we have the elements of a deeper civilization; yet, the 'Christian was in its infancy; the Greek in its maturity; 'nor could she look on the expression of a great nation's 'intellect, as insignificant. These fables of the Gods 'were the result of the universal sentiments of religion, 'aspiration, intellectual action, of a people, whose politi-'cal and æsthetic life had become immortal; and we 'must leave off despising, if we would begin to learn.'"

The reporter closes her account by saying: — "Miss Fuller's thoughts were much illustrated, and all was said with the most captivating address and grace, and with beautiful modesty. The position in which she placed herself with respect to the rest, was entirely lady-like, and companionable. She told what she intended, the earnest purpose with which she came, and, with great tact, indicated the indiscretions that might spoil the meeting."

Here is Margaret's own account of the first days.

TO R. W. E.

'*25th Nov.*, 1839. — My class is prosperous. I was so 'fortunate as to rouse, at once, the tone of simple earnest-'ness, which can scarcely, when once awakened, cease to 'vibrate. All seem in a glow, and quite as receptive as I 'wish. They question and examine, yet follow leadings; 'and thoughts, not opinions, have ruled the hour every 'time. There are about twenty-five members, and every 'one, I believe, full of interest. The first time, ten took 'part in the conversation; the last, still more. Mrs '——— came out in a way that surprised me. She 'seems to have shaken off a wonderful number of films. 'She showed pure vision, sweet sincerity, and much tal-'ent. Mrs. ——— ——— keeps us in good order, and takes 'care that Christianity and morality are not forgotten. 'The first day's topic was, the genealogy of heaven and 'earth; then the Will, (Jupiter); the Understanding, '(Mercury): the second day's, the celestial inspiration 'of genius, perception and transmission of divine law, '(Apollo); the terrene inspiration, the impassioned aban-'donment of genius, (Bacchus). Of the thunderbolt, 'the caduceus, the ray, and the grape, having disposed 'as well as might be, we came to the wave, and the 'sea-shell it moulds to Beauty, and Love her parent 'and her child.

'I assure you, there is more Greek than Bostonian

'spoken at the meetings; and we may have pure honey 'of Hymettus to give you yet.'

To another friend she wrote: —

'The circle I meet interests me. So even devoutly 'thoughtful seems their spirit, that, from the very first, 'I took my proper place, and never had the feeling I 'dreaded, of display, of a paid Corinne. I feel as I 'would, truly a teacher and a guide. All are intelli- 'gent; five or six have talent. But I am never driven 'home for ammunition; never put to any expense; 'never truly called out. What I have is always 'enough; though I feel how superficially I am treat- 'ing my subject.'

Here is an extract from the letter of a lady, who joined the class, for the first time, at the eighth meeting, to her friend in New Haven: —

"Christmas made a holiday for Miss Fuller's class, but it met on Saturday, at noon. As I sat there, my heart overflowed with joy at the sight of the bright circle, and I longed to have you by my side, for I know not where to look for so much character, culture, and so much love of truth and beauty, in any other circle of women and girls. The names and faces would not mean so much to you as to me, who have seen more of the lives, of which they are the sign. Margaret, beautifully dressed, (don't despise that, for it made a fine picture,) presided with more dignity and grace than I had thought possible. The subject was Beauty. Each had written her definition, and Margaret began with reading her own. This called forth questions, comments, and illustrations, on all sides. The style and manner, of course, in this age, are different, but the question, the high point from which it was considered, and the earnestness and simplicity of the discussion, as well as the gifts and graces of the speakers, gave it the charm of a Platonic dialogue. There was no pretension or pedantry in a word that was said. The tone of remark and question was simple as that of children in a school class; and, I believe, every one was gratified."

The conversations thus opened proceeded with spirit and success. Under the mythological forms, room was found for opening all the great questions, on which Margaret and her friends wished to converse. Prometheus was made the type of Pure Reason; Jupiter, of Will; Juno, the passive side of the same, or Obstinacy; Minerva, Intellectual Power, Practical Reason; Mercury, Executive Power, Understanding; Apollo was Genius, the Sun; Bacchus was Geniality, the Earth's answer. "Apollo and Bacchus were contrasted," says the reporter. "Margaret unfolded her idea of Bacchus. His whole life was triumph. Born from fire; a divine frenzy; the answer of the earth to the sun, — of the warmth of joy to the light of genius. He is beautiful, also; not severe in youthful beauty, like Apollo; but exuberant, — liable to excess. She spoke of the fables of his destroying Pentheus, &c., and suggested the interpretations. This Bacchus was found in Scripture. The Indian Bacchus is glowing; he is the genial apprehensive power; the glow of existence; mere joy."

Venus was Grecian womanhood, instinctive; Diana, chastity; Mars, Grecian manhood, instinctive. Venus made the name for a conversation on Beauty, which was extended through four meetings, as it brought in irresistibly the related topics of poetry, genius, and taste. Neptune was Circumstance; Pluto, the Abyss, the Undeveloped; Pan, the glow and sportiveness and music of Nature; Ceres, the productive power of Nature; Proserpine, the Phenomenon.

Under the head of Venus, in the fifth conversation, the story of Cupid and Psyche was told with fitting beauty, by Margaret; and many fine conjectural interpretations suggested from all parts of the room. The ninth conversation turned on the distinctive qualities of poetry, discriminating it from the other fine arts. Rhythm and Imagery, it was agreed, were distinctive. An episode to dancing, which the conversation took, led Miss Fuller to give the thought that lies at the bottom of different dances. Of her lively description the following record is preserved: —

'Gavottes, shawl dances, and all of that kind, are 'intended merely to exhibit the figure in as many atti- 'tudes as possible. They have no character, and say 'nothing, except, Look! how graceful I am!

'The minuet is conjugal; but the wedlock is chiv- 'alric. Even so would Amadis wind slow, stately, 'calm, through the mazes of life, with Oriana, when he 'had made obeisances enough to win her for a partner.

'English, German, Swiss, French, and Spanish 'dances all express the same things, though in very 'different ways. Love and its life are still the theme.

'In the English country dance, the pair who have 'chosen one another, submit decorously to the restraints 'of courtship and frequent separations, cross hands, 'four go round, down outside, in the most earnest, 'lively, complacent fashion. If they join hands to go 'down the middle, and exhibit their union to all spec-'tators, they part almost as soon as meet, and disdain 'not to give hands right and left to the most indifferent 'persons, like marriage in its daily routine.

'In the Swiss, the man pursues, stamping with 'energy, marking the time by exulting flings, or snap-'ping of the fingers, in delighted confidence of succeed-'ing at last; but the maiden coyly, demurely, foots it 'round, yet never gets out of the way, intending to be won.

'The German asks his *madchen* if she will, with 'him, for an hour forget the cares and common-places 'of life in a tumult of rapturous sympathy, and she 'smiles with Saxon modesty her *Ja.* He sustains her in 'his arms; the music begins. At first, in willing mazes 'they calmly imitate the planetary orbs, but the melodies 'flow quicker, their accordant hearts beat higher, and 'they whirl at last into giddy raptures, and dizzy evolu-'tions, which steal from life its free-will and self-collec-'tion, till nothing is left but mere sensation.

'The French couple are somewhat engaged with one 'another, but almost equally so with the world around 'them. They think it well to vary existence with plenty 'of coquetry and display. First, the graceful rever-'ence to one another, then to their neighbors. Exhibit 'your grace in the *chassé*,— made apparently solely for 'the purpose of *déchasséing*,— then civil intimacy be-'tween the ladies, in *la chaine*, then a decorous prom-'enade of partners, then right and left with all the world, and balance, &c. The quadrille also offers opportunity 'for talk. Looks and sympathetic motions are not 'enough for our Parisian friends, unless eked out by 'words.

'The impassioned bolero and fandango are the dances 'for me. They are not merely loving, but living; they 'express the sweet Southern ecstasy at the mere gift of 'existence. These persons are together, they live, they 'are beautiful; how can they say this in sufficiently 'plain terms?—I love, I live, I am beautiful!—I put 'on my festal dress to do honor to my happiness; I 'shake my castanets, that my hands, too, may be busy; 'I *felice,—felicissima!*'

This first series of conversations extended to thirteen, the class meeting once a week at noon, and remaining together for two hours. The class were happy, and the interest increased. A new series of thirteen more weeks followed, and the general subject of the new course was "the Fine Arts." A few fragmentary notes only of these hours have been shown me, but all those who bore any part in them testify to their entire success. A very competent witness has given me some interesting particulars:—

"Margaret used to come to the conversations very well dressed, and, altogether, looked sumptuously. She began them with an exordium, in which she gave her leading views; and those exordiums were excellent, from the elevation of the tone, the ease and flow of discourse, and from the tact with which they were kept aloof from any excess, and from the gracefulness with which they were brought down, at last, to a possible level for others to follow. She made a pause, and invited the others to come in. Of course, it was not easy for every one to venture her remark, after an eloquent discourse, and in the presence of twenty superior women, who were all inspired. But whatever was said, Margaret knew how to seize the good meaning of it with hospitality, and to make the speaker feel glad, and not sorry, that she had spoken. She showed herself thereby fit to preside at such meetings, and imparted to the susceptible a wonderful reliance on her genius."

In her writing she was prone to spin her sentences without a sure guidance, and beyond the sympathy of her reader. But in discourse, she was quick, conscious of power, in perfect tune with her company, and would pause and turn the stream with grace and adroitness, and with so much spirit, that her face beamed, and the young people came away delighted, among other things, with "her beautiful looks." When she was intellectually excited, or in high animal spirits, as often happened, all deformity of features was dissolved in the power of the expression. So I interpret this repeated story of sumptuousness of dress, that this appearance, like her reported beauty, was simply an effect of a general impression of magnificence made by her genius, and mistakenly attributed to some external elegance; for I have been told by her most intimate friend, who knew every particular of her conduct at that time, that there was nothing of special expense or splendor in her toilette.

The effect of the winter's work was happiest. Margaret was made intimately known to many excellent persons.* In this company of matrons and maids, many tender spirits had been set in ferment. A new day had

* A friend has furnished me with the names of so many of the ladies as she recollects to have met, at one or another time, at these classes. Some of them were perhaps only occasional members. The list recalls how much talent, beauty, and worth were at that time constellated here: —

dawned for them; new thoughts had opened; the secret of life was shown, or, at least, that life had a secret. They could not forget what they had heard, and what they had been surprised into saying. A true refinement had begun to work in many who had been slaves to trifles. They went home thoughtful and happy, since the steady elevation of Margaret's aim had infused a certain unexpected greatness of tone into the conversation. It was, I believe, only an expression of the feeling of the class, the remark made, perhaps at the next year's course, by a lady of eminent powers, previously by no means partial to Margaret, and who expressed her frank admiration on leaving the house: — "I never heard, read of, or imagined a conversation at all equal to this we have now heard."

The strongest wishes were expressed, on all sides, that the conversations should be renewed at the beginning of the following winter. Margaret willingly consented; but, as I have already intimated, in the summer and autumn of 1840, she had retreated to some interior shrine, and believed that she came into life and society with some advantage from this devotion.

Of this feeling the new discussion bore evident traces.

Mrs. George Bancroft, Mrs. Barlow, Miss Burley, Mrs. L. M. Child, Miss Mary Channing, Miss Sarah Clarke, Mrs. E. P. Clark, Miss Dorr, Mrs. Edwards, Mrs. R. W. Emerson, Mrs. Farrar, Miss S. J. Gardiner, Mrs. R. W. Hooper, Mrs. S. Hooper, Miss Haliburton, Miss Howes, Miss E. Hoar, Miss Marianne Jackson, Mrs. T. Lee, Miss Littlehale, Mrs. E. G. Loring, Mrs. Mack, Mrs. Horace Mann, Mrs. Newcomb, Mrs. Theodore Parker, Miss E. P. Peabody, Miss S. Peabody, Mrs. S. Putnam, Mrs. Phillips, Mrs. Josiah Quincy, Miss B. Randall, Mrs. Samuel Ripley, Mrs. George Ripley, Mrs. George Russell, Miss Ida Russell, Mrs. Frank Shaw, Miss Anna B. Shaw, Miss Caroline Sturgis, Miss Tuckerman, Miss Maria White, Mrs. S. G. Ward, Miss Mary Ward, Mrs. W. Whiting.

Most of the last year's class returned, and new members gave in their names. The first meeting was holden on the twenty-second of November, 1840. By all accounts it was the best of all her days. I have again the notes, taken at the time, of the excellent lady at whose house it was held, to furnish the following sketch of the first and the following meetings. I preface these notes by an extract from a letter of Margaret.

TO W. H. C.

'*Sunday, Nov. 8th*, 1840. — On Wednesday I opened 'with my class. It was a noble meeting. I told them 'the great changes in my mind, and that I could not be 'sure they would be satisfied with me now, as they were 'when I was in deliberate possession of myself. I tried 'to convey the truth, and though I did not arrive at 'any full expression of it, they all, with glistening eyes, 'seemed melted into one love. Our relation is now per-'fectly true, and I do not think they will ever interrupt 'me. —— sat beside me, all glowing; and the moment 'I had finished, she began to speak. She told me after-'wards, she was all kindled, and none there could be 'strangers to her more. I was really delighted by the 'enthusiasm of Mrs. ——. I did not expect it. All 'her best self seemed called up, and she feels that these 'meetings will be her highest pleasure. ——, too, was 'most beautiful. I went home with Mrs. F., and had a 'long attack of nervous headache. She attended anx-'iously on me, and asked if it would be so all winter. 'I said, if it were I did not care; and truly I feel just 'now such a separation from pain and illness, — such a consciousness of true life, while suffering most, —

'that pain has no effect but to steal some of my 'time.'

CONVERSATIONS ON THE FINE ARTS.

"Miss Fuller's fifth conversation was pretty much a monologue of her own. The company collected proved much larger than any of us had anticipated: a chosen company, — several persons from homes out of town, at considerable inconvenience; and, in one or two instances, fresh from extreme experiences of joy and grief, — which Margaret felt a very grateful tribute to her. She knew no one came for experiment, but all in earnest love and trust, and was moved by it quite to the heart, which threw an indescribable charm of softness over her brilliancy. It is sometimes said, that women never are so lovely and enchanting in the company of their own sex, merely, but it requires the other to draw them out. Certain it is that Margaret never appears, when I see her, either so brilliant and deep in thought, or so desirous to please, or so modest, or so heart-touching, as in this very party. Well, she began to say how gratifying it was to her to see so many come, because all knew why they came, — that it was to learn from each other and ourselves the highest ends of life, where there could be no excitements and gratifications of personal ambition, &c. She spoke of herself, and said she felt she had undergone changes in her own mind since the last winter, as doubtless we all felt we had done; that she was conscious of looking at all things less objectively, —more from the law with which she identified herself. This, she stated, was the natural progress of our individual being, when we did not hinder its development, to advance from objects to law, from the circumference of being, where we found ourselves at our birth, to the centre.

"This advance was enacted poesy. We could not, in our individual lives, amid the disturbing influences of other wills, which had as much right to their own action as we to ours, enact poetry entirely; the discordant, the inferior, the prose, would intrude, but we should always keep in mind that poetry of life was not something aside, — a path that might or might not be trod, — it was the only path of the true soul; and prose you may call the deviation. We might not always be poetic in life, but we might and should be poetic in our thought and intention. The fine arts were one compensation for the necessary prose of life. The man who could not write his thought of beauty in his life, — the materials of whose life would not work up into poetry, — wrote it in stone, drew it on canvas, breathed it in music, or built it in lofty rhyme. In this statement, however, she guarded her meaning, and said that to seek beauty was to miss it often. We should only seek to live as harmoniously with the great laws as our social and other duties permitted, and solace ourselves with poetry and the fine arts."

I find a further record by the same friendly scribe, which seems a second and enlarged account of the introductory conversation, or else a sketch of the course of thought which ran through several meetings, and which very naturally repeated occasionally the same thoughts. I give it as I find it: —

"She then recurred to the last year's conversations;

and, first, the Grecian mythologies, which she looked at as symbolical of a deeper intellectual and æsthetic life than we were wont to esteem it, when looking at it from a narrow religious point of view. We had merely skimmed along the deeper study. She spoke of the conversations on the different part played by Inspiration and Will in the works of man, and stated the different views of inspiration, — how some had felt it was merely perception; others apprehended it as influx upon the soul from the soul-side of its being. Then she spoke of the conversation upon poesy as the ground of all the fine arts, and also of the true art of life; it being not merely truth, not merely good, but the beauty which integrates both. On this poesy, she dwelt long, aiming to show how life, — perfect life, — could be the only perfect manifestation of it. Then she spoke of the individual as surrounded, however, by *prose*, — so we may here call the manifestation of the temporary, in opposition to the eternal, always trenching on it, and circumscribing and darkening. She spoke of the acceptance of this limitation, but it should be called by the right name, and always measured; and we should inwardly cling to the truth that poesy was the natural life of the soul; and never yield inwardly to the common notion that poesy was a luxury, out of the common track; but maintain in word and life that prose carried the soul out of its track; and then, perhaps, it would not injure us to walk in these by-paths, when forced thither. She admitted that prose was the necessary human condition, and quickened our life indirectly by necessitating a conscious demand on the source of life. In reply to a remark I made, she very strongly stated the difference between a poetic and a *dilettante* life, and sympathized with the sensible people who were tired of hearing all the young ladies of Boston sighing like furnace after being beautiful. Beauty was something very different from prettiness, and a microscopic vision missed the grand whole. The fine arts were our compensation for not being able to live out our poesy, amid the conflicting and disturbing forces of this moral world in which we are. In sculpture, the heights to which our being comes are represented; and its nature is such as to allow us to leave out all that vulgarizes, — all that bridges over to the actual from the ideal. She dwelt long upon sculpture, which seems her favorite art. That was grand, when a man first thought to engrave his idea of man upon a stone, the most unyielding and material of materials, — the backbone of this phenomenal earth, — and, when he did not succeed, that he persevered; and so, at last, by repeated efforts, the Apollo came to be.

"But, no; music she thought the greatest of arts, — expressing what was most interior, — what was too fine to be put into any material grosser than air; conveying from soul to soul the most secret motions of feeling and thought. This was the only fine art which might be thought to be flourishing now. The others had had their day. This was advancing upon a higher intellectual ground.

"Of painting she spoke, but not so well. She seemed to think painting worked more by illusion than sculpture. It involved more prose, from its representing more objects. She said nothing adequate about *color.*

"She dwelt upon the histrionic art as the most complete, its organ being the most flexible and powerful.

"She then spoke of life, as the art, of which these all

were beautiful symbols; and said, in recurring to her opinions expressed last winter, of Dante and Wordsworth, that she had taken another view, deeper, and more in accordance with some others which were then expressed. She acknowledged that Wordsworth had done more to make all men poetical, than perhaps any other; that he was the poet of reflection; that where he failed to poetize his subject, his simple faith intimated to the reader a poetry that he did not find in the book. She admitted that Dante's Narrative was instinct with the poetry concentrated often in single words. She uttered her old heresies about Milton, however, unmodified.

"I do not remember the transition to modern poetry and Milnes; but she read (very badly indeed) the Legendary Tale.

"We then had three conversations upon Sculpture, one of which was taken up very much in historical accounts of the sculpture of the ancients, in which color was added to form, and which seemed to prove that they were not, after all, sufficiently intellectual to be operated on by form exclusively. The question, of course, arose whether there was a modern sculpture, and why not. This led us to speak of the Greek sculpture as growing naturally out of their life and religion, and how alien it was to our life and to our religion. The Swiss lion, carved by Thorwaldsen out of the side of a mountain rock, was described as a natural growth. Those who had seen it described it; and Mrs. —— spoke of it. She was also led to the story of her acquaintance with Thorwaldsen, and drew tears from many eyes with her natural eloquence.

"Mrs. C. asked, if sculpture could express as well as painting the idea of immortality.

"Margaret thought the Greek art expressed immortality as much as Christian art, but did not throw it into the future, by preëminence. They expressed it in the present, by casting out of the mortal body every expression of infirmity and decay. The idealization of the human form makes a God. The fact that man can conceive and express this perfection of being, is as good a witness to immortality, as the look of aspiration in the countenance of a Magdalen.

"It is quite beyond the power of my memory to recall all the bright utterances of Margaret, in these conversations on Sculpture. It was a favorite subject with her. Then came two or three conversations on Painting, in which it seemed to be conceded that color expressed passion, whilst sculpture more severely expressed thought: yet painting did not exclude the expression of thought, or sculpture that of feeling, — witness Niobe, — but it must be an universal feeling, like the maternal sentiment.

"*March* 22, 1841. — The question of the day was, What is life?

"Let us define, each in turn, our idea of living. Margaret did not believe we had, any of us, a distinct idea of life.

"A. S. thought so great a question ought to be given for a written definition. 'No,' said Margaret, 'that is of no 'use. When we go away to think of anything, we never 'do think. We all talk of life. We all have some thought 'now. Let us tell it. C——, what is life?'

"C—— replied, — 'It is to laugh, or cry, according to our organization.'

"'Good,' said Margaret, 'but not grave enough. 'Come, what is life? I know what I think; I want 'you to find out what you think.'

"Miss P. replied, — 'Life is division from one's principle of life in order to a conscious reörganization. We are cut up by time and circumstance, in order to feel our reproduction of the eternal law.'

"Mrs. E., — 'We live by the will of God, and the object of life is to submit,' and went on into Calvinism.

"Then came up all the antagonisms of Fate and Freedom.

"Mrs. H. said, — 'God created us in order to have a perfect sympathy from us as free beings.'

"Mrs. A. B. said she thought the object of life was to attain absolute freedom. At this Margaret immediately and visibly kindled.

"C. S. said, — 'God creates from the fulness of life, and cannot but create; he created us to overflow, without being exhausted, because what he created, necessitated new creation. It is not to make us happy, but creation is his happiness and ours.'

"Margaret was then pressed to say what she considered life to be.

"Her answer was so full, clear, and concise, at once, that it cannot but be marred by being drawn through the scattering medium of my memory. But here are some fragments of her satisfying statement.

"She began with God as Spirit, Life, so full as to create and love eternally, yet capable of pause. Love and creativeness are dynamic forces, out of which we, individually, as creatures, go forth bearing his image, that is, having within our being the same dynamic forces, by which we also add constantly to the total sum of existence, and shaking off ignorance, and its effects, and by becoming more ourselves, *i. e.*, more divine; — destroying sin in its principle, we attain to absolute freedom, we return to God, conscious like himself, and, as his friends, giving, as well as receiving, felicity forevermore. In short, we become gods, and able to give the life which we now feel ourselves able only to receive.

"On Saturday morning, Mrs. L. E. and Mrs. E. H. were present, and begged Margaret to repeat the statement concerning life, with which she closed the last conversation. Margaret said she had forgotten every word she said. She must have been inspired by a good genius, to have so satisfied everybody, — but the good genius had left her. She would try, however, to say what she thought, and trusted it would resemble what she had said already. She then went into the matter, and, true enough, she did not use a single word she used before."

The fame of these conversations spread wide through all families and social circles of the ladies attending, and the golden report they gave, led to a proposal, that Margaret should undertake an evening class, of four or five lessons, to which gentlemen should also be admitted. This was put in effect, in the course of the winter, and I had myself the pleasure of assisting at one — the second — of these soirées. The subject was Mythology, and several gentlemen took part in it. Margaret spoke well, — she could not otherwise, — but I remember that she seemed encumbered, or interrupted, by the headiness or incapacity of the men, whom she had not had the advantage of training, and who fancied, no doubt, that, on such a question, they, too, must assert and dogmatize.

But, how well or ill they fared, may still be known; since the same true hand which reported for the Ladies' Class, drew up, at the time, the following note of the Evenings of Mythology. My distance from town, and engagements, prevented me from attending again. I was told that on the preceding and following evenings the success was more decisive.

"Margaret's plan, in these conversations, was a very noble one, and, had it been seconded, as she expected, they would have been splendid. She thought, that, by admitting gentlemen, who had access, by their classical education, to the whole historical part of the mythology, her own comparative deficiency, as she felt it, in this part of learning, would be made up; and that taking her stand on the works of art, which were the final development in Greece of these multifarious fables, the whole subject might be swept from zenith to nadir. But all that depended on others entirely failed. Mr. W. contributed some isolated facts, — told the etymology of names, and cited a few fables not so commonly known as most; but, even in the point of erudition, which Margaret did not profess, on the subject, she proved the best informed of the party, while no one brought an idea, except herself.

"Her general idea was, that, upon the Earth-worship and Sabæanism of earlier ages, the Grecian genius acted to humanize and idealize, but, still, with some regard to the original principle. What was a seed, or a root, merely, in the Egyptian mind, became a flower in Greece, — Isis, and Osiris, for instance, are reproduced in

Ceres and Proserpine, with some loss of generality, but with great gain of beauty; Hermes, in Mercury, with only more grace of form, though with great loss of grandeur; but the loss of grandeur was also an advance in philosophy, in this instance, the brain in the hand being the natural consequence of the application of Idea to practice, — the Hermes of the Egyptians.

"I do not feel that the class, by their apprehension of Margaret, do any justice to the scope and depth of her views. They come, — myself among the number, — I confess, — to be entertained; but she has a higher purpose. She, amid all her infirmities, studies and thinks with the seriousness of one upon oath, and there has not been a single conversation this winter, in either class, that had not in it the spirit which giveth life. Just in proportion to the importance of the subject, does she tax her mind, and say what is most important; while, of necessity, nothing is reported from the conversations but her brilliant sallies, her occasional paradoxes of form, and, sometimes, her impatient reacting upon dulness and frivolity. In particular points, I know, some excel her; in particular departments I sympathize more with some other persons; but, take her as a whole, she has the most to bestow on others by conversation of any person I have ever known. I cannot conceive of any species of vanity living in her presence. She distances all who talk with her.

"Mr. E. only served to display her powers. With his sturdy reiteration of his uncompromising idealism, his absolute denial of the fact of human nature, he gave her opportunity and excitement to unfold and illustrate her realism and acceptance of conditions. What is so noble is, that her realism is transparent with idea, — her human nature is the germ of a divine life. She proceeds in her search after the unity of things, the divine harmony, not by exclusion, as Mr. E. does, but by comprehension, — and so, no poorest, saddest spirit, but she will lead to hope and faith. I have thought, sometimes, that her acceptance of evil was *too great*, — that her theory of the good to be educed proved too much. But in a conversation I had with her yesterday, I understood her better than I had done. 'It might never be sin to us, at the moment,' she said, 'it must be an excess, on which conscience puts the restraint.' "

The classes thus formed were renewed in November of each year, until Margaret's removal to New York, in 1844. But the notes of my principal reporter fail me at this point. Afterwards, I have only a few sketches from a younger hand. In November, 1841, the class numbered from twenty-five to thirty members: the general subject is stated as "Ethics." And the influences on Woman seem to have been discussed under the topics of the Family, the School, the Church, Society, and Literature. In November, 1842, Margaret writes that the meetings have been unusually spirited, and congratulates herself on the part taken in them by Miss Burley, as 'a presence so positive as to be of great value to me.' The general subject I do not find. But particular topics were such as these: — "Is the ideal first or last; divination or experience?" "Persons who never awake to life in this world." "Mistakes;" "Faith;" "Creeds;" "Woman;" "Dæmonology;" "Influence;" "Catholicism" (Roman); "The Ideal."

In the winter of 1843–4, the general subject was "Education." Culture, Ignorance, Vanity, Prudence,

Patience, and Health, appear to have been the titles of conversations, in which wide digressions, and much autobiographic illustration, with episodes on War, Bonaparte, Goethe, and Spinoza, were mingled. But the brief narrative may wind up with a note from Margaret on the last day.

'28*th April*, 1844. — It was the last day with my 'class. How noble has been my experience of such 'relations now for six years, and with so many and so 'various minds! Life is worth living, is it not?

'We had a most animated meeting. On bidding me 'good-bye, they all, and always, show so much good-will 'and love, that I feel I must really have become a friend 'to them. I was then loaded with beautiful gifts, accom'panied with those little delicate poetic traits, of which 'I should delight to tell you, if we were near. Last 'came a beautiful bouquet, passion-flower, heliotrope, 'and soberer blooms. Then I went to take my repose 'on C——'s sofa, and we had a most serene afternoon 'together.'

APPENDIX.

APPENDIX.

A.

THOMAS FULLER AND HIS DESCENDANTS.

[From the New England Historical and Genealogical Register for October, 1859.]

In 1638 Thomas Fuller came over from England to America, upon a tour of observation, intending, after he should have gratified his curiosity by a survey of the wilderness world, to return. While in Massachusetts, he listened to the preaching of Rev. Thomas Shepard, of Cambridge, who was then in the midst of a splendid career of religious eloquence and effort, the echo of which, after the lapse of two centuries, has scarcely died away. Through his influence, Mr. Fuller was led to take such an interest in the religion of the Puritan school, that the land of liturgies and religious formulas, which he had left behind, became less attractive to him than the "forest aisles" of America, where God might be freely worshipped. He has himself left on record a metrical statement of the change in his views which induced him to resolve to make his home in Massachusetts. These verses were collected by the Rev. Daniel Fuller of Gloucester from aged persons, who declare that the author was urged, but in vain, to publish them. Now, after the lapse of two centuries, we will favor the world with a few of them, which will serve as a sample: —

"In thirty-eight I set my foot
On this New England shore;
My thoughts were then to stay one year,
And here remain no more.

But, by the preaching of God's word
By famous Shepard he,
In what a woful state I was,
I then began to see.

Christ cast his garments over me,
And all my sins did cover:
More precious to my soul was he
Than dearest friend or lover.

His pardoning mercy to my soul
All thought did far surmount;
The measure of his love to me
Was quite beyond account.

Ascended on his holy hill,
I saw the city clear,
And knew 'twas New Jerusalem,
I was to it so near.

I said, My mountain does stand strong,
And doubtless 'twill forever;
But soon God turned his face away,
And joy from me did sever.

Sometimes I am on mountains high,
Sometimes in valleys low: —
The state that man's in here below,
Doth ofttimes ebb and flow.

I heard the voice of God by man,
Yet sorrows held me fast;
But these my joys did far exceed;
God heard my cry at last.

Satan has flung his darts at me,
And thought the day to win;
Because he knew he had a friend
That always dwelt within.

But surely God will save my soul!
And, though you trouble have,
My children dear, who fear the Lord,
Your souls at death he'll save.

All tears shall then be wiped away;
And joys beyond compare,
Where Jesus is and angels dwell,
With every saint you'll share."

If these verses do not give evidence of the highest poetical culture and finish, they yet prove genuine Puritan blood, and hand down through the centuries the very laudable reason which induced Lieut. Thomas Fuller (so we find him styled in the probate proceedings on his will) to purchase and settle upon a large tract of land in New Salem, (afterwards Middleton;) and this land, we will say in passing, is still mainly owned and improved by his descendants. He built a house on it near a stream, about half a mile below Middleton Pond, and about the same distance west from Will's Hill. He did not reside continuously at Middleton; but for some years dwelt in Woburn, and was one of the first settlers and most active citizens of that town, as its records manifest. He died in the year 1698, bequeathing his remaining land to his youngest son, Jacob, having previously, in his lifetime, conveyed lands to his other children, by way of advancement. The last named (Jacob) was born in 1655, and continued to reside on the farm in Middleton till his death in 1731. He married Mary Bacon, and they had five children. His fifth child and second son was likewise named Jacob, who was born in 1700, and died October 17, 1767. He married Abigail Holton, and they had ten children — six sons and four daughters.

TIMOTHY FULLER, the sixth child and third son of the second Jacob Fuller, was born at Middleton, on the 18th of May, 1739. He entered Harvard University at the age of nineteen, and graduated in 1760. His name over that date may still be seen on the corner-stone of one of the college buildings. He applied himself to theology; and in March, 1767, received from the church and town of Princeton, Mass., a nearly unanimous invitation to become their pastor, having previously supplied their pulpit for two years. Here he was ordained the first minister of Princeton, 9th September, 1767. In 1770 he married Sarah Williams, daughter of Rev. Abraham Williams, of Sandwich, Mass. He was successful as a preacher, and his people were united in him till the war of the revolution broke out. He declared at the time, and ever afterwards, that he was friendly to the principles of the revolution, and anxiously desired that his country should be liberated from its dependence on the British crown; but he was naturally a very cautious man, and believed this result would be certain to come, if the country reserved itself for action till its strength was somewhat matured, and its resources in a better state of preparation. Resistance at the time he believed to be premature, and hazarding all by too precipitate action. Such views, however, were by no means congenial to the heated zeal of his townsmen. He first gave dissatisfaction by a discourse he preached to the "minute men," at the request of the town, choosing for his text 1 Kings xx. 11: "Let not him that girdeth on the harness boast himself as he that putteth it off." He was not a man to swerve from his own cool and deliberate views through the pressure of public opinion; and his persistence in them led to his dismissal, in 1776, from the pastorate by an ex parte council, his parish refusing to agree with him upon a mutual council. He removed soon after to Martha's Vineyard, and preached to the society in Chilmark till the war was ended. He then removed to Middleton, and brought a suit against the town of Princeton for his salary. His dismissal had been irregular, and the law of the case was in his favor; but the jury had too much sympathy with the motives that actuated the town to render a verdict in his behalf. It was supposed this result would be crushing to him, and that he would not be prepared to pay costs recovered by the town; and some were malignant enough to anticipate with pleasure the levy of the execution. But they were disappointed; for, when the sheriff called upon him, he coolly counted out the amount of the execution in specie, which, in his habitual caution, he had carefully hoarded to meet this very exigency. He soon after returned to Princeton, where he applied himself to the careful education of his children, in connection with the cultivation of a large farm, which embraced within its bounds the Wachusett mountain.

None of his children attended any other than this family school; all were carefully taught, and several fitted for college at home. Those in the town who had been opposed to him, soon became reconciled, and even warmly attached. He was very active in town affairs, and represented Princeton in the convention which approved and adopted the present federal constitution. He himself, with his characteristic firmness, voted against the constitution, mainly on the ground of its recognition of slavery; and he has left his reasons on record. In 1796, he removed to Merrimac, N. H., where he continued to reside till his decease, on the morning of the 3d of July, 1805, at the age of sixty-seven, leaving a wife and ten children to mourn his loss. His wife deserves more than a passing notice, as she must have had no small influence in moulding the character of the children. Her father, Rev. Abraham Williams, was a person of genuine piety, a warm patriot, and an ardent friend of the revolution. His letter accepting his call at Sandwich, which is still carefully preserved, breathes a pure Christian spirit; as also a subsequent communication, in which he kindly expresses a willingness to dispense with a portion of his salary to accommodate himself to the narrow means of his people. His will is likewise very characteristic. He emancipates his slaves, and requires his children to contribute to their support if they shall be destitute; and "deprives any child who may refuse to give bonds to perform this duty of his share of the estate, giving to such child in lieu thereof a new Bible of the cheapest sort, hoping that, by the blessing of Heaven, it may teach them to do justice and love mercy." He married Anna Buckminster, of Framingham, aunt of the distinguished clergyman, Rev. Joseph Buckminster, D. D., of Portsmouth, N. H., who was father of Rev. Joseph Stevens Buckminster, of Boston. Rev. Mr. Williams graduated from Harvard University in 1744, and died 12th of August, 1784, aged fifty-seven. His daughter Sarah, wife of Rev. Timothy Fuller, possessed a vigorous understanding and an honorable ambition, which she strove to infuse into her children. She died in 1822. Rev. Timothy Fuller left five daughters and five sons. The sons were Timothy, Abraham Williams, Henry Holton, William Williams, and Elisha; of these we shall speak more in detail.

TIMOTHY FULLER, the fourth child and eldest son, attained great distinction. The chief steps in his career may be thus summarily stated: He was born in Chilmark, Martha's Vineyard, 11th of July, 1778: graduated at Harvard University with the second honors in his class, 1801. He was a member of the Mass. Senate from 1813 to 1816; Representative in Congress from 1817 to 1825; Speaker of the Mass. House of Representatives in 1825; a member of the Executive Council in 1828; and died suddenly of Asiatic cholera, at his residence in Groton, Mass., October 1, 1835. In the narrow circumstances of his father, he was obliged to work his way through college, and be absent much in teaching; but such were his talent, industry, and scholarship, that it is believed he would have borne off the first honors had he not countenanced a rebellion of the students, caused by certain college rules regarded as oppressive. He was always an ardent advocate for freedom and the rights of man, and even while in college made himself marked as a Democratic Republican, in contradistinction to the Federalist party. After graduating, he taught in Leicester Academy, till he had acquired funds to complete his professional study of the law, which he did in the office of Hon. Levi Lincoln, of Worcester, and afterwards practised law in Boston. We copy the following description of the monument erected to his memory in Mount Auburn, which is taken from the Mount Auburn Memorial: —

"In the centre of the foreground, on Pyrola Path, is the chaste and beautiful marble sarcophagus, on which are inscribed the names of Hon. Timothy Fuller and two of his children, who departed life in infancy. This is a fitting memorial of a distinguished man. Mr. Fuller was a member of Congress from Massachusetts from 1817 to 1825, and was noted for reasoning power and eloquence. Among his marked speeches are his addresses upon the Seminole war, and in opposition to the Missouri Compromise, in 1820. Mr. Fuller was eminent among the Democratic Republicans of his time, and very influential in securing the election of John Quincy Adams to the presidency. His services as chairman of the Committee on Naval Affairs are not forgotten. Mr. Fuller had great distinction at the bar, and a large professional practice. He was untiring in his industry, grudged the hours nature demands for sleep, was a fine classic scholar, and an extensive reader. These were traits in his character which won much public honor; but there were others — a strict integrity, a warmth of heart, and a liberal benevolence, endearing him to the humble and needy, and a tender and faithful attachment to his children and friends, which make his memory widely cherished. In the pressure of business, having to prepare many briefs by his evening fireside, he yet found time to instruct his daughter Margaret, to cultivate her rare intellect, and to incite her to a noble ambition. Having practised many years in Boston, with his residence in Cambridge, he in later years removed to Groton. Here, in his beautiful residence, he designed to write a history of his country, for which he had been long collecting materials, and to educate his younger children with the advantages of due physical development. Perhaps, too, in the afternoon of his life he was drawn, as many are, nearer the scenes of his childhood and youth, attracted towards the blue Wachusett and the range of New Hampshire hills. Here he died the 1st of October, 1835. Circumstances prevented his daughter Margaret from completing a memoir of him which she designed, and which, we believe, would have been a worthy record of a high-minded and distinguished man."

Mr. Fuller's published writings are, "An Oration delivered at Watertown, July 4, 1809;" "Address before the Massachusetts Peace Society, 1826;" "The Election for the Presidency considered, by a Citizen;" Speeches on the Seminole War, Missouri Compromise, &c.

Hon. Timothy Fuller married Margaret Crane, daughter of Maj. Peter Crane, of Canton, Mass., May 28, 1809. She died Sabbath morning, July 31, 1859. A character like hers — so sweet and amiable, gifted, yet unpretending, with a rare intellect and ardent imagination, with warmth of sentiment and affectionate benignity of heart, together with tender susceptibilities and the love of a sympathetic nature for flowers and every beautiful type of the great Creator — is, indeed, one of the fairest ornaments of existence. Her life was one of habitual self-denial and devotion to duty in the various relations of her lot. We know not that she ever made an enemy; and, on the contrary, we believe that she has drawn towards herself the heart of every one with whom she has come in contact. In youth she was possessed of great personal beauty, and was much admired in the Washington circles when her husband was in Congress. She had a rare conversational gift, aided by a lively fancy and a well-stored mind, which made her society much valued by the educated and the gifted. Above all, she was a sincere and devoted Christian.

Margaret Fuller, the first child of this union, is well known to fame. After her father's death she was her mother's chief stay; for, though of very little business experience, and with a natural aversion to financial affairs, she had a strength of mind and courageous firmness which stayed up her mother's hands when the staff on which she had leaned was stricken away. It had been the life-long desire of the daughter Margaret to go to Europe and complete her culture there, and arrangements with this view had been matured at her father's death. Her patrimony would have still sufficed for the destined tour; but she must have left her mother sinking under a sense of helplessness, with young children to educate. Margaret, after a struggle between a long-cherished and darling project and her sense of duty, heroically resolved to give up her own brilliant hopes, and remain with her mother. She applied herself personally to the academic training of the children, who learned from her the rudiments of the classic languages and the first reading of some of its great authors. We extract from the "Mount Auburn Memorial" the following brief sketch of her and of the monument erected to her memory: —

"We have not yet mentioned the monument forming the chief attraction of the lot, and that by which so many feet are drawn thither: we allude, of course, to that commemorative of Madame Ossoli, her husband, and child. It contains a medallion likeness of Margaret Fuller Ossoli, a star, which was the signature to many of her literary contributions, and a sword, indicative of the Italian struggle, in which her husband fought, and where she herself ministered to the wounded, the whole surmounted by the cross, indicative of their Christian faith. It would certainly be foreign to our purpose, and quite inconsistent with the limits of this sheet, to attempt any sketch of her life. Nor is it necessary. She lives, and will, while life lasts, in the memory of a large circle of friends and admirers. Her journey in a foreign land, and what she did and suffered there, engaged the attention and sympathy of a large number of still living witnesses. Her melancholy death with her husband and child, returning home, just entering the haven of her native land, sent a thrill through this country, and caused tears to flow in other lands, and has not been, nor is to be, forgotten. The brightness of her genius, the nobleness and heroism of her life, are set forth in two volumes of Memoirs from the pens of R. W. Emerson, Horace Greeley, W. H. Channing, J. F. Clarke, and other friends, which have been widely circulated, and have presented the story of an extraordinary life. Her thougths, committed to paper by her own eloquent and industrious pen, not only through the columns of the New York Tribune, for a series of years, but in several literary works, still express her genius, and breathe her noble aspirations. 'Woman in the Nineteenth Century,' 'At Home and Abroad,' 'Art, Literature, and the Drama,' 'Life without and Life within,' embalm much of the mind of Margaret Fuller; but her wonderful power of conversation lives in memory alone. It is said that there has been no woman like her in this respect since Madame de Stael; but while Margaret Fuller's conversation, in eloquence and effect, in sparkle and flow, was fully equal to that of the gifted French woman, it had, superadded, a merit which the latter could not claim. There is hardly upon record one with her power to draw out others. She not only talked surprisingly herself, but she made others do so. While talking with her they seemed to make discoveries of themselves, to wonder at their own thoughts, and to admire the force and aspiration of their character — hitherto latent to their own consciousness. She made those who conversed with her forget to admire her in wondering at themselves. As a friend, Margaret Fuller Ossoli is, and must be, tenderly and devoutly remembered by the very large and miscellaneous class who knew and loved her. What an assemblage they would make if gathered together! The rich and the refined, the poor and the humble, the men and women of genius struggling with destiny, and demanding audience for new and noble thoughts; the poet, with his scorned and broken lyre, to whose lays how few would stop and listen, and still fewer echo in sympathy, — all these found in her a confidant to soothe their sorrows, and a friend to encourage and point onward. She had a wonderful way of winning unsolicited confidence. All ran to her with their secrets; and she was a storehouse of confidential disclosures. The servants about her, and all with whom she came in contact, found her a ready friend. There was but one thing needed to admit to the friendship of Margaret, and that was a pure purpose and a noble aim. Those who did not possess this instinctively shunned her. She had a penetrating eye to see through, and a power of satire to strip off, masks and pretences. She hated shams, hypocrisies, falsehoods, and outside show. Characters artificial and not genuine strove to keep at a safe distance from her; they dreaded the sting of her satire, the eagle look of her eye, and the eloquence of her tongue.

"Margaret Fuller Ossoli lived above the world, while she lived in it. She was one of those *exaltadas* who are described in her 'Woman in the Nineteenth Century;' which description has been thus thrown into a poetical dress:—

"'Who are these that move below,
Often glancing as they go,
With their homage-speaking eyes,
Rapt looks upward to the skies?'
Such *exalted ones* they name —
Characters of heavenly frame,
Walking on the pilgrim road,
Living, moving still in God.
'Tell me why their eye intent
Fastens on the firmament;
Or where, in the gilded sky,
Embers of the daylight die.'
'In this world another lies,
Glorious as paradise;
And their souls have eyes to see,
Vision, undisclosed to thee.'

'Tell me why they oft appear
Listening with attentive ear,
While emotions seem to glance
On the speaking countenance,
Though no being breathes a word,
Nor has aught the stillness stirred.'
''Tis because their ears have caught
Hidden harmony of thought,

Music high, and deep, and broad,
Making melody to God!
World of sight and world of sound,
Close that clasp the earth around,
These exalted ones discern,
And with heavenly ardor burn.'

"We have not yet spoken of Margaret as the representative of woman. Nor can we, in these limits, allude to what she said, and what she strove to do, to vindicate the honor of her sex. We cannot close, however, without quoting the lines of the celebrated Walter Savage Landor. Her husband, the Marquis Ossoli, was captain of the Civic Guard during the Italian revolution, in 1848, and was not only a Roman noble, but, what is much higher, a noble Roman.

ON THE DEATH OF MARQUIS OSSOLI AND HIS WIFE, MARGARET FULLER.

"Over his millions death has lawful power;
But over thee, brave Ossoli! none — none!
After a long struggle, in a fight
Worthy of Italy to youth restored,
Thou, far from home, art sunk beneath the surge
Of the Atlantic; on its shore; in reach
Of help; in trust of refuge; sunk with all
Precious on earth to thee — a child, a wife!
Proud as thou wert of her, America
Is prouder, showing to her sons how high
Swells woman's courage in a virtuous breast.
She would not leave behind her those she loved:
Such solitary safety might become
Others — not her; not her who stood beside
The pallet of the wounded, when the worst
Of France and Perfidy assailed the walls
Of unsuspicious Rome. Rest, glorious soul,
Renowned for strength of genius, Margaret!
Rest with the twain, too dear! My words are few,
And shortly none will hear my failing voice;
But the same language with more full appeal
Shall hail thee. Many are the sons of song
Whom thou hast heard upon thy native plains,
Worthy to sing of thee; the hour has come;
Take we our seats, and let the dirge begin."

Of EUGENE FULLER, the second child, the following notice, taken from the annual obituary college record, by Joseph Palmer, M. D., published by the Boston Daily Advertiser, gives some account: —

"Eugene Fuller, the eldest son of Hon. Timothy and Margaret (Crane) Fuller, was born in Cambridge, Mass., May 14, 1815. After leaving college in 1834, he studied law, partly at the Dane Law School in Cambridge, and partly in the office of George Frederick Farley, Esq., of Groton, Mass. After his admission to the bar, he practised his profession two years in Charlestown, Mass. He afterwards went to New Orleans, and was connected with the public press of that city. He spent several summers there, and, some two or three years ago was affected by a sun-stroke, which resulted in a softening of the brain, and ultimately in a brain fever, which came very near proving fatal, and left him in a shattered condition. His friends hoping that medical treatment at the north might benefit him, he embarked, with an attendant, on board the Empire City for New York. When one day out, June 21, 1859, his attendant being prostrated with seasickness, Mr. Fuller was left alone, and was not afterwards seen He must have been lost overboard. The New Orleans Picayune of the 30th June, with which he was some time connected, says, 'His industry, reliability, and intelligence were equalled only by his invariably mild, correct, and gentlemanly demeanor, and he was liked and respected by all who knew him.'"

The second son of Hon. Timothy Fuller was WILLIAM HENRY FULLER. He applied himself to mercantile pursuits, first in New Orleans, afterwards in Cincinnati; and at present resides in Cambridge, Mass. He married Miss Frances Elizabeth Hastings, February 28, 1840.

The third* daughter was ELLEN KILSHAW FULLER, who married William E. Channing, author of several volumes of

* An older daughter, Julia Adelaide, died in childhood.

poetry. In the account of the Fuller lot in Mount Auburn, already quoted from, we have the following in reference to her: —

"Near by, on a simple and elegant monument, is inscribed 'Ellen Fuller Channing.' These words may mean little to a stranger, but they speak volumes to all who knew her, and are capable of loving and admiring an elevated and ideal character. Of great personal beauty, she was herself a poem. With a nature largely ideal, her whole life was a beautiful and poetic composition. In family love, in the refinement and elegances of domestic life, in the tender nurture and care of her children, she had a charm like music. The following lines, written by one who honored her, but faintly portray her to the mind: —

'Hers were the bright brow and the ringlet hair,
The mind that ever dwelt i' the pure ideal;
Herself a fairer figure of the real
Than those the plastic fancy moulds of air.'"

Rev. Arthur Buckminster Fuller,* the third son of Hon. Timothy Fuller, was born August 10, 1822. He was early instructed by his father and his sister, Margaret Fuller. At the age of twelve, he spent one year at Leicester Academy; and, subsequently, studied with Mrs. Ripley, the wife of Rev. Samuel Ripley, of Waltham. In August, 1839, he entered college, at the age of seventeen, and graduated in 1843. During his college course he united with the church connected with the University. Immediately on graduation he purchased Belvidere Academy, in Belvidere, Boone Co., Illinois, which, assisted by a competent corps of instructors, he taught for the two subsequent years. During this time, Mr. Fuller occasionally preached, as a missionary, in Belvi-

* Rev. Mr. Fuller has collected most of the ancient records pertaining to the Fuller family. He has also in his possession an ancient chair, which tradition declares to have been brought from England to this country by the first Thomas Fuller, in 1638; and also a chair owned by Rev. Abraham Williams, of Sandwich.

dere and destitute places, and also to the established churches, having been interested in theological study during his senior year at college. He was a member of the Illinois Conference of Christian and Unitarian ministers, and by them licensed to preach. His first sermon was preached October, 1843, in Chicago, to the Unitarian church then under the charge of Rev. Joseph Harrington. In 1845 Mr. Fuller returned to New England; entered, one year in advance, the Cambridge Theological School, whence he graduated in August, 1847. After preaching three months at West Newton, to a society of which Hon. Horace Mann was a principal founder and a constant attendant, Mr. Fuller accepted a call to the pastorate of the Unitarian Society in Manchester, N. H., and was subsequently ordained, March 29, 1848. In September, 1852, Mr. Fuller received a call from the New North Church, on Hanover Street, in Boston, one of the most ancient churches in the city, being founded in 1714, and a church built that year on the spot where the present one now stands. This call Rev. Mr. Fuller refused, the relation between himself and the Manchester Society being a most happy one. The call was, however, renewed, and ultimately accepted, and Mr. Fuller was installed in Boston, June 1, 1853. Failing health, and the fact that the Protestant population was rapidly leaving the North End, induced Mr. Fuller to resign his city pastorate, and close his labors there July 31, 1859. He accepted at once, however, a call for a six months' charge of the Unitarian Church in Watertown, Mass., having preferred this temporary settlement to one of longer duration. In November, 1853, Mr. Fuller was chosen by the citizens of Ward 1, in Boston, a member of the School Committee, then a much smaller body than now, consisting of only twenty-four members. In January, 1854, Mr. Fuller was chosen by the Massachusetts House of Representatives chaplain of that body. In 1858 he was elected by the Massachusetts Senate their chaplain, both of which appointments he accepted, and discharged their duties. In 1855 Rev. Mr. Fuller was selected by the citizens of Groton, Mass., to deliver a bi-centennial oration, it being the two hundredth anniversary of the settlement of that ancient town. This oration was delivered October 31, 1855. In 1857 Mr. Fuller was nominated, by the republicans of Suffolk District No. 2, for the Massachusetts Senate, but, with the other candidates of his party in that district, failed of an election. In 1858 Mr. Fuller was chosen by the State Temperance Convention a member of the Executive Committee, and in the same year was elected a director of the Washingtonian Home, better known as the Home for the Fallen. Mr. Fuller's published writings are, "A Discourse in Vindication of Unitarianism from popular Charges against it," Manchester, 1848; "Sabbath School Manual of Christian Doctrines and Institutions," Boston, 1850; "A Discourse occasioned by the Death of Hon. Richard Hazen Ayer, delivered in the Unitarian Church, February 18, 1853;" "An Historical Discourse, delivered in the New North Church, October 1, 1854;" "A Discourse occasioned by the Death of Miss Mercy Tufts, delivered in the Unitarian Church in Quincy, Mass., January 24, 1858;" "Liberty versus Romanism, or Romanism hostile to Civil and Religious Liberty, — being two Discourses delivered in the New North Church, Boston," Boston, 1859. Mr. Fuller has also edited four volumes of his sister Margaret's works, and has prepared for the press a complete and uniform edition of her works and memoirs.*

RICHARD FREDERICK FULLER was the fourth son. He graduated at Harvard University, 1844, studied law in Greenfield, Mass., afterwards a year at the Cambridge Law School, and, having completed his studies in the office of his uncle, Henry H. Fuller, Esq., in Boston, was admitted to the bar on examination in open court, December, 1846, at the age of twenty-two, and became, and continued for two years to be,

[* These volumes are now published simultaneously with these memoirs. They are Woman in the Nineteenth Century, At Home and Abroad, Art, Literature, and the Drama, and Life Without and Life Within. — ED.]

the law partner of his uncle; and has subsequently practised law without a partner, in Boston. Having been fitted for college, at the age of sixteen he entered a store in Boston, at the solicitation of his family; but mercantile life proving distasteful to him, he relinquished it at the end of one year. By severe application, he in six months made up for this lost year, at the same time keeping pace with the studies of the Sophomore class, and was admitted to college in the middle of the Sophomore year. He graduated the second or third scholar of his class.

This ends our account of those who have been noted in the family of Hon. Timothy Fuller. His brothers likewise attained distinction, and deserve now to be mentioned.

Abraham Williams Fuller, the second son of Rev. Timothy Fuller, applied himself, on reaching manhood, to mercantile life. His strict application to business, his sagacity and integrity, speedily won the confidence of his employer, who, retiring from business about the time Abraham became of age, lent him an adequate capital, and set him up as his successor. The embargo, occurring at this time, caused a great rise in prices, and Abraham very soon acquired a large fortune. He at once relinquished mercantile business, and studied the law, and had an office in Boston till he died, April 6, 1847, unmarried, leaving a large property. A granite obelisk has been erected to his memory, near the tower, in Mount Auburn.

The third son was Henry Holton Fuller, who graduated at Harvard College, 1811, the second scholar in his class, Edward Everett being the first, and was admitted to the Suffolk bar September 19, 1815. He went into partnership with his brother Timothy, and attained great distinction at the bar. He was a thorough and careful lawyer, a sound logician, and had a sparkling flow of wit and humor, which made him a great favorite with juries. When he could not answer arguments, he could almost always throw a grotesque coloring over them, and bring them into ridicule, possessing a vein of very cutting satire. He had a great run of business in court almost immediately; and at thirty years of age it was said that he had argued more cases than any lawyer of his age in Massachusetts. He himself remarked that he never was counsel in a case where the jury did not wish to give him the verdict, if they could find a fair way to do so. In conversation he was genial and sprightly, affable and pleasant to all about him, and a universal favorite with his juniors. He was several years a representative from Boston in the Massachusetts legislature, and very efficient in its debates and the transaction of the public business. At his death, September 15, 1852, the bench and bar joined in a public tribute of eulogy to his memory. A granite obelisk in Mount Auburn, near the tower, beside the monument of Abraham W. Fuller, is erected to his memory.

WILLIAM WILLIAMS FULLER likewise graduated at Harvard University, in 1813, and studied law. He practised several years in Hallowell, Me., afterwards in Lowell, Mass., and ultimately in Oregon, Ill. His mind was cool and deliberate, his judgment sound and reliable, and he obtained a very favorable reputation in his profession. He died at Oregon, Ill., 1849, leaving an infant child, who survived but a few months.

ELISHA FULLER, the youngest son, graduated at Harvard University, 1815, and studied law. He practised at Lowell, and afterwards at Worcester, Mass. He had a keenness of perception, a ready wit, and a sound knowledge of law, which won for him much success in practice. He was a person of remarkably buoyant temperament, and so cheerful and social a companion, that his advent was sure to banish gloom and low spirits, as sunshine dissipates the darkness. In person he closely resembled Henry, whose vivacity of discourse he also shared. Both were of rather small stature, with lively black eyes, and great sprightliness of manner. Elisha died the last of the five lawyers, 1855. Seldom, in one generation has a family numbered so many successful professional men as were the five brothers we have described.

B.

[From the Quarterly Jcurnal.]

MEMORIAL OF MRS. MARGARET FULLER,

BY HER SON, RICHARD F. FULLER.

[The following interesting memoir of an excellent Christian woman was not prepared with any reference to being printed. It was written by one of her sons for the use of his children; but, having had the privilege of reading it, I requested to be allowed to print it in the Quarterly Journal, and my request was granted. I think the readers of the Journal will be interested in this sketch. — EDITOR JOURNAL.]

MARGARET FULLER, the daughter of Major Peter Crane, was born in Canton, Mass., February 15, 1789. Her father, though an artisan of moderate circumstances, was quite scholarly for his day and condition in life, and possessed an original turn of mind, as well as marked independence of character. He left some disquisitions, preserved by his family, of no literary excellence, but indicative of a strong and untutored mind, coping with the intellectual problems of life, and feeling after truth by the unaided light of individual thought. He was noted for going on in his own course, with utter disregard of popularity, and of the view which others might take of his conduct. He served in the revolutionary war, and at one time, when there was no chaplain, performed the duties of that office for his regiment. Though belonging to no church, and entertaining, perhaps, rather crude views of his own in religious things, yet he had an influence over the minds of others, which induced his counsel and his prayers to be sought for in circumstances of distress. He died before I was born; but my grandmother lived till after I attained manhood. My father and mother often visited her at Canton, riding in a chaise, and carrying one of the chil-

32

dren, sitting on a cricket at their feet; and my turn for these journeys came often. My father was an ardent lover of nature, which he doubly enjoyed in his escapes from the pressure of public and professional business; and his enjoyment of it, and the points of interest he called attention to, heightened my relish for this pure gratification. He drove slowly, and sang with my mother on the way. These journeys are ever memorable with me; and the visits were always celebrated in sacred song among the Canton kindred, which my father accompanied with the flute, enjoying music with almost passionate delight. Arriving at Canton, we were always joyously greeted by the bright and sunny face of my aged grandmother, who lived with a maiden aunt, and the uniformity of whose life was very agreeably varied by these visits, while my father never neglected to bring generous supplies for her rather meagre larder. She was a very pious woman, in the simplicity and devotion of the Baxter school, whose "Saint's Rest," as well as the works of Watts and Doddridge, were very familiar and precious to her, and formed, with her ever-diligently conned and well-worn Bible, almost the whole range of her literary acquirement. She was very fond of singing devotional hymns. Among others, I remember "China" was a great favorite, sung even with her last failing voice upon her death bed. As she sang it, the minor cadence and its reference to the grave rather affrighted and repelled my childish taste; but I have since been able to appreciate the sentiment which made it attractive. My grandmother had great sweetness of temper and a sunshine of disposition, which may have been received by my mother as an hereditary gift.

In childhood and youth, my mother was marked not only for rare bloom and personal beauty, but for an almost irrepressible gayety and buoyancy of temper. She was as full of the elasticity of life, and her heart as overflowing with the music of nature, as the early songsters of spring. She was above the medium height of woman, being in stature about five feet and nine or ten inches, and considerably taller than my father. She had blue eyes, a fair, white complexion, not liable to tan or freckle, and a rich bloom, like that of the peach, in her cheeks. This bloom was a very marked characteristic of her face, and one that she retained to quite mature life. It was transmitted to her daughter Ellen, and its rose has reappeared undiminished in the blooming cheeks of some of her grandchildren.

My mother had a very happy childhood. Her own temper, with its rare elasticity, was then, and ever through life, a fund of happiness for herself as well as others. As a child and maiden, she had a wild exuberance of spirits, regulated, however, by as strong a benevolence, and a tenderness of feeling and sympathy, which made her generally beloved. Her fondness for flowers was ever a passion with her, if so gentle and refined a sentiment may be thus denominated. I have heard her speak of her mother as one who, though sweet and loving, was determined not to spoil the child by sparing the rod, when occasion required its exercise, which, happily, was seldom. On one occasion, however, her mother had forbidden the children to eat certain grapes, and Margaret had yielded to the temptation of the luscious fruit, and despoiled the vine of some of its clusters. Her mother inquired of Abby, a younger daughter, if she had done it, and was answered, "No." On being further interrogated if she knew the offending party, Abby would not reply; and her mother attempted with the rod to compel her to answer. Abby bore it with heroic endurance, and continued mute, till Margaret, unable to endure the sight of this vicarious suffering, confessed the deed, and thereby transferred the rod to her own more deserving shoulders. Before she was out of her teens, she taught school in the district where she resided. One large boy presumed upon his familiar acquaintance and her well-known playfulness of disposition, which he could hardly believe it possible for her to lay aside, and showed a disinclination to submit to her sceptre in the school room. She displayed her characteristic energy and courage, called the boy out upon the floor, and, ere he could collect his forces for resistance, ferruled him soundly. The dismayed youth quailed and submitted, and her authority was afterwards unquestioned.

My mother has given some rather grotesque accounts of riding to church on a pillion; and of being sometimes taken up behind a rustic cavalier, whose invitation she had unwillingly accepted, to spare him the mortification of a refusal. It was at church that my father first saw her, she happening, through some chance, to be in Cambridge on the Sabbath. He loved, and his love was returned. He soon led her to the altar, a blooming girl of twenty, and ten years younger than himself. Father was not blind to worldly advantages of family and position; and such were readily within the reach of a rising young lawyer, whose talents had already become favorably known. But it was well for him that he yielded to a softer and a better sentiment. "His love for my mother," says Margaret in her autobiographical sketch, "was the green spot on which he stood apart from the commonplaces of a mere bread-winning, bread-bestowing existence." She adds, in describing her mother, "She was one of those fair and flower-like natures which sometimes spring up even beside the most dusty highways of life — a creature not to be shaped into a merely useful instrument, but bound by one law with the blue sky, the dew, and the frolic birds. Of all persons whom I have known, she had in her most of the angelic — of that spontaneous love for every living thing, for man, and beast, and tree, which restores the golden age." Not only was this union a blessing to father, but favorable to the character of his children. Margaret used to say that we derived our ideal sentiment mainly from our mother. And certainly she had a good store of refined fancy and delicate feeling, though coupled, as they but rarely are, with a ready hand and a willing mind for useful effort, graced by uninterrupted benignity and sweetness, and not marred by the moody and irritable temperament which are not unfrequently the blemish of an imaginative mind. None of her sons can fail to be grateful for sentiment, from whichever parent derived, since it is not only the most satisfactory evidence of a divine and immortal germ within, but affords that purer gratification of thought and fancy, which, better than any thing in life, deserves the name of pleasure, being a satisfaction to which memory can ever revert without self-reproach. It is true that such a temperament is apt to be more sensitive to the thorns in life's pathway; but, when religiously developed, which is its best and most congenial bias, it furnishes itself a corrective for its fault, and opens to the soul fountains of even heavenly consolation.

My mother's Cambridge years rather antedate my recollection; but in Groton her character and life are fresh in my memory. A picture of her is very prominent in my mind, as she stooped over her flower-bed, and toiled long sunny hours over its extensive border. Her unwearied labors in the heat attracted the admiration even of the hardy farmers. Her expression, as she knelt by the flower bed and bent her near-sighted gaze close to a plant, and, discovering some new unfolding promise of beauty, turned round to announce it with a child-like simplicity and a delighted smile, I think can never fade from the memories of her children. This image has often been renewed; and though latterly her hair, no less beautiful than before, has been gray, yet never thinned by years, her smile has gleamed ever with the same sunshiny, child-like triumph, her countenance never hardened or saddened by life's experience, nor her joy abated with the declining vigor of life. The flowers were ever new and ever young, and they kept her spirit still child-like in freshness of sentiment, simplicity of taste, and purity of soul, showing her ever guileless, single-hearted, and such as are of the kingdom of heaven.

My father's death was a dreadful stroke to my mother. It bowed her to the earth; but it did not break her spirit, and she rose again, leaning on the arm of her beloved Lord. My father had been a man of strength and of success, and on him she had entirely relied, never cognizant of the practical financial problems of life. His property was in unproductive real estate, and, with young children to be educated, it was necessary to change and straiten our style of living. The arithmetic of the business appalled my mother; she was as naturally inapt for it as the lilies that neither toil nor spin. But she was always remarkable for indefatigable industry; and she applied herself to the dairy, and the farm, and the economy of the table with heroic determination, while she was aided and encouraged by Margaret's firm and courageous, though far from financial or business-like, mind. She ever rose early, and her voice with the morning birds roused the rest of the household. Well do I remember the night of my father's death, when I was ten years of age. The solemn tones of the minister's voice in prayer, in the chamber of death, have not been — can never be — forgotten. Very soon after I was confined to my bed for a fortnight, with fever. Mother feared it might prove fatal. She never faltered; she was with me night and day. I remember well her voice as she called me her "dear lamb." Her soothing, gentle hand had no ornament but her simple wedding-ring of gold, without any stone, which she always wore, and which was buried with her. After my father's death she devoted every energy, with untiring self-sacrifice, to her children. Her economy in respect to herself was most rigorous. Her dress was as plain and simple as propriety would permit, and it was preserved with great care. She always persevered in this self-denial, wishing to husband what was hers for others. Her annual income from her share of the property was five or six hundred dollars, and she invariably saved about half of it, till the lot was purchased at Mount Auburn, which was obtained to commemorate the dear departed, and to testify her perennial remembrance. She contributed largely and principally toward its marble memorials, and adorned it with flowers, whose growth she assiduously fostered with her own hand. We think this was a great solace to her; and it evidently furnished her satisfaction, not merely to keep green and fresh holy memories, but to express in the language of flowers her never doubting Christian faith.

At Groton she was active in the efforts of the religious society to which she belonged. Indeed, from the time she united with the Unitarian Church in Cambridge, soon after her marriage, till her last sickness, and even during it, as far as possible, she was much and actively engaged in religious effort. Loving and full of charity towards those of every Christian name, she was herself an earnest and devoted Unitarian, through evil report and good report. She was among the first who formed the Lee Street Church and Society, in Cambridge; nor can her efforts in its behalf be soon forgotten. When her son, Rev. Arthur B. Fuller, was settled in Manchester, N. H., she was, with him, actively devoted to the interests of his society, and tenderly loved by all its members. When he left Manchester, to accept the call of the New North Church in Boston, she accompanied him, and there continued till her last sickness. Her sympathy for all, her teaching in the Sabbath school, her interest, always cordial and as laborious as her years would permit, in the benevolent organization of the society, and her Christian graces, which shone with so mild and lovely a light, won affection as well as respect from all who came in contact with her, no matter how variant their theological creed from her own.

Benevolence, of a sympathetic and hopeful cast, overflowed from the pure fountains of her Christian heart. The bad awoke in her much pity and little reproach. No one could desire a kinder judge than she to pass upon character or determine destiny. In the large charity of her soul, she hoped from the divine benignity a place for repentance would ever be preserved for all. She never spoke against others — dwelt much upon their virtues, gently and charitably upon their faults. She reproved her children if they spoke unfavorably of the absent, and always advocated their cause, and endeavored to excuse what was alleged against them. We sometimes held up the faults of others merely to notice the ingenuity with which she would seek for excuse, or strive to throw the veil of charity over them. I shall never forget her efforts by the bedside of a large, coarse man, a tenant of ours in Groton, who lived "without God and without hope in the world," until he took opium to end his wretched existence. Mother used every exertion to rescue him from death, and staid by him during the hours of fearful struggle between a powerful frame and the working of the poison. In the early part of it, before his mind entirely wandered, he said, "It will be all in vain; but you may try all means." The memory of this scene is in one view appalling, as representing a gross and sensual nature meeting the fearful fate itself had invoked; but, on the other hand, is beautiful as exhibiting one, like an angel, exerting every power to snatch him from his self-elected doom.

Mother's sympathy was sometimes taken advantage of to induce her to lend money which she could ill spare. One case in particular we used to jest a little about, of a man who induced her to lend him, on the plea that he "wanted to pay his debts, and become an honest man." We thought it would only change his creditor, and doubted if it would not make him a less honest man, not only by the pretext he used, but by his employing the money for other objects than that alleged. But in her readiness of sympathy she exhibited the charity that "believeth all things."

My mother's piety was as truly genuine as any I have ever

witnessed. It was meek and unpretending; it had a faith which buoyed her up in all the stormy passages of life, which drew the gleam of heaven down upon the earth, and surrounded her with its sanctifying light. Duty was her daily food — not a burden, nor an artificial action, but the spontaneous movement of her life. Self-sacrifice was as natural to her as self-gratification is to many others. When I say *natural*, I refer to that acquired nature which was the fruit of her Christian experience. She never attached any merit to self-sacrifice, nor regarded herself as having any claim to consideration with God or man founded on it. She took spiritual nourishment as regularly as physical. Prayer was habitual — a frequent, regular, and delightful exercise to her. God was her best friend. His book was read and re-read, to her last hours, with ever fresh satisfaction; it was not only inscribed on her memory, but written on the tables of her heart. The Psalms and the Gospel of John were, perhaps, especial favorites, though not to the disparagement of the rest. What I say of her Christian character may seem like extravagant eulogy to those who did not know her; but it will not to those who knew her well, (for whom this is especially written,) since her religion was not only sentimental and devotional, but lived out in all the little and large things of life, which ever showed her mindful of the things of others, and not of her own, and always denying herself and taking up the cross. What heightened it was her humility, she having no idea that she had any such grace of character, and the sunshiny cheerfulness with which she constantly bore the crosses of life, without the gloom or austerity which sometimes stamp the Christian self-conquest with something like servitude.

Early in the year 1839, our family moved to Jamaica Plain, a part of Roxbury, having succeeded in selling our Groton farm. My brother Arthur had, the autumn previous, gone to Waltham to complete his college preparatory studies, under the teaching of Mrs. Ripley. At Jamaica Plain, Margaret had two pupils from Providence in the house. I attended the school of Mr. S. M. Weld, in Jamaica Plain. I think mother had a good deal of rest here, now the cares and responsibilities, as well as the drudgery, of the farm were over. She had ever great enjoyment in Margaret's society. It was beautiful to see the relation between them — the noble, strong-minded, and courageous daughter sustaining and cheering the heart of that holy and loving parent. Our house in Jamaica Plain was elevated, with a fine view, near a brook, then called Willow Brook; and in the rear were rocks, at times almost covered with the wild columbine.

After I entered college, Margaret, to have me at home, as well as to be with my mother, took a house in Ellery Street, Cambridge. As I record this, memory seems to rush back upon me like a mighty wind, freighted with a mother's and sister's love. Here we resided till I graduated; and in the constant intercourse of my mother and sisters, I enjoyed a noble and elevating society, such as rarely can be expected this side of heaven. Not but there are many pure and noble natures, and often side by side; but they are not often fluent and expressive. Their souls rarely speak and flow forth from one to the other with benignant activity, as they might and should. We kept house in Cambridge till I graduated, in 1844. On my entering the Law School, we purchased the Prospect Street House, in Cambridge, and there resided till I went into the practice of my profession in Boston. This sojourn in Cambridge is marked in memory by the farewells we here took with Margaret on her departure for Europe. O, such a mother and sister! May life be so unselfish, noble, and aspiring that we may obtain admission into such companionship, when these years of fleeting change are passed away!

On my brother Arthur settling in Manchester, N. H., our mother went to live with him, and subsequently, after five years' residence there, removed with him to Boston, residing with him and her loving daughter-in-law * till the departure of the latter to "the better land," in 1856. During this mournful year, our pure and noble sister Ellen was also called to the higher divine life of heaven. Excepting these bereavements, these were sunny years for our mother. She was able to do much good in the parish, and she was the object of much attention. Mother had, for Margaret's sake, a particular sympathy for Italians. She would hear the poor man with his organ, and invariably give; which made the street of my brother's residence quite a common resort for these poor sons and daughters of the land of music. She also visited the suffering Italian women in their homes of penury, more, perhaps, than those of other poor, though she delighted to "lend to the Lord" by bestowing her widow's mite to the destitute of whatever kindred and nation.

We notice in the above narrative that mother had three different successive homes while father lived, and after his death five. But her flowers went with her every where; they were certain to spring up and bloom around her wherever she was. From first to last, as types of the Creator's infinite goodness, beauty, and perfection, she loved them with ardent and undiminished tenderness. Washington said his biography could not be written without the history of his country. Neither could mother's be expressively written without the history of flowers. Families and generations of plants adhered to her, year after year, like the tenantry of a feudal lord. When she left one residence, they accompanied her, or perhaps were set out in the hospitable garden of a friend till she acquired another home. There was a family of lilies, in particular, which adhered to her fortunes for a quarter of a century; and some of them she left in my garden. Mother felt much this frequent change of home. No longer, God be praised! is she tossed to and fro. She is

* Mrs. Elizabeth G. Fuller.

now in an eternal mansion — a home never to change — in the heavens. She is with her Saviour, her loved ones. Shortly before her death, when she could hardly articulate, she joined me in singing, —

> "There, at my Saviour's side,
> I shall be glorified —
> Heaven is my home!
> There are the good and blest,
> Those I love most and best;
> There, too, I soon shall rest —
> Heaven is my home."

Even later, she sang with Arthur, —

> "We are passing away, passing away!
> Let us hail the glad day."

Another favorite and oft-repeated hymn with her was that beautiful one by Montgomery, commencing, —

> "Forever with the Lord!
> Amen, so let it be!
> Life from the dead is in that word —
> 'Tis immortality.
> Within this body pent,
> Absent from thee I roam,
> Yet nightly pitch my moving tent
> A day's march nearer home."

Mother had the truest delight in sacred music. When she taught our infant lips to pray, she also encouraged us to join her sweet voice in singing. She accompanied the tune with a gentle motion of one hand. Her love for tunes, like her affection for friends and flowers, was constant and unchanging. "Safely through another week," how often, from my first to my last recollection of her, did I hear her sing! "While with ceaseless course the sun," was another favorite. "Softly now the light of day," she sang constantly. "Brattle Street," "While thee I seek, protecting Power," she loved to sing, especially because Margaret sang it often on her home voyage. Tappan's beautiful hymn, "There is an hour of peaceful rest," she seemed to feel a rest in singing. She was not exclusive, but loved all beautiful hymns, and often bade me sing by the bedside in her last sickness.

In September, 1858, mother came to our house in Wayland to pass her last days. She was suffering from most painful disease, and a fatal result was inevitable. She was sick from that time, and confined to her bed seven months, till she left us on Sabbath morning, July 31, 1859, at half past eight o'clock. Such faith I never witnessed. She had a trust in her Saviour which took away every sad aspect from mortality. She rested in his love. Every day she pursued the even tenor of her Christian life, till she at last "fell asleep" as peacefully as an infant, so that the moment of departure was hardly distinguishable. She told Arthur, shortly before her decease, that she felt she had done with earth, and wanted to go home now. She was only solicitous lest her sickness should be a burden to others. She thanked even the hired nurse for what she did. She took the same *heavenly* interest in the world — that regard which those have for it who live above it — to the last. All that interested others, their plans, their hopes, their improvement, interested her to the very end of life. She suppressed groans and sighs of weariness, and rarely yielded to her pains any outward manifestation. She said she "believed God would give strength to a firm mind to bear whatever he imposed." Her sweetness, resignation, trust, and sympathy were such as to draw to her bedside young children, instead of frightening and repelling, as such scenes usually do. They loved to resort to her sick room. She sought to be useful after she could sit up no longer, by encouraging them in their studies; and as we had a family school, she had them study in her room. When she died, I felt that she had gone to be with Christ, which is far better. But such a spirit as hers enriched life, made it elevated and noble. To live was Christ, and to die was gain. Fitting was it that on that calm and beautiful Sabbath morning her endless day, her glorious Sabbath, her peaceful rest should begin. Fitting that, as gently she had lived, she should as gently die.

"We watched her breathing through the night,
Her breathing soft and low,
As in her breast the wave of life
Kept heaving to and fro.

. . . . .

Our very hopes belied our fears,
Our fears our hopes belied;
We thought her dying when she slept,
And sleeping when she died."

C.

[The following poetical tributes, by Mrs. J. H. Hanaford, to the memory of Margaret, of our mother, and our noble and true-hearted brother Eugene, seem to me deserving of a place in this Appendix. No such tribute of affection and honor can fail to be grateful to those who cherish in holy remembrance the members of my family now so fast gathering on the eternal shores. In the closing part of "At Home and Abroad" I have collected other tributes to my sister, both in prose and verse, which the reader who desires can there find. — Ed.]

THE ASCENDED SAINT.

[Suggested by the recent death of Mrs. Margaret Fuller, the honored mother of the late Margaret, Countess d' Ossoli.]

Brightly the morning of the Sabbath dawned,
And swiftly vanished all the stars of night;
Like them to be unseen, but still shine on,
A Christian spirit took its upward flight.

Her years on earth were many, and those years
All filled with usefulness and holy love;
Sorrow had disciplined her soul for heaven,
And trials fitted her for rest above.

Shall we in sackcloth mourn when such depart—
Freed spirits, like fair uncaged birds, to soar
Far up and on toward wisdom infinite,
'Mid glories mortal minds may not explore?

O, no! we'll lift on high a triumph song;
Jubilate! all her griefs are o'er.
Loved ones are left; but O! she greeteth now
The loved and wept for who had gone before.

Death hath removed each dark veil from her eye,
And radiant spirits walk with her in white;
No sea in heaven shrouds their beloved forms,
No sorrow there, no weary, gloomy night.

Strike, strike your harps! sing loud, ye angel choir,
And welcome gladly this companion new,
New in the courts of heaven, with youth renewed,
But long ago, it may be, known to you.

The saint ascending to her own "sweet home"
Claims from no sorrowing hearts a tear or sigh;
We mourn for those who tread earth's pathway still,
But not for saints triumphant called to die.

Peace to the weary dust whose pain is o'er!
Joy to the spirit whose long race is run!
God comfort those who wait the summons home,
Hoping to meet her when their work is done!

EUGENE FULLER.

[Lines suggested by the recent death by drowning of Eugene Fuller, Esq., brother of Margaret, Countess d' Ossoli.]

I knew him not; mine eye had never gazed
Upon his thoughtful brow:
His name, so musical, I scarce had heard
To recognize till now.

But neither years nor space will now erase
From out my heart his name,
For with his sister's it will e'er be linked
And share her deathless fame:

Since both have found, when homeward tending, rest
Beneath the foamy wave,
Whereon no marble monument may stand
To mark their watery grave.

O Sea! wert thou not satisfied to take
The sister, good and wise,
And bear her with her loved ones to their home,
Above the starry skies?

Why shouldst thou rend again those mourning hearts,
O dark and treacherous Sea?
Why bid those hearts forevermore be sad,
Ocean! at sight of thee?

Hush! gentle voices to my soul are calling,
And, whispering, they tell —
"The Ocean is the Lord's; it doth His bidding.
Repine not; all is well."

Beyond the confines of terrestrial regions
There is a better shore;
God's love unfathomed, as the only sea,
Flows round it evermore.

There parted friends shall meet, and Death's dark wing -
Like sea-birds, screaming shrill —
Shall never flap above the drowning forms
Of friends belovéd still.

God speed the dawning of that glorious day,
When, sin-freed, we shall be
Where tears are wiped from every grief-dimmed eye,
And where is no more sea.

MARGARET FULLER OSSOLI.

Friend of humanity! whose warm, true heart
Throbbed ever to redeem a fallen race, —
Alas! that thou from earthly scenes shouldst part,
Ere thou hadst reached in joy thy native place.

Thy noble husband, too, whose manly soul
Longed for fair Freedom in *his* native land, —
Alas! that ocean's waves o'er him should roll,
Ere he could view, in peace, Columbia's strand.

And that sweet "bud of promise," whose fair bloom,
Evoked from out thy paradise of love,
Once made so fragrant thine Italian home,
He, too, went with thee to the land above.

An undivided circle! nevermore
Will tears of sad farewell your cheeks bedew;
For on that other, that celestial shore,
Our God unites for aye pure hearts and true.

Margaret! thy name hath long been to my soul
A talisman of influence pure and strong;
Though born a woman, born to have control
O'er human hearts for virtue far and long.

Thy name shall be remembered when shall die
  The name of many a warrior of renown,
For thou on nobler fields gain'dst victory,
  And won from history a glorious crown.

O for the day when Italy shall know
  How to be truly free, in virtue strong! —
We wonder not that thou didst love her so —
  Home of the classics, and the land of song!

When dawns that day on fair Italia's shore,
  Thou shalt be well remembered by the free;
America and Europe evermore
  Shall, as the friend of Freedom, think of thee.

And happier thought! where souls, from every chain
  Made free, forever sing redeeming grace,
There shall thy loved ones hear thy voice again,
  And look with deepest joy upon thy face.

They who love man love God; and they who toil
  To break the chains from men and minds below,
Win, through the Lamb, a right to heaven's soil,
  Where boundless progress each glad soul may know.

God make me worthy, Margaret, to meet thee,
  And list to thy rich converse on the shore
Where holy love from heart to heart flows free,
  And weary spirits rest forevermore.

www.ingramcontent.com/pod-product-compliance
Lightning Source LLC
LaVergne TN
LVHW011159110826
845150LV00006B/1268

9781425573225